HERBERT FEIS, economist and Pulitzer Prize winner in History, has had a distinguished career as a scholar, a writer, and as an influental adviser to the U. S. government. He was graduated from Harvard in 1916 and took his Ph. D. there in 1921. He taught at Harvard, at the University of Kansas, and from 1926 to 1929 he was head of the Economics Department at the University of Cincinnati. From 1930 to 1931 he was on the staff of the Council of Foreign Relations. In 1931 he began a period of government service, as Adviser on International Economic Affairs to the Department of State (1931-1943), chief technical adviser for the American delegation at the World Economic and Monetary Conference in London (1933), special adviser at the Conference of American Republics (1936, 1938, 1939), Special Consultant to the Secretary of War (1944-47), and member of the State Department's policy planning staff (1950-51). He has been a member of the Institute for Advanced Study and a Guggenheim fellow.

Mr. Feis has written many books, including: *Europe: The World's Banker 1870-1914* (1930); *The Spanish Story* (1948); *The Road to Pearl Harbor* (1950); *The Diplomacy of the Dollar* (1950); *The China Tangle* (1953); *Churchill-Roosevelt-Stalin* (1957); *Between War and Peace: The Potsdam Conference* (1960); *Japan Subdued* (1961); and *Foreign Aid and Foreign Policy* (1964).

Also in the Norton Library
by Herbert Feis

THE DIPLOMACY OF THE DOLLAR
(1919-1932)

EUROPE: THE WORLD'S BANKER (1870-1914)

The Spanish Story

FRANCO AND
THE NATIONS AT WAR

BY

HERBERT FEIS

The Norton Library
W · W · NORTON & COMPANY · INC ·
NEW YORK

PREFACE TO THE NORTON LIBRARY EDITION

RECENT sojourns among the Spanish people have enabled me to mark more confidently some of the feelings and reflections which made them resist the pressure to come into the war and the temptation thereby to secure the return of Gibraltar and expand their African empire.

Remembrance of the agonies of war suffered during the Napoleonic period, graven so compellingly by Goya, had never faded out. It was more deeply dyed in the black of mourning by the sufferings during the Civil War, which ended in 1939, only a few months before the great second World War began. Most of the Spanish people wanted to be left alone and to stand alone. The war had not only brought sorrow, but had also consumed their provisions for living. Many of their towns and villages were in ruins, and they lacked food, clothing, medicines, and oil. They had hardly enough to live on from day to day, nothing to spare for combat.

Satiation with war and distress and recoil from the thought of having foreign military forces again in Spain were conjoined. Few wanted the Germans back, if only for a short time, if even to extend the realm of Spanish nationalism. (Mindful and appreciative of the aid given by the British when Spain was invaded by Napoleon's armies, Spaniards have always wryly noted that their War for Independence is known of in British histories merely as the "Peninsular War." Today, although followers of Franco acknowledge the value of Italian and German aid during the Civil War, they wish to allow it to drop out of mind; for most of them it is unhappily associated with the terrible division among the Spanish people.) The governing groups turned even more devoutly to the Church they had defended, seeking solace and justification in their faith. Even ardent Nationalists were repelled by the thought of associating again with the vulgar, sacrilegious Nazi Germans, preachers of Aryan superiority. Though at one with Germany and Italy in their denunciation of Communism, many Spaniards were fearful of having Germans as neighbors in Africa and along the Pyrenees.

These memories and sentiments favored the caution that led them — and Franco in their name — to refuse Hitler's urgent pleas to enter the war and to reject his assurances that the fight would be short and victory sure and easy.

Without their assent Hitler did not dare thrust down through Spain to Gibraltar and the Straits. Further travel in Spain makes Hitler's hesitation quite understandable to me; in those long, harsh mountain ranges of Spain, on the dry, bare plateaus, along the narrow, curving roads and defiles, a hostile people could make life dangerously hard. Thus, while geography lured the Germans toward Spain, topography gave them pause.

These retrospective surmises explain the trail of events followed in this narrative. Still, conjectures about the "conditionals" of history remain extremely provocative — conjectures about what would have occurred and what the present international situation would be, had decisions other than the actual ones been taken, had some elements of reckoning, or items of circumstance, or traits of character been different from what they were. If General Franco had agreed to permit the Nazis to march through Spain and assault Gibraltar, close the Straits, and possibly move into Morocco, would the Spanish people have rebelled and civil war in Spain been renewed? If the Germans had come into control of the Western Mediterranean, could the British have continued to fight on unless the United States had immediately entered the war? With Gibraltar in German hands and the Straits closed, would the Americans and British have attempted the invasion of North Africa; and if they had, would they have succeeded?

Suppose that, despite General Franco's evasion of his proposals, Hitler had listened to Goering and some other advisers and marched into Spain; would Franco have capitulated? Or would the Germans have found themselves in a protracted and frustrating struggle, and would this have caused Hitler to desist from — or at least postpone — his invasion of the Soviet Union? If events had taken that turn, would the Soviet government have taken advantage of circumstance and pushed into the Balkans and down toward the Persian Gulf?

Suppose that during the closing period of the war, when victory was in sight, the American government had pinched off the oil supplies sent into Spain; would Franco have rallied the Spanish people around him and perhaps attacked Gibraltar? Or would the consequent decline in Spanish industry and the hunger of the Spanish people have resulted in their casting Franco out of office?

The temptation to the historian to roam through the caverns of the past in which such protean possibilities shimmer is great. He has to be either strong or dull not to lose himself in the vapors of the philosophy of history. I draw back from that inviting realm.

But it is perplexity, not prudence, that compels me to refrain also in this note from trying to peer into the future. Franco alone among the European dictators has survived. In the two decades since World War II, although political repression has been continually harsh and social injustices are still marked, the differences among the Spanish people have quieted down and their conditions of life have bettered. But what will happen when Franco passes on? Will the transition be peaceful or will divisive tendencies flare forth and Spain become again the arena of an internal and international struggle?

I hope that the fact that such lively conjectures about both the past and future sprout out of and around the narrative in this book justifies its republication.

Herbert Feis

December 1965
York, Maine

* PREFACE *

In the cement edging the French end of the International Bridge between Hendaye and Irún the curious eye can still detect footprints of the German guards who tramped there during the war years. They were made in 1940 when the road to the span was widened—the more freely to permit divisions being trained in France to pass over. Once across into Spain, the road lay open to Gibraltar, the Atlantic, the shores of the Mediterranean, and the African coasts. But the footprints stopped there. The Germans did not cross. Though expected each day, the word of invitation or shout of command to do so was never given. This is the story of what took place, and why, and what came after.

It is an interpretative account of the diplomacy that focused on Spain during the years 1939–44. Hitler included Spain in his millennial vision of a Europe and Africa organized and controlled by Germany. At a time best suited to his schedule of conquest, he did his utmost to bring Spain into the war. The United States and Britain did their utmost to defeat his efforts. This story tells of the diplomatic battle and of Franco's conduct throughout its course.

* CONTENTS *

The Spanish Story

✣

FRANCO AND
THE NATIONS AT WAR

I

FRANCO SPAIN—A SICK SPECTER

The Specter over the Rock

THE summer of 1939 Franco was master in Spain. The remnants of the broken Republican forces took refuge in wretched camps across the Pyrenees, while their leaders scattered the world over. The small elements of opposition remaining in Spain were repressed without mercy.

Germany and Italy had given Franco vital aid in the battle; Germany had flown Franco's troops into Spain and then provided tanks, planes, instructors, and technicians. Italy had smuggled a large army into the field. These forces from abroad had enabled Franco finally to break the resistance of the ill-equipped Republican forces, exhausted by their struggle against the Moors. Their contribution created a lien to Hitler and Mussolini, a lien which the Fascist leaders sought to spin into an eternal bond. Thus Serrano Suñer, the leader of the Executive Committee of the Falange (and Franco's brother-in-law), waved off the Italian legions on the quay at Cádiz on May 31st with the words:

"Every time the war- or battle-cry resounds on the Italian shores of the Mediterranean, the Spanish people from the Iberian shores of that sea will answer with the shout of 'Rome, Rome, Rome'; in this immortal word is our common destiny both Latin and Mediterranean. If Italy were threatened, a forest of Italo-Spanish bayonets would defend our common spiritual inheritance. . . ."

Still, all in all, Franco had no real reason to resent the way that Great Britain and the United States had behaved during the years of his war. Neither had put obstacles in his way. Rather the contrary. The British government had evaded all claims of the Republican government for aid by a deceptive program of "non-intervention." The United States, in a hasty action, had prevented the government under assault from buying arms in the United States. Despite some distress of spirit the two governments had allowed the Republic to be destroyed. At the time, it had seemed to them part of the price of peace. And for the Conservative British government the prelude to friendship. Chamberlain wrote on the eve of Franco's victory (February 1939):

"I think we ought to be able to establish excellent relations with Franco who seems well disposed to us. . . ."[1]

He was self-deceived. Franco and his circle felt no thanks for the helpful conduct of the democracies. A forced tribute—it was taken to be—to the virtue of their cause and the power of their allies. If any thanks were due, it was to Germany and Italy for recognizing his valiant fight against the evil movements that threatened the whole world. Of all forms of popular rule the new ruler of Spain felt a passionate distrust—as a wild seed-bed of opposition, anarchy, Communism, as it so often had been in Spain. Only as long as Hitler and Mussolini lived to dominate these forces could he feel safe. The obverse of this fact of fortune was that he might share in the triumph of the others.

The governments of the Allies came, in the midst of the war, to rue their consent to Franco's victory. For Spain became a specter—a dark, brooding form that might, in their time of weakness, pounce upon Gibraltar and the coast of Africa. But not until the fall of France. Before then it was sentenced to watch and tend its weakness. The Spanish islands in the Atlantic and even in the Mediterranean were exposed to attack by the British and French fleets. The Spanish colonies in Africa could not long have been defended. The invasion of Spain itself from the sea or across the Pyrenees was possible. The imports of food, fuel, and raw materials into all parts of the Spanish Empire were subject to an effective sea and land blockade. By these facts, as long as France was in the battle, the Allies were protected against any vital wound. Spain was a suspect center of enemy action but not a menace.

[1] Keith Feiling: *Life of Neville Chamberlain,* page 394. The biographer adds: "On no conclusions was Conservative opinion more united than on these: that this had been a civil war, that 'non-intervention,' with all its falsity had stopped it from becoming European, that recognition was a question not of ideology but of fact, and that Franco was, if we allowed him to be, well disposed." Ibid., page 392.

But when France fell, the specter was released, or so it seemed in that fearful period. All of Britain's strength was needed in the desperate struggle to defend its island and to keep the sea lanes open. There was none to spare to meet an attack by or through Spain. A strong and free German Army camped along the Pyrenees frontier. Gibraltar could not defend itself against a well-organized assault. Even though the Rock was held, the airfield and naval base could be made useless and passage through the western Straits impossible. If Britain lost the entry into the Mediterranean, the battle for Malta, Suez, and the whole of the East would be lost.

Thus the Spanish government seemed possessed of the power to decide whether Britain could continue to resist outside its island—perhaps even of the power to decide whether it could continue to fight at all. For if Germany could use the Spanish coasts in Africa and the Spanish islands in the Atlantic, the sustaining flow from the United States might be broken.

The British and American governments took the measure of these dangers. The struggle to influence or control Spanish action became crucial to their battle plans and hopes. To quiet the specter, or keep it confined, they used all their arts and powers. Spain became the focal point of their diplomacy. Every day the Rock remained unsurrounded was a day gained—until there was no further need to count the days gained. Their allies were Spanish misery and the internal divisions over which the Franco government ruled.

The Plight of the Country—1939

On May 19th Franco celebrated his entry into Madrid. The sun was warm and the crowds in the Plaza Mayor were moved with thanks. The gruesome Civil War was at an end; those who were unharmed and free could hope that life would again become calm and orderly. But entwined between the places at the official feast, dislike ran like a table decoration. Spaniards, within and outside the government, were bitterly separated from one another. Many senior officers in the Army despised their new political associates. They were scornful of the ruffian and vulgar spirit of the Falange, being wont to say in private that the Army did the fighting while the Falange did the cheering and the profiteering. The industrialists, bankers, and merchants opposed the doctrines of state control of economic life, propounded by the political professors. Most of the aristocracy had little regard for the upstart government; even though it had returned their lands, they wished the monarchy restored. Elements in the Catholic clergy were openly or silently out of sympathy, being repelled by the intimate association between members of the new government and the un-Christian band of National Socialists. But most telling of all was the widespread covert hostility among the workers and the peasants. Add to these the sectional differences such as those which kept the Basques, the Catalonians, and the miners of Asturia apart from the rest of Spain. As Sir Samuel Hoare has said:

"Franco and Franco alone held together these differing elements."

In every move he had to take care not to lose the support of any large faction, not to displace or displease any too greatly. The sustaining combination was like a country stone wall; undisturbed it might long endure and contain the land; but if a few large stones fell out, the whole might tumble.

Among the people of Spain there was but one common wish—that there be no renewal of fighting. They were tired and grieving, weary of killing and destruction. The crowd that stood beneath the brightly colored banners were mostly clothed in black. Proud Spaniards they were, but in no mood to suffer war again in pursuit of lost glories or lands. Like Sancho Panza, if asked they would have said:

"Not for me, for I have been bombasted by more than four hundred Moors, which have hammered me in such sort as the bruising of the pack-staves was gilded bread and spice cake in comparison of it."

They had been glad to see the foreign legions depart. Their grim memory still contained tales of the cruel conduct of Napoleon's men, etched forever by Goya. They had found nothing to like about the Italian and German auxiliaries. Now the struggle was over, and they were gone. Useful as they had been, none wished to have them come back.

Many had been hungry for a long time and were still hungry. There was a serious shortage of bread; those who stood in the long bread lines, which formed hours in advance of the opening of the stores, were often turned away. They did not know from one day to the next whether they could get enough bread, olive oil, beans, or rice. Meat and milk were scarcer still.

Nor was the production of such essentials increasing. Many farms were still vacant and on others there were still not enough hands to do the work. Few had the fertilizer and tools needed to produce fully. Many factories were closed or half idle, since the machinery was out of order, or they lacked the cotton, copper, leather, rubber, or steel. The street cars and buses on which they rode to work were old, dirty, unrepaired. On some railroads the bridges were still down and the rails worn out; the cars were too few and the engines so old that they broke down on each trip. There was not enough room in the passenger coaches even to carry the wounded veterans back to their homes; nor enough room on the freight cars to carry necessities.

The Spanish government lacked the means of buying what it needed from other countries. It had few surpluses to export and no gold.

The Franco regime entered office with an intellectual wardrobe borrowed from Italy—tissue-paper patterns of state direction of economic life. One of the features was that Spain should be made self-sufficient in food, raw materials, and manufactures. During the first spell of office an attempt was made to shape Spanish life according to this pattern. Obscure decrees filled the columns of the badly printed newspapers. The main results were to hinder private efforts and to cram everyday life with paper forms. The production of food, coal, cloth, shoes, and fertilizers, all remained very low. Whatever propaganda can do, it cannot plow or fertilize the soil. Coal seams cannot be broken down by police standing in the entrance to the mines; broken locomotives and trucks cannot be made to run by the dirty grease of oratory; cotton mills cannot spin threats. These things the ministries under Franco began to find out.

They soon found themselves compelled to look outside again for help. They were forced to ask foreign governments to supply Spanish needs on credit, to seek goods in return for promises. The

German and Italian governments were not pleased that Spain was so necessitous. They were not willing to regard their previous aid to Franco merely as a gift to a joint cause. They had kept careful accounts of the cost. Germany had deformed its economic life to accumulate the means for war. The rulers of Germany were not willing to give away any of these reserves; they expected rather that the Spaniards would sweat and hunger to pay for the glorious revolution. The same was true of Italy, though that country had little to spare.

Thus the Spanish government had to turn toward the detested democracies, to make advances to the overseas world. It had to seek ways of obtaining products from the British Empire, the United States, and South America. These countries, and these countries alone, had the cotton, the wheat, the oil, the fertilizers, the rubber, and the machinery that were wanted. The simple law of need cut across the kinship of the conniving dictators.

Thus in the summer of 1939, even before the war had commenced, Spanish representatives in Britain and the Dominions, in the United States, Argentina, and Brazil, were asking for goods and for credit. The Spanish question facing the democracies took the form which it was to have throughout the war years: whether they wished a hungry or a thriving Spain, whether they dared trust the Spanish government enough to help its people.

NEED CLOTHED BY PRIDE AND PREJUDICE

Spain Turns to the Land of Cotton

THE American government had recognized Franco as the ruler of Spain in April of 1939. The spacious Spanish Embassy on Sixteenth Street changed occupants. The black-bearded former professor of literature, Fernando de los Ríos, whom the Republic had sent, left the house in which he had pleaded the popular cause to a circle of liberal journalists and officials. He had never pleased the State Department and was never at ease with it. The career diplomat, Juan Cárdenas, returned with an air of easy habitude. In the patio of his well-graced home the influential and the social had spent many congenial hours. Their friendship had served him well in serving Franco well. During the years of the Civil War he had remained in the United States, pleading with quiet effectiveness the cause against the Republic and gaining material help for Franco's forces. With none of the brutal or domineering airs of Fascism in or about him, and at heart drawn more to Britain than to Germany, he was a well-selected agent for Madrid within the Washington diplomatic circle.

His first important errand was to secure American cotton on credit for the Spanish mills. This errand took him upon a visit to the Under Secretary of State on May 18th. He entered the Department with a complaint in hand. His government, he told Welles, wished him to make known its displeasure over the fact that the wife and the mother of the President had permitted their names to be used as sponsors for an exhibition of Picasso paintings in New York. This exhibit was for the benefit of Spanish refugees in the Civil War. One of the paintings expressed the terror of the bombing of Guernica. The exhibition, Cárdenas asserted, was being used to stir up and organize opposition to his government.

9

That it was bringing together many who detested the cruelty through which Franco had gained power, he was correct in perceiving. That Picasso's picture created repulsion against the regime of which he was the official defender, many visitors would attest. But most Americans would have told him that it was the deed, not the evocation of the deed, that should be suppressed.

Welles kept his lips dry. He did not apologize for the conduct of the Roosevelt ladies. He also refused to discuss the political propriety of the exhibition. The Ambassador had registered his protest and therefore performed his official duty; the Under Secretary had ignored the protest and therefore performed his.

Cárdenas then turned to the real business that had brought him to the State Department. He asked if it was possible for the Spanish government to secure a two-year credit from the Export-Import Bank to buy 300,000 bales of American cotton. A loan of this kind, he calmly remarked, would improve the sentiment of the Spanish government and reopen the channels of normal trade between Spain and the United States.

The Ambassador was aware that there might be angry objections within the American government—particularly the Treasury. For the Franco government had brought an irritating lawsuit in the American courts to recover some fifteen million ounces of silver bought by the Treasury from the Bank of Spain in 1938. These purchases had provided dollars for the Republican government when in the utmost straits. It had had to pay cash for everything. The Ambassador entered into explanations of why the Franco government thought itself in the right. Welles refuted the justifying points and added that he was certain that the American courts would also reject them.[1]

The State Department dealt with the loan request gingerly, with a wish to turn it into a trifle of no account except to the cotton trade. The men at the desks were divided between those who regretted that we had permitted Franco to come into power and those who were convinced that we had acted wisely. But they had

[1] He was correct. The United States District Court for the Southern District of New York decided against the Spanish government on July 14, 1939. But the Spanish government stubbornly carried forward the matter on appeal, which was quashed only in January 1941.

entered into an armistice of opinion in regard to the event; all were, by then, willing to avoid an antagonizing revival of the argument.

Thus, the request was transmitted to the Export-Import Bank with the simple comment that the State Department had no objections if the bank found the business attractive. The credit seemed to fit the trade advantage of both countries. The American government controlled a large amount of cotton of which it was eager to be rid; the Spanish people needed to be clothed. The Spanish mills had almost no cotton and were equipped to use American growths. They were located in sections of Spain in which the masses had been supporters of the Republican government and remained unreconciled. If given work, they would have less time to nourish their sullen regret, and more to eat.

The officials of the bank were ready to do the business. This was the type of loan they preferred—short-term financing for the export of an American farm product. But a contrary will entered the meeting of the Board of Directors. Even though a spokesman for the State Department made known that the President approved the credit, as he had, the Treasury flatly refused approval. No loan would be granted—if it could prevent—to a foreign government that was bringing it before the bar for a transaction so just and legal. The silver suit was baseless and some of the language of the accusations insolent. Who was Franco to appeal to—and by so doing misuse—the American courts?

The Board did not act in the face of so intense an objection, knowing it would flare back from outside. Jesse Jones, the Federal Loan Administrator, who mostly ran the bank, tried to compose the question. He suggested to Cárdenas that the Spanish government agree to drop the suit if the bank made the requested advance. But the Ambassador evaded by saying that this was a political matter. Perhaps he was made bold to reject Jones's terms by some tip that the loan would be made anyhow.

For on June 12th Welles informed the Ambassador that the President had decided the cotton loan should not be connected with the question of the silver suit. The thought was that this legal question should be permitted to take its course in the courts. The Secretary of the Treasury had evidently been rebuffed. But, as both the Ambassador and the State Department were to learn, he was not fazed.

The shunting of the silver suit, however, did not at once clear the way for the cotton loan. Another obstacle was now advanced, this time by the State Department. The Spanish government was being unfriendly to American business interests. It was hindering their efforts to restore trade connections, ignoring debts owed to them, and on the verge of casting out the most important of them —the telephone company. Why, it is now easy to understand, since we know that the Spanish government had promised to reserve all the good economic chances for Germany.[2]

To ignore this situation would have been almost equal to consent. The State Department therefore decided to require assurances of fair treatment for American business interests before the cotton loan was given. Welles so stated in a talk with Cárdenas on June 12th. His remarks bore upon the troubles of the largest American venture in Spain, the National Telephone Company, a subsidiary of the International Telephone and Telegraph Company. The system which it had built and run was, by common testimony, efficient and honest. Throughout the Civil War the whole working organization had, as several officers of the State Department could personally attest, conducted itself with caution and impartiality. Yet the Franco government had taken control of the property and would not permit the owners even to enter the country. Welles pointed out that if the American government gave credit to Spain while American property was being taken away, criticism, and just criticism, would follow.

The Ambassador skillfully wondered aloud whether the troubles of the Telephone Company might not be of a special kind rather than a Spanish policy towards the United States. Stories were mentioned for which, the Ambassador said, he would not vouch. Had not the president and other officials of the American-owned Telephone Company been on congenial terms with the leaders of the Spanish Republican government, and had not the company building in Madrid been put to use defending that city against

---

[2] Under an Economic Agreement signed in July 1937 at Burgos and the Pact of Friendship, March 1939.

Franco's attack? [3] Welles dismissed both the stories and their meaning. The talk made clear that the American government intended to give protection but left the issue for another day. The fight to reclaim this American property turned out to be long and underground.

Thus the loan was held up and again (during June) Jones, after talking with the President and the Secretary of State, tried to find a way to free the business from the clamps of circumstance. This might be done by shrinking it and cutting it into sections. He suggested to the Ambassador that the credit be limited to the amount needed to pay only for Spain's most proximate need for cotton—some forty to sixty thousand bales. Who could raise a hue and cry about so small a sum; who would promote questions of principle? But the Spanish government did not hurry to grasp this way out of the difficulty. No answer was made to the American request to be assured that American interests in Spain would be given fair and friendly chances. The State Department waited, saying nothing more. The Spanish government professed not to understand why; as so often later, it tried to appear completely unaware of any possible reason for our difficult behavior. Spanish diplomacy often cultivated an air of innocence.

On June 28th Cárdenas returned to the theme. This talk with Welles was a delicate minuet in which each knew well the steps

[3] Later talks between the American Ambassador in Madrid and officials of the Spanish government revealed the variety of reasons that influenced the Spanish government in its refusal to restore the property to the control of the International Telephone Company. Among those that emerged were: (1) that during the Civil War Franco had asked Sosthenes Behn, president of the company, for various forms of help and Behn had not acceded; (2) the company had continued to furnish service to Madrid throughout the Civil War; (3) various government officials and members of the Falange longingly eyed the important and profitable posts within the company; (4) the German government was urging the Spanish government to expel the American company and to transfer the property to a Spanish company in which Germany could count upon having important influence; (5) Serrano Suñer, Minister of the Interior, was eager to destroy any and all American influence in Spain.

The property was, as will be told in later pages, presently restored to American ownership. This action was followed by an offer of the Spanish government to buy the property with gold, which could only have come from German sources. At the request of the American government, the company refused to sell.

and turns. He said that he was instructed by his government to state that if the reasons for the delay could be solved by action on its part, the action would be taken; but otherwise it would have to change greatly the whole of its cotton-buying policy. The Ambassador gave point to this remark by recalling that the Spanish mills were equipped to use those lengths of cotton which were grown in the United States, especially in Texas. However, if Spain could not secure American cotton, it would begin to modify the looms and the United States might lose the Spanish market permanently. The American fear of loss of export markets, it may be observed, was one upon which all the dictators of Europe at one time or another wrongly counted. They mistook our eagerness to do business for a readiness to put aside both justice and patriotism in order to do business.

Then Cárdenas progressed to another type of appeal. By making the loan, he suggested, we could influence the direction of Spanish political policy. For, he said, if the Foreign Minister, Count Jordana, and other moderate colleagues could point to this cotton loan as proof, they would be the more able to defend their view that it was best for Spain not to cling to the Axis. Lessen the necessity to do so, was the essential argument, so often to be repeated later, and those many elements in Spain who wished to remain outside the Axis orbit might be helped to prevail. The reference to the Foreign Minister's purposeful effort was valid; he was at this time rebuffing Italian proposals for military and political pacts. Shortly thereafter (August 11th) he was dismissed from office, but will reappear again as a leading figure in this narrative—a fighter for Spanish independence.

Welles, who in previous talks had been inclined to take an easy, friendly view of the matters under discussion, became more formal. But his response did not follow Cárdenas's traces into Spanish foreign policy. It stayed within the bounds of direct American concern as then conceived. He said that obstacles had arisen of which only the President could dispose and added the hope for a quick decision. He then once again repeated our misgivings in regard to the treatment of American interests in Spain. The Department was being currently advised by the Embassy in Madrid that the German government had submitted a program for entrusting the telephone-telegraph system to a company to be manned by Germans. Cárdenas, who was about to leave for Madrid, promised that he would make another effort to obtain the assurances asked by us.

It may be presumed that he did his best. But the diplomatic minuet went on through July. The Department was determined that it would not permit the American enterprise in the communications field to be despoiled and possibly replaced by a German one. It was a test of whether Spain was prepared to ignore our just rights and interests. And besides, it was a test of whether Serrano Suñer and other intimates of the Axis were strong enough to lead Spain into the coming conflict. Further, the American government now began to want something else before it would make the loan. Americans who had fought in the Republican Army were still being held as prisoners. Our repeated requests that they be permitted to return home had been evaded.

The American Ambassador in Madrid, Weddell, alertly took up our cause. He made the circuit of the Spanish Cabinet— with the exception of the member who was causing the trouble, Serrano Suñer, the Minister of the Interior. That official controlled internal communications and was plainly bent on taking the property over. Weddell made his tour under formal orders from Washington not to bargain. The American government maintained the formal position that its requests were just in themselves and that we would not buy satisfaction by promising a loan. If the Spanish government wished to obtain the loan, it would be well advised to remove legitimate causes for objection. Thus there was no bargain. There was merely a related succession of actions— some to be taken by the Spanish government, some by the American.

For the need for cotton prevailed. On July 24th Ambassador Weddell talked with Franco and the new Foreign Minister, Beigbeder. Franco agreed to release the former American members of the Republican Army. He also agreed to permit the American owners of the telephone company to enter Spain; this gave them at least the chance to fight for their property. It also meant that the danger that Germany might gain control was postponed and probably ended. The company officials were admitted at the end of July. Shortly thereafter the loan was approved. The first consignments of cotton left New Orleans for Spain. The way seemed to have been opened to the resumption of regular trade between the United States and Spain. The Export-Import Bank announced on August 7th that it would provide 80 per cent of the credits, totaling 13,700,000 dollars. This sum was to be used to buy 250,000 bales of American cotton to be shipped in ten monthly lots.

The State Department made as little as possible of the transaction. Secretary of State Hull had passed by all earlier queries of the press, with an annoyed glance at those who implied that a loan might have a moral and political tinge. This attitude was maintained. Welles, then Acting Secretary, at his press conference of August 7th, disposed of questions by stating that the matter was entirely a commercial transaction. The State Department would not be drawn out further. Pretense or obtuseness? But not grave or without reason. The deal was small; it might incline Spain to a friendlier course; if it failed to do so, little would be lost; the Spaniards under Franco would have a few more shirts, dresses, tablecloths, while to give an account of what had been obtained in return might put our Spanish friends in a corner. So the reasoning ran.

But within a few weeks the world was at war. Much as the American government might, for a while longer, wish our trade with Spain to remain a matter of only commercial significance, it could not be so. Each item became a factor in the war strength of nations. By what standards or purposes should the exchange henceforth be guided? How, under the unsettled circumstances within Spain, could we best achieve them? These questions lay in wait. They were to become, after the fall of France, knotted strings around papers that grew damp with fingering. But before trying to unravel them, it is in order to follow Spain's career, as a restless neutral, through the winter of 1939-40.

SPAIN THE RESTLESS NEUTRAL
(SEPTEMBER 1939—JUNE 1940)

The Clamp of Circumstance

DURING the first period of the war Juan Beigbeder was Foreign Minister for Spain. He was a voluble and supple man, bold in his beliefs that Britain would win and that Spain must be kept out of the conflict. These became the more determined as he found the authority of his office usurped by a colleague, whose longing it was then to make Spain part of the Axis. Serrano Suñer had been a provincial lawyer from Saragossa. An avid gift for political agitation, power to hate in a time of hate, and marriage to the sister of Franco's wife had brought him to the top of the heap. He was head of the Executive Council of the Falange, the sole political party in Spain, and Minister of the Interior. The first office put him in working companionship with the leaders of the Fascist Party in Italy and the National Socialists in Germany, a figure in their celebrations. The second office placed him in control of the press and the police of Spain. Franco used him, not his Foreign Minister, as liaison with the rulers of Germany and Italy. The lines of attraction and repulsion between Spain and these men wove through the sheaves of his nature.

In June 1939 Serrano Suñer drove through the streets of Naples with his friend Ciano, the Italian Foreign Minister. The latter has left behind an impression of his companion as he then appeared in Axis eyes:

"He is a slender, sickly man—one of those creatures notable for study and reflection; a very conscientious man, honest and full of enthusiasm. Having been caught in the whirlpool of the revolution, he has become both actor and author, and brings to his task a passionate faith. Intelligent, but still somewhat inexperienced, he wavers in his judgment between the results of the practical knowledge he has acquired and the vague and metaphysical expression of his reflections. But it is always feeling that dominates him: he hates and loves impetuously." [1]

On this man (and the elements about him) the Axis leaders based their policy in Spain. They relied upon him to prod Franco into the making of a government fit and eager for their kind of revolution and war. His ambition—to become Minister for Foreign Affairs—sought its path through them. It was to be the clasp by which Spain and the Axis would be joined together. Pleasing by tribute and promise, he sought their help in getting the chance to please them more. Ciano advised his chief that Serrano Suñer wished to become Foreign Minister and that it was in the interest of the Italians that this should happen, adding that Serrano Suñer would be grateful if Mussolini persuaded Franco to that end. Before the war was over, the Axis leaders—particularly Hitler— came to think themselves bitterly deceived by this Spanish agent. For he turned out to be more daring in word than in deed; giving as a suitor, but ungiving when Spain's help was wanted; an independent and scornful Spaniard in his crooked way; and quite unable to make the Spanish people feel as he felt about the Axis cause. Neither actor nor author, but an upstart guardian of his own career.

Serrano Suñer, on this June visit to Italy before the war, described to Ciano the elements in the Spanish situation that doomed it for the time being to the role of neutral.

"We touch on many points: *war*. Spain fears a war in the near future because she is today at the end of her resources. In certain regions there is famine. If she can have two or preferably three years' time, she can reconstitute herself and complete her military preparations. Spain will be on the side of the Axis because she will be guided by feeling and reason. A neutral Spain would, in any event, be destined to a future of poverty and humiliation. Furthermore, Franco Spain intends to solve the problem of Gibraltar; as long as the British flag flies on Gibraltar, Spain will not be a completely free and sovereign nation. The youth of Spain lives in the desire and hope of pushing the English into the sea, and is getting ready to do so. Spain also has accounts to square with France, that 'dishonest and dishonorable France,' and

[1] The Ciano Diaries 1939–43, entry for June 5, 1939.

these accounts are called Morocco and political and economic independence." [2]

Thus Ciano paraphrased Serrano Suñer, recording at the same time that

"Serrano Suñer was very happy to learn that we and the Germans also wish to postpone the conflict for some years."

In July Ciano returned Serrano Suñer's visit. Dinners, receptions, parades, and toasts all seemed to point to the conclusion of a full military and political alliance. But when the emptied orators and soldiers parted, and the uniforms were put away, talk had not been turned into troth. Franco held aloof from any decisive engagement. He had expressed a wish for five years of peace—during which Spain might recover and prepare to identify herself with the system of the Axis—and had welcomed Ciano's confirmation of Serrano Suñer's report. Thus Spain remained unengaged, though far from free.

For Franco had joined the Anti-Comintern Pact and sworn common cause. He had, during the maturing time of victory, entered into a Pact of Friendship with Germany. This provided that in case one of the contracting parties got into war, the other would avoid everything in the political, military, and economic spheres that could accrue to the disadvantage of the treaty partner or to the advantage of the latter's opponent.[3]

This accord was supplemented by various secret pacts which provided for close co-operation with Germany in the direction of the Spanish police, press, and propaganda. An agreement between the navies provided for help to German naval and blockade-running operations. In short, the Spanish government was pledged to observe, should war come, a favorable, a more than favorable neutrality. So, in any case, these pacts were taken by the Italian and German governments to mean, as confirmed by Ciano after his talk with Franco on July 19th.

But though placing himself in this fashion on the Axis side if war should come, Franco's real and dominating wish—as has been

[2] Ciano, op. cit.
[3] Article VI, German-Spanish Pact of Friendship, signed March 31, 1939, ratified November 29, 1939.

said—was for a long period of peace, so that Spain might recover and his regime become well enough established to stand the stress of war, perhaps to profit by it. Spain—he let Berlin and Rome clearly know—was unhappy over the danger of war in Europe and unready to enter into it. Hitler permitted him to go through the summer with the consoling belief that war would be avoided; and that the vows of loyalty and help for Germany would not be soon tested.

The event was in shocking disregard of these hopes. The Spanish government could only watch and wait. Geography, economic conditions, and the misery of the people would have defeated even an ardent wish to enter on the Axis side. But the wish was reserved and tinged with bitterness. Hitler had ignored the requests for time. He, for his own ends, had entered into a pact with the Communists, deeply feared and hated by many of the Spanish leaders. The vaunted paladin in that crusade had turned out to be no paladin at all.

On September 4th the Spanish government announced its neutrality in the most correct language:

"Officially recognizing the state of war which unfortunately exists between Poland, Britain and France on the one hand and Germany on the other, I ordain by the present decree the most strict neutrality on the part of Spanish subjects in accordance with contemporary laws and principles of international law."

Franco accompanied this announcement by an appeal "to the common sense and the responsibility of the rulers of the nations" to direct the efforts of all to the localization of the conflict. American policy at the time is reflected in Secretary Hull's quick and warm response to this plea for neutrality, which said that Franco's "moving appeal" had been read with "deep interest." [4]

The German government did not protest or complain. Franco gave assurances that he would do what he could, within the practical limits of the situation, to show his friendship. Germany could be sure, he sent word, that Spanish neutrality would be benevolent. The German Ambassador in Madrid assured the Foreign Minister that Germany also had a great interest in the

[4] State Department Press Release No. 393, September 5, 1939.

observance of Spanish neutrality and wished only that the Spanish government would shut its eyes from time to time.

But it was not easy during the first months of the war to deviate from an honest, neutral course. The Spanish government did not dare, even if it had truly wished, to serve Germany. British sources in Spain seemed to learn of most projects before the anchor was hoisted or the disguise completed. British and French ships kept most vigilant watch along the Spanish coasts and among the Spanish islands. They sometimes failed to gauge closely the limits of Spanish territorial waters, without serious reproof. Extensive plans, drawn up by Germany before the war, to outwit the blockade and supply German submarines with Spanish aid, had mainly to be deferred. Irked and depressed, Franco devoted himself to the urgent tasks of getting the means needed by the Spanish people to live and work, order within his government, and the suppression of his domestic enemies.

IV

ALL SIDES DEAL WITH A HUNGRY SPAIN

First Germany, then the Allies, then the United States

THE Spanish government had also pledged itself to show special regard to Germany in economic matters. In their Pact of Friendship (March 1939) the two governments had written that they were unified in the wish to increase the economic relations between their two countries as much as possible.[1]

The Spanish government did not disclaim this wish, but it found it necessary to subordinate it. After the advent of war Germany was not able to supply the products that Spain most wanted. The Spanish government was compelled to seek francs, sterling, and dollars and the goods they would buy. For a time after the outbreak of the war it tried to reward special allegiance with special favor—sending to Germany goods that the Spanish people needed. But there was no easy and safe transport route from Spain to Germany. Then, frightened of a revolt of hunger, it began to bargain with Germany in the same way as with the Allies.

The trade missions of all countries were welcomed in Madrid; no suitor was rejected because of early vows. But the banns with Germany were drawn up first. A series of economic accords was signed on December 22nd. The German officials were able to report at the end of their mission that the Spanish government pursued a policy that was basically friendly to Germany. But they also observed that among the Spanish negotiators there were some who opposed ideas of joining the Spanish economy too closely with Germany.

---

[1] This supplemented the provision in the Secret Protocol of July 16, 1937, signed at Burgos, which provided for German collaboration in the economic reconstruction of Spain, especially in the development of minerals and raw materials.

In these accords the Spanish government agreed to take pains to reserve to Germany the greatest possible margin of exports, especially of those products in the delivery of which Germany was particularly interested.[2] It also promised to try to comply with Germany's import demand for Spanish commodities, except those needed by Spain and those which in view of the foreign-exchange situation Spain felt it had to reserve for export to other countries. But these loose promises were hedged around.

The needs of Spain were so many and so great, its representatives insisted, that it had to obtain goods of the same value as it sent to Germany; and at the same time. This was expressed in a provision that the trade was to be in balance. The German government took this blend as the best procurable and set its state trading organization (Sofindus) to work to extract the utmost. For several years it secured far more than it gave; Germany was until 1942 a drain upon Spanish economic life.[3]

The French and British trade missions were just as industrious as the German. In January 1940 the Spanish government signed an agreement with France which stipulated an extensive trade in designated goods, some of which Germany wanted. This accord had two attractions for the Franco regime; it contained a promise of greatly needed goods, and it was a kind of assurance that France would not support domestic enemies.[4] To the French government the accord was a payment for Spanish quiet and a means of reducing the volume of products that Spain might send to Germany. These aims smothered doubts as to whether a fire was being kindled for the devil.

The talks with Britain were longer drawn out despite the fact

[2] Among the more important products designated were iron ore, zinc, lead, mercury, wool, hides and skins, and wolfram.

[3] This conclusion is based on scattered records and the increase in the German debt under the German-Spanish clearing accord. Bernhardt, the head of Sofindus, told American interrogators that during the years 1940-4 Germany shipped to Spain 450 million gold pesetas of merchandise, while Spain shipped to Germany 693 million gold pesetas. The difference was mainly in the first years of the war.

[4] Earlier in 1939 Spain and France had signed an accord restoring to Franco all the Spanish assets—mainly gold—which had been sent to France by the Republican government. At the time, Franco had explained to Ciano that he had to cajole France for some time longer in order to obtain these assets, which he valued at an absurdly high figure.

that the Civil War had not cut established trade ties with Spain. The British bargained patiently for the war supplies they wanted, counting on Spanish needs of goods from the Empire. Unlike the French, they would not accept an accord with patches of Spanish sky; they wanted to know just how it would work, because the French agreement was failing. Without success, they tried to get promises that Spain would use its ships to carry products to Britain through dangerous waters.

The British-Spanish agreements were concluded on March 18, 1940. They formed a mechanism for trade rather than an exact program of trade.[5] Old debts were adjusted and Britain agreed to advance Spain 2,000,000 pounds for future purchases. Spain promised not to re-export products secured from the sterling area and to limit or prohibit the export of certain other goods to the Axis.

The British government was, no doubt, aware that this war trade agreement might later make it possible for Spain to give Germany greater help. It decided to overlook this aspect of the deal and to use the resources of the British Empire as a weight in the future struggle for influence.

Churchill, on becoming Prime Minister, did not dispute this policy.[6] Indeed, after the disaster in France he clung to it tenaciously. For the economic bond became the only substitute for divisions of tanks and squadrons of planes. Thus, when in May 1940 Sir Samuel Hoare was rushed to Madrid on the anxious errand of keeping Spain out of the war, he was told particularly to press forward with the trade arrangements envisaged in these agreements. There was no other way in which Britain at the time could so clearly show its usefulness, its command over the seas, and its power to carry on.

In these ways, then, the poor neutral, Spain, arranged to obtain essentials from the nations at war. Each found it best to give that

[5] Many parts of the agreement between Germany and Spain were kept secret. In contrast these British agreements were published in full. *Board of Trade Journal*, March 30, 1940. A good interpretative analysis is to be found in *Hansard Debates*, House of Commons, Volume 358, March 18, 1940.

[6] But in May 1940 Chamberlain lost his faith. When, shortly after his displacement as Prime Minister, Hoare consulted him about accepting the special mission to Spain, Chamberlain told him not to expect success in the midst of defeat. Sir Samuel Hoare: *Complacent Dictator*, page xii of the Introduction.

it might get, and to keep Spain out of the clutches of the others.

During this cycle of negotiation the American government pursued a semi-detached course. It did not interfere with the flow of private trade between the United States and Spain. This was limited only by Spain's power to pay and the Allied naval control. A few American exports, oil above all, grew greatly, but they passed through the British blockade. The State Department was still trying, during this period, to sustain rights claimed as a neutral. As late as January-February 1940 it lurched into and out of a series of quarrels with the British government over what we chose to regard as infringements of these rights, especially the rough handling of American mails and ships. The American government was not ready to control trade with other neutrals to serve the defense of Britain and France. The Executive had no legal authority to do so; Congress had refused to grant it. Besides, were these countries not trading with Spain?

But the State Department abstained from attempts to foster American trade with Spain by negotiating a trade agreement. The traffic was unpopular. In any newspaper office tales could be heard of secret funneling to the Axis. Further, the Spanish government was still punishing American commercial and investment interests. The fight for control over the Spanish telephone system was not at an end. The Spanish government, despite the gesture it made while the cotton loan was being arranged, prevented the American group from resuming actual direction of their property.

Weddell pleaded with patience but he was put off time and again. The State Department made clear through the Spanish Ambassador in Washington that Spain could expect no economic help until right was done in this matter. The tedious dispute was relieved a bit in December (1939) by a turn in Spanish tactics. The Minister of Finance hinted broadly that if the American government would expedite (by an advance or otherwise) the minting of a great quantity of Spanish coins in the United States, the telephone company might get a favorable hearing. The operation would have yielded the Spanish Treasury a good profit. Upon Weddell's advice, the hint was ignored.

For the American government had concluded that it could not count on goodwill to produce justice. That, it was gradually realized, would come into sight only if and when Spain could not get along without us. Economic conditions within Spain were growing worse as winter went on. Wheat, cotton, and oil became scarcer. Spanish reserves of foreign exchange became smaller. Franco had foreseen that this was likely to be so.

In a radio broadcast on New Year's Eve of 1940 Franco tried to clear himself of any blame because the sacks and stores were empty. He passed it out with virtuous complacency. Most of all to blame were the countries which had refused to bow to the regenerative doctrines of Germany and Italy, and thus brought about the war. Next were the Spaniards who had fought him with consequent harm to the nation's economy. And next were those

"unscrupulous merchants who trade on the miseries of others."

Here he took a fling in defense of the anti-Semitism of his friends:

"You will now understand the persecution of certain races which other countries, to safeguard their historic destinies, were forced to persecute and isolate because they had become a national peril. Thanks to God and clear vision of our Catholic King and Queen Ferdinand and Isabella, we were once freed of such a dangerous burden as all those speculators attached to easy gains and sinister speculations."

The Spanish people were not moved to join in the praise of persecution, for they knew that the most talented traders in misery were members of the Falange.

By speeches such as this the Spanish leaders sought to teach their people to endure their troubles. They thought to make hunger less gnawing by spicing it with hatred and contempt for the well-fed plutocracies. But as they became aware that the next harvest was not going to be good, pride fell before fertility. In the spring of 1940 the Spanish government began to hint that it would be greatly pleased to obtain succor from the United States.

V

FRANCO ASKS US FOR A LOAN, THEN PAUSES
(MAY–JUNE 1940)

The Request

DURING the spring of 1940 the protests over the shortage and dearness of food in both the cities and the provinces of Spain became louder. Imports had just made it possible to maintain a too small ration, which was poorly distributed. The harvest prospects were bad. It became clear that Spain would have to secure from overseas at least a million tons of wheat as well as other foodstuffs.

The government was so absorbed with these problems of need and internal order that it was glad to stay on its edge of the war. Both civilian and military leaders repeatedly affirmed that Spain would maintain its position of neutrality unless directly attacked. They continued to do so during April and even into early May, while the German armies conquered Norway and began to sweep over Belgium, Holland, and France. In fact, these swift successes at first seemed to alarm rather than exalt the Spanish government. A sudden fear appeared that Italy might not only strike against France, but also seize the Balearic Islands. At the same time, so the current of fear expanded, the large German Fifth Column in Spain might spring into action to gain control of the government. The dictators had not yet had a full chance to become familiar with each other's ways; but what knowledge they had was enough to make them watchful.

Under these combined trials—hunger, weakness, and fright—the Spanish government was impelled to improve its relations with the United States. Early in May Serrano Suñer at last seemed to relent in regard to the telephone company. On the 15th he signed an agreement with the American owners whereby they would be permitted to regain control of the property and management. Or so both they and Weddell, the American Ambassador, construed the deed. In reporting progress on this matter Weddell had let the State Department know that both Franco and Serrano Suñer had broadly hinted that the time was ripe for the United States to give further help to Spain, but that he had said nothing.

The German economic delegation had written in the January (1940) report upon their return to Berlin that Franco did not wish to borrow from any belligerent government since Spain was pursuing a neutral policy and did not wish to impair its painfully acquired independence.

But now he felt compelled to turn, not to a belligerent, but to another neutral whose sympathies were plainly on the other side. On May 15th Cárdenas told Welles, with a veiled air, that he had received a rather vague and indefinite instruction to find out if the Spanish government could secure in the United States a credit of between 120 and 200 millions of dollars. Welles replied at once that it was out of the question that the American government could extend a credit of anything like this size in view of the limited resources of the Export-Import Bank.

But this call left agitation in its wake. The answer did not dispose of the issue within the American government. It was not easy, even for a participant like myself in the agitated discussion, to know what was going on. The sense prevailed, when our relations with Spain were in question, of watching a sleight-of-hand act from the second row. Now the hat was empty; now the ears of the rabbit were visible; now they were out of sight. At one moment the performance took place on the right of the stage. The next it took place on the left. And all the time the performers were anxiously watching the audience.

To all except a few of the officials concerned, the idea of helping Franco was unpleasant—to be avoided if possible. But there were a few, chiefly in or about the European Division of the State Department, who did not seem to mind this concession to his power to survive; while aligned against them were others who would not grant him aid, no matter what the consequences. The Secretary of State was more the arbiter than judge. The attitude of the President seemed to quiver between distaste and the tales of caution that were carried to him. Until the United States was almost in the war, Britain's wishes often swayed the uncertain quorum.

But besides the matter of judgment there was a question of popular feeling. The Franco regime was disliked; suspect to most and hated by many. The liberal press was excitedly alert to every rumor of intended American aid, suspicious of the State Department, and skeptical of the idea that such aid could serve the Allied cause. Sources within the government kept this section of the press well supplied with "dope," which was at times more arousing than accurate.

In retrospect, as the following narrative will show, the prevailing judgment of the press that it would have been foolish to have substantially helped Franco at that particular time (May–June 1940) seems correct. But much of the press comment was unfair in one respect. It tended to view the willingness of the State Department to consider such action as indicative of a positive design to help Franco to remain in power. No wish of this kind was avowed even in closed and discreet sessions; and if it had been, it would have been disregarded. The central question that engaged attention was different; would help, or the mere prospect of help with conditions, serve to guard against the danger of Spanish entry into the war on the side of the Axis? That was the only focus of debate. But it is true that advisers tended to cluster around the answer that matched their feeling about Franco and his fate.

The failure of Cárdenas to receive any encouragement on his first call did not cause the Spanish government to quit the attempt to get a loan. The Minister of Finance, who had hitherto shown no interest in trade with the United States, took the matter up next.[1] After admitting on May 24th that there had been a difference of opinion within the government as to whether to resort to borrowing, he said it was now recognized to be necessary. Without foreign credits Spain would not recover. Howard Bucknell, the Chargé d'Affaires, remarked that our response was certain to be influenced by Spain's course in the war. The Minister

---

[1] The Spanish shortage of dollars at this time was shown by the fact that the proceeds of the Spanish gold shipments to the United States were spent even before the gold reached this country. The gold itself was assayed at only about 60 per cent and included a lot of old gold and jewelry.

stated earnestly that Spain was determined to maintain her neutrality and had given no contrary promises. There is every reason to think him sincere, a worried Secretary of Treasury trying to get money to pay for supplies. France was not yet at this date clearly beaten. The rich Moroccan lands had not yet fallen on the gaming table of war.

The officials in the State Department argued, under the cool guidance of the Under Secretary, about the response to be made to the Minister of Finance. They were reading with dismay that series of cables in which Ambassador Bullitt vividly told—often with news and insight in advance of the press—of the crumbling of French resistance. When the forecast end came, who could foresee how Spain would behave? But all agreed that until the situation was clearer, it was wise to hold out hope that we might take care of Spanish needs. It seemed foolish to put Franco in a position to justify entry into the war by telling the Spanish people that it was essential if they were to live and work. Later, the intention was reserved, we could give further thought to the conditions of aid.

Ambassador Weddell was then on his way to Washington. The State Department therefore cabled the Chargé on May 27th to tell the Spanish government that the loan request was before us, that Weddell would fly back at once with our reply, and to ask Franco to see him as soon as he arrived in Madrid. With quickness unusual in Madrid, the answer was given that Franco would see the Ambassador between June 6th and 10th.

Weddell found that the State Department was disposed to grant aid if Spain behaved well. But it was not ready—pending further knowledge of Spain's intention—to talk dollars and cents, or bushels of wheat and bales of cotton. There was a wish to reserve any firm or clear promise, and a groping for a form of help least open to popular criticism. These thoughts shaped Weddell's instructions. He was authorized to inform the Spanish government that we were ready to consider credits, particularly for the purchase of products such as cotton and corn of which the American government itself possessed a surplus. We were also willing to give sympathetic attention to such further proposals as the Spanish government might care to make. This guarded tender—if it may be so called—was trimmed with cautions and conditions.

The kind and amount of help, it was specified, would depend upon our available surpluses and credit facilities. The Spanish government in return was to be asked to promise to treat our trade fairly. And, above all, Weddell was told that he should make it daylight clear that credit in any form could only be arranged if Spain remained neutral. This notice was not merely a careful word from a lender to a borrower, lest the proceeds of the loan be wastefully used. It was the center of purpose.

This instruction, as the reader may have gathered, was as tangled a ditty of yeses and noes as puzzled group talent could produce. The State Department added a verse while Weddell was on his way back—a discursive postscript which said that we would make a loan only if Spain entered into a trade agreement with us, and that it was improbable that Spain could do so.

Weddell held his head in perplexity. But the swift movement of events relieved him of the task of unraveling the tangle. For by the time that his talk with Franco came around, the whole outlook of the world had changed, and with it Spanish policy. Franco ceased to care about the American response. Other chances beckoned, other golden gates seemed about to open.

The Ominous Pause

At about the same time (June 1) that Weddell was rushing back to Madrid, Britain's new Ambassador to Spain, Sir Samuel Hoare, arrived. The haze of anxiety over the western Mediterranean was reflected in the questions that he asked himself while flying to his post:

"What could now stop the Mediterranean from becoming the *Mare Nostrum* of Mussolini and Hitler? Was it not inevitable that our communications with the Far East would be completely severed, and an irreparable breach made in the British front? Could Malta and Suez hold out, and would the fortress of Gibraltar be of any value if the naval and air bases under the shadow of the rock now became untenable? Would not Hitler seize this unique opportunity of pushing through Spain and North Africa and of creating for himself an impregnable base from which to dominate the African continent and threaten the Atlantic highway?" [2]

As Hoare stood by the windows of the Embassy he could hear the organized cry of the Falange mob:

"Gibraltar for Spain."

He could see the bright posters that were being pasted over the blank street walls with the messages:

"So that Spain may be great: Gibraltar, Tangier, Casablanca, Fez, Oran, Algiers."

Those elements in Spain that stood in with the Axis were certain that the hour had come; they were calling out for a military action that seemed all but begun. Could they fail in their attempt to force an actual beginning?

Weddell, while waiting to get clearer instructions, tried to find out if there was any sense left in an offer of American aid conditioned on the maintenance of Spanish neutrality. He asked the Foreign Minister on June 10th whether the United States could assume that this would be so. The Minister replied in the language of indirection that it was to be presumed. But was it? The formal Italian declaration of war was in the morning's newspapers.

Two days later, on June 12th, Franco announced that Spain henceforth would be a "non-belligerent." Italy had once said the same, interpreting it to mean all aid to Germany without declaring war; then, when it saw a chance that seemed safe, hitched on to victory. The Spanish government was plainly excited by this example.

Yet even so, both the British and American governments decided that it might be persuaded to wait, if not to desist. Spain was still an invalid, an invalid of divided mind and body. It could not move more than a short step by its own strength, and could not face strain. An offer of aid in recovery might still attract, and keep it quiet if only the better to act later on. Therefore, it seemed best not to show alarm, to impress by going forward as though nothing of final account had happened.

So (on the 13th) Weddell was told to talk with Franco as arranged, taking guidance from the Caudillo's answers. But Franco

[2] Sir Samuel Hoare: *Complacent Dictator*, pages 9–10.

was otherwise engaged. Weddell's appointment was put off from the 15th to the 22nd. Even Beigbeder, the hitherto helpful Foreign Minister, ceased to be in any hurry to know what the American government might or might not do for Spain. The reasons for this delay and the lapse of interest have since become known. The finality of French defeat had become clear. The German troops were on their way to the Pyrenees. Franco was turning to hail them. He was poring over France's collapse and qualifying Spain as heir to its African lands. Germany was being asked whether it would supply the goods Spain needed, as the first part of a joint plan for the capture of Gibraltar and the Straits. If the reply was generous, Spain would no longer need to beg of the United States and the British Empire.[3]

While Weddell was still waiting, the French Army surrendered. Weddell cabled on June 17th that the Spanish reaction to the news was quick and jubilant. On the part of many Spaniards this was relief at the prospective ending of the war that touched and isolated Spain. On the part of others, however, it was an excited sense that the collapse of the democracies would bring Spain the chance to become great again.

Weddell was granted an interview with Franco for the 22nd. Just before the scheduled hour, Serrano Suñer asked him to call —before going on to see the Chief of the Government. Hardly had Weddell taken his chair when the Minister of the Interior remarked that he regarded the agreement with the telephone company as invalid. In fact, he said, while drawing in the smoke of his cigarette, none existed. Weddell calmly affirmed the opposite, without arguing the matter through. The intent was obviously to provoke. Serrano Suñer wanted us to be out of the way, sulking and distant, when the expected bid arrived from Berlin. He wished to leave Spain no chance to go on except at Germany's side.

Weddell, undeterred, went on to his appointment with Franco. The Caudillo did not like talk that contained questions and answers. A mind reputed to be slow revealed a gift for enigmatic reply, for phrases of several meanings. Thus when Weddell inquired

[3] The dealings between Spain and Germany during this period are told in detail in Chapters xii and xiii.

about the import of the declaration of non-belligerency, he said it was as a form of national sympathy with the cause of the Axis. When Weddell then asked bluntly whether Spain would enter the war, he remarked that the United States was nearer war than Spain. The rest of the talk did not make it easy to interpret these answers. Franco said German victory was certain and imminent. With a steady tone of satisfaction he exposed the troubles in store for England and France. The division of these empires among Germany and other countries, he avowed, would promote the general good. Hitler, he said, was a very human (*sic*) man and would be reasonable in his demands. This was, we now know, the blithe hour of Franco's hopes.

Weddell edged toward the matter of possible American aid by observing that European food needs would soon become critical. No longer, Franco said. It was plain that the compass of his economy had swung; that he thought he had located food close by. The deviation could not be corrected by the dull instructions Weddell carried in his briefcase. But he left behind a message that might help to correct it later; that if Spain should decide to remain out of the war, the American government would be glad to listen to Spanish suggestions for an extension of their trade relations.

The disturbing impression left by this talk was deepened by word of an immediately following talk between Hoare and Franco. True, the Caudillo explained to Hoare also that Spain's announcement of non-belligerency did not mean a change in the policy of staying out of the war. But when the chance was given to discuss terms with Britain, Franco was silent. Hoare's bid was in the form of a remark that there was no question between the Allies and Spain which could not be settled by negotiation, even if the agreement could only be made effective after the coming of peace. This was almost an invitation to Franco to discuss Gibraltar, French Morocco, and similar subjects. But Franco did not accept the chance. The reason, it seemed probable, was that Germany had already promised satisfaction of Spanish wishes. This we now know was not so. Franco had asked to be given, but Germany had not yet responded to his request. One other point in the talk seemed to confirm the fear that Spain was about to join the Axis. Franco brushed aside Hoare's mention of the economic situation and said that Spain needed nothing from the British Empire.[4]

Still the British government continued to cling to the thin edge of hope. Like a trained mountain-climber, it would hold harder and not look down. Hoare concluded that while Spain might enter the war, Franco's first hope was that the war might end quickly and that he might play a main part in the peace negotiations.

The American government thought otherwise, that he had about decided to better his claims by joining the action. On June 24th the whole staff of the American Embassy in Madrid, military included, joined in a report on the situation, which stated that the probability of Spain's entry into the war was increasing and outweighed, if it did not preclude, the contrary view. The complete indifference, this message concluded, of all elements in the Spanish government from Franco down, toward potential and conditional help from us pointed, if not to an actual accord, at least to the belief that Spanish needs would be met by Germany. This message marked the low point in the belief of the State Department that Spain could be induced to stay out of the war; lower even than in later days when Franco was openly meeting with Hitler. For Britain's defense in the western Mediterranean seemed so weak, Germany's attacking forces so strong.

But almost at once a reason for believing the situation was not yet settled and could not easily be settled emerged. Germany showed its fear of losing control over Morocco and of having the French fleet join Britain. A promise to satisfy the aims flaunted in Spanish propaganda would carry the risk of French revolt. Failure to satisfy them might cause the Spanish government to be resistant. Perhaps disputes over the disposition of the French Empire among France, Italy, and Spain would yet prevent the combination of all of these countries in a joint assault upon Britain.

In this connection, attention may be drawn to one of those paradoxes which so often in history have made leaders look foolish. There can be no doubt that Franco, during that middle period of June when France was going down, was intent upon snatching French Morocco for Spain in some way or other. The better to

[4] Hoare, op. cit., page 30.

seize any chance that came along, he increased the Spanish armed forces in Morocco. But the action destroyed his prospects. For it discouraged the French Military Commander in Morocco, General Nogues, from carrying on the fight against Germany. He concluded that resistance was impossible, since the weak French armies would be attacked at once on the Riffian front.[5] Had the war spread to Morocco, it is almost certain that Spain and Germany would have come to terms. But this is all surmise in the light of later knowledge.

The State Department at the end of June studied its contradictory collection of estimates and guesses—without reaching any firm conclusion as to whether Spain was about to enter the war or not. It was not to be known at first sight, nor at second sight; and none had second sight. But all agreed that the United States could not then bribe Spain to refrain from joining in what might be the fatal blow against England. Nor could it threaten Spain. This country was not ready, willing, or equipped to plunge into the vortex of what might be an already lost war. But it was no longer reconciled to having events take their course. Thus the government searched for some form of action that might be telling but safe. It stumbled upon one suddenly. We began to pinch off the flow of oil from this hemisphere to Spain and its colonies. Begun with the wish to absolve ourselves from possible criticism, this measure hindered the fusion of German and Spanish desires.

[5] *Le Procès du Maréchal Pétain*, page 304, testimony of Commandant Le Roch.

VI

THE FLOW OF OIL IS PINCHED

Why did Spain Want So Much?

ON MAY 12th of this year 1940 the President told the British Ambassador in Washington that he would be willing to consider any other ways, beyond those already in use, by which the American government might assist the Allied governments. Among the wishes expressed in the British response of May 20th was that the United States deny supplies to the enemy direct or through neutral channels. By June we were ready to try to do so, ready to lay aside the mask of neutrality.

The gaze of suspicion fell upon the flow of oil from the United States and the Caribbean to Spain. That country had been permitted to secure as much oil as it was able to pay for and have transported. With the consent of the nations at war, the cargoes moved untroubled through the blockades. The Spanish government oil monopolies in Spain (Campsa) and in the Canary Islands (Cepsa) were amply and smoothly served under contracts with American companies. The volume of imports grew and grew again.

About the middle of June the French and the British governments both placed a finger upon that fact. On the 14th of June the French Ambassador called to Under Secretary Welles's attention the fact that twenty-one ships, mostly of American registry, were then on their way to Spain with oil; some of this oil, the French government believed, was en route to Italy. A few days later the British government, in a note passed on by its Ambassador in Washington, expressed great concern over this concentration. The figures cited traced the recent abnormal rise in Spanish imports. They were taken to prove that Spanish reserve stocks were excessive, and rapidly increasing. The statistical graph had an

37

ominous hook; it curved toward the Straits of Gibraltar.

Here it may be commented that the figures then in hand were necessarily rough estimates. When, much later, the actual record was compiled, the bulge in shipments was greater than had been surmised. In June American exports of fuel to Spain were triple the usual rate, and of lubricants an ample half year's supply. But the estimate of the size of Spanish reserve stocks was much too high and later corrected by the British.[1]

A substantial part of the oil for Spain was carried in neutral tankers, mostly American. The Texas Company arranged many, if not most, of the shipments. The British note stated that the British government had the clearest possible evidence that the chairman of the Texas Company had arranged with the manager of the company's Italian affiliate to assist Spain in every possible way to charter neutral tonnage for the transport of oil—part of which seemed to be intended for Italy. This charge, it may be interjected, had a basis in fact.[2]

The British government asked us, in view of these facts, first, to restrict the use of American tankers for the transport of oil to Spain; second, to limit shipments from the United States to Spain of lubricants and aviation gasoline. These latter products were carried by ordinary cargo vessels. The British government had no sure way of checking them, even if it were to try; and it feared that any try might cause unwanted trouble with the Spanish government.

The First Furtive Turns of the Valve

The French and British requests were first put in the cooler of routine. There they were treated merely as minor complaints by the Allies concerning evasions of their blockade. As such they might long have been ignored, since some branches of the State Department, particularly a corner of the Legal Adviser's Office,

[1] During June 1940 (according to unpublished figures of the Department of Commerce) the United States exported to peninsula Spain 446,000 barrels of fuel oil as compared with 830,000 during the whole second half year

were still bent upon preserving our neutral trade and supporting the "neutral" rights enumerated in the textbooks of an earlier era.

But after a few days the papers were taken away from the lawyers. It was perceived that the size of the shipments to Spain itself and of the Spanish stocks was the main question of interest —not that of diversion to the Axis. A search began for means by which the excess flow might be prevented without noise or detection. Secretary Hull was not eager to hear a cry from Congress that the Administration was taking sides in the war. He was even less eager to incite an internal row over our relations with Franco. Therefore the British suggestion that we openly control the export of oil to Spain was rejected, as too likely to cause a fight. It was not foreseen that all the oil of Texas would soon be needed for our own defense.

But a number of other steps were taken to serve the same end. First, the Maritime Commission ruled that this trade with Spain was a dangerous one, and that American tankers should not engage in it. Even tankers chartered to foreign buyers of oil were included in this order. Second, the Department arranged with the Treasury to have all oil cargoes labeled for Spain inspected—in order, it was said, to guard against diversion to other destinations. The Secretary of the Treasury, who knew of the British and French notes, had been urging stiff control. His Department at once set about inspecting every tanker in reach, including those already loaded, from keel to cabin. The crews of ships calling at Port Arthur, Texas, to secure oil for Spain became very well acquainted with the look of the harbor.

These measures were put into effect as quietly as possible. The Secretary of State in the few troubled moments that he gave to the matter had shown his hope that the purpose could be achieved without admitting the intent. But the Spanish government quickly sensed that someone was shutting the valve. Spain had no dollars to spare. Behind the decision to use so much of the short supply to buy oil, there was a pressing reason. Whether for peace or for

---

of 1939; and 50,000 barrels of lubricants as compared with 34,000 during the whole second half year of 1939.

For analytical comment on the state of Allied knowledge on the subject and a summary of the real situation, see Supplementary Note II.

[2] See Supplementary Note I on the activities of Thorkild Rieber, chairman of the Texas Company.

war, no one in Washington, and perhaps in Madrid, could then be certain. Probably the enlarged buying orders were first placed as a cautionary economic move; they were in part intended for Italy. Then when the German assault on the western front surged forward, new great values were seen in having large stocks. They were the fee for opportunity—the ticket for Gibraltar and Africa. Germany was being asked to supplement, as a condition for entering the war, what Spain could buy elsewhere.[3]

The Spanish government took swift heed of the delays in tanker sailings from the United States and the cancellation of contracts. The head of the Petroleum Monopoly inquired of the American Embassy in Madrid at once. The Spanish Ambassador in Washington tried to quiz the Under Secretary of State on June 18th. His answer was opaque—consisting merely of a statement that the Maritime Commission was of the opinion that it would be dangerous for American tankers to enter European waters at that time.

[3] See Chapter xii.

VII

THE PINCH GROWS TIGHTER

What Next and How?

SECRETARY HULL relapsed into a relieved belief that the needs of the situation had been met. But he soon learned otherwise. On July 10–11 the Treasury refused to clear two tankers of the Texas Company loaded with oil for Spain on the ground that it was safer for the preservation of American neutrality that they should not be seized carrying contraband.

In accounting for this action to Secretary Hull, the Secretary of the Treasury, Morgenthau, referred to reports that Spanish imports were still excessive. This was so; the rate of flow had been reduced, but it was still enough to enable Spain to add to reserves. Morgenthau then asked orders in regard to the future clearance of tankers for Spain—in such a way as to seem to give orders. The Secretary of State did not welcome this pushful interest. The cut in his skin left by the quarrel over our denial of arms to Spain during the Civil War still pained. He felt ill-treated and was quick to take offense at any hint, no matter how soft or indirect, that there was anything to regret in our record. Were critics, ignorant of his worries, again to force the same quarrel upon him in regard to oil? Britain would bear the brunt of the consequences of whatever was done, let it take the lead! All these ideas could be glimpsed in the comments that he dispersed with tired irritation.

After they had failed to agree on the matter in talk over the telephone, the two Cabinet officers met, only to part in sulky anger. Secretary Hull resented the pressure to act—sustained by those who would not be held responsible for error—without more time and chance to gauge the situation. He disliked quick decision. Secretary Morgenthau was convinced that there was no time to wait, since Spain was on the verge of joining Germany. Secretary

Hull tried to shake himself free by proposing that Morgenthau should act as he saw fit. But then the latter seemed to become afraid that if Spain rebuked us or entered the war, he would be exposed to blame.

Relations between the two departments were unhappy. Differences in policy separated them, and mistrust made the separation angry. The State Department was aroused over stories in the press and on the radio which were thought to originate in the Treasury. These gave inaccurate accounts of action and prejudiced views of motive. Thus the State Department participants in any meeting with their colleagues from the other side of the White House came to fear the experience. For it was all too likely that when it was over, versions that did them no credit would shortly circulate. The State Department, it should be added, was not defenseless. Journalists also called there, and the more faithful ones at the Carlton Hotel as well.

While the departments argued, tankers moved, though not in the same numbers as before. The President was consulted, but he would offend neither one nor the other of his Cabinet. The thought of reducing the flow of oil further was encouraged, but the Secretary of State was left to decide how. Within the next fortnight (in the first part of July) his slowly traveling judgment arrived at the next action station. But he remained anxious lest a mistake be made, and possibly a grave one. We might incite or hurry the Spanish government to do what it otherwise might not do. We might be accused in Congress of thrusting the country toward war; for if Spain entered we could not ignore the fate of her Atlantic islands. We did not know, but could guess (and correctly) that Hitler had his eye upon them.[1] Therefore the hunt continued for an unobtrusive means. The Secretary conveyed to his staff, as a kind of pendant to his talk, his assent to the idea that the oil companies might secretly be asked to reduce shipments.

For about a fortnight longer this idea hung suspended in the void of doubt. Secretary Hull's hints of action seemed to dissolve in mid air. The political officers concerned, who had handled this question of Spanish oil since it first came up, were dubious of the finality of the Secretary's wish and avoided the chore. It was suggested to me, on a holiday in New York (on July 19th),

[1] See Chapter xiii.

that I drop in on the oil companies and let them know that the Department would be pleased if they sent less oil to Spain. This seemed to be a futile step. In view of the size of the trade and the contracts under which it was conducted, I argued, upon my return to Washington, for more impressive action by the State Department. The Texas Company would surely want to be certain that the government was in earnest, and almost as surely would have to explain to the Spanish government why it did not fill orders.

At this point the situation might have had a dramatic solution. For the question of oil for Spain became mingled with the greater question of oil for Japan. We were pouring into that aggressive Empire increasing quantities of oil, including great quantities of those grades used in aviation. This nourishment of a likely enemy became in July the subject of anguished talk between the members of the Cabinet and with Lord Lothian, the British Ambassador. Congress, on July 2nd, had given the Executive legal authority to control all exports.[2] We had informed the British government that we did not feel that we could justify the use of this power to control the flow of oil to Spain—on the grounds of defense. But on July 25th the President signed an order to do so, as part of a program to regulate the supply to all countries except Britain and its Allies.

All the night before, the cables and wires had sluiced their reports of battle and anxiety into the receiving room on the fourth floor of the State Department. On the morning of the 25th the stream was of exhausting dimensions and, save for the report of England's courage, all of it of bad meaning for the United States. Acting Secretary Welles was intently reading through the neat stack of cables on his desk when an assistant entered. The White House, she explained, asked that he countersign the Presidential proclamation that she held in her hand. One glance was sufficient to extract the essential meaning from its formal phrases; the American government would thereafter subject all exports of oil, scrap iron, and other metals to license. The cables were thrust aside and colleagues hastily summoned to discuss the meaning of this order.

While they were on the way down to Welles's office, it was learned that the White House had already announced the is-

[2] National Defense Law, July 2, 1940.

suance of the proclamation. The group took their chairs with perturbed wonder, especially those who were immersed in the crisis in the Far East. Almost at once they learned that it would be of little use to ask the urgent questions that were in their minds. For Welles said that he had not known how it was to be applied. If he could surmise, he did not choose to. His habitual coolness resisted the contagion of excitement. He was not inclined to retell tales out of the Cabinet or White House until they were condensed into succinct orders.

Thus he listened with blank expression to the points and queries of his staff. Of these the Chief of the Control Division, Joseph C. Green, was the most obviously disturbed. That was not unusual, since this harassed official was by nature easily aroused. Further, his place within the government subjected him to all the detailed consequences of the sudden moves above. He knew that within the hour every oil company in the United States would be on the other end of his telephone asking what the order meant. This was a spur to his detective faculties. They led him to the conclusion that the manner and form of action had been conceived within the Treasury. His evidence for that opinion was not bad. Clipped to the draft proclamation was a small piece of paper on which the word "Treasury" was typed. Further, he asserted that in response to his inquiry the White House told him that it thought that the Treasury had cleared the proclamation with the other branches of the government, including the State Department. The basis of this impression remains even today obscure. With whom the matter might have been discussed, no one present knew or could find out.

Whatever the originating source and intention, the questions presented were urgent and of consequence. What would the regulations be and how would they be applied? How the President decided to end, or greatly curtail, the shipment of vital materials to all whom we regarded as aggressors and potential enemies? Were we about to take this crucial step? Both the manner and the language of the proclamation seemed to indicate that we were.

Like observers of an atomic bomb test stretched out on the ground, the conferring officials sought to discern what shape the fiery cloud took. Upon the meaning of this order depended the chances of war with Japan and of Spanish entry into the war against Britain. The more safely to face the glare, some put on the dark glasses of discretion. The Secretary of State, they knew, doubted whether it was wise, as yet, to invite the strains and dangers that would follow if we directly denied vital supplies to countries not included in the British blockade. His mouth had seemed to sag at the corners with worry whether Congress or public opinion would support him in that course, and whether the American Army and Navy were prepared for the struggle. But he was absent.

Welles, after hearing the review of anxieties felt in various divisions of the Department, said that he would try to persuade the President to confine the order to oil of grades useful in aviation, and to scrap iron of the highest type only. That afternoon he did so. Whether or not this was a reversal of the idea that the President had in mind when he signed the order was not discussed. But it probably was. The Treasury's slip was removed, the State Department's appended.

The currents toss and twist where fast rivers join. Now one, made turbulent by the night's rainfall, runs more swiftly and strongly than the other and dashes over it with high foam; now the other, having washed away some obstacle, suddenly pours out in greater depth. So the streams of desire within the government clashed and whirled about in the years before the war; the will to prevent Axis victory, the wish to remain out of war, and the longing for time in which to strengthen ourselves for whatever struggle was ahead. The breakers of decision constantly foamed as they rolled on.

The reduced order (issued on July 26th) was of little importance—except to Japan. It did not affect the question of whether and how we would further reduce the flow of oil to Spain. Welles decided to consult with the heads of the oil companies concerned. They came to Washington around August 1st. They were asked to keep their shipments to Spain within previous customary limits and cautioned to be sure that none of it was passed on to Germany or Italy. This caution was directed particularly at Captain Thorkild Rieber, head of the Texas Company. His close associations with Nazi Germany were at that very time being exposed in the public press.[3]

Thus by some quiet turns of the wrench of authority during the summer of 1940, the flow of oil to Spain was reduced. At first the hands that grasped the tool had been lax and doubtful. But they grew firmer as American policy evolved into one of open opposition to the Axis. During the next few months, while Britain's fate was being decided, the tanker sailings were few; the quantities of gasoline, fuel oil, and lubricants were insufficient even for ordinary needs. Spain had to begin to empty its tanks and to worry about what would happen if the shrinkage went further.[4]

[3] See Supplementary Note I, already cited.

[4] The extent of reduction is shown by the following table:

Exports from U.S. to Spain

THOUSANDS OF BARRELS

	Gasoline	Fuel Oils	Lubricants
Second half year 1939	1,267	830	34
First half year 1940	1,165	1,403	110
Second half year 1940	357	891	76

From unpublished records of the U.S. Department of Commerce.

VIII

THE SPANISH GOVERNMENT PIVOTS

The Failure of a Threat

THE Spanish government tried to loosen the valve by reviving the threat against the American-owned telephone company. Serrano Suñer, it will be recalled, had on June 22nd, in an attempt to irritate, denied his promise to allow the owners to resume control. Weddell took up the case again with zeal, but Franco took no notice of his scattered appeals. Weddell concluded that the Spanish government was trying to use our protective concern to force us to supply all the oil wanted. The State Department instructed him to make clear that it would not consider any such bargain. He was told to insist upon the restoration of American control as a matter of right and given promise, and to let it be known that the American government would not discuss any other matter of interest to Spain (meaning a loan) until this was done.

Weddell expounded these views in a number of rasping talks with Beigbeder, Serrano Suñer, and Franco. On July 29th, August 3rd, and again on August 6th the Ambassador and the Foreign Minister exchanged complaints. Each of these talks roamed far. Beigbeder said that the attitude of the Spanish government was misunderstood. Spain, he averred, had no thought of entering the war unless attacked; the time for any such action in conjunction with Germany had gone by. These comforting words were wholly unlike the versions of the ideas of the Spanish government —since become known—which the German Ambassador in Madrid was making to Berlin. For example, in a memorandum that Stohrer prepared for the German Foreign Office on August 8th, he stated that the Spanish Foreign Minister had several times reminded him of the offer made by Spain in June to enter the war.[1] The only

[1] Stohrer wrote as follows: "The Spanish Foreign Minister and also the

way to acquit Beigbeder of duplicity at this juncture is to believe that he believed that the offers to Germany were not genuine.

These avowals were spread like a carpet to deaden the tread of suspicion, but they did not do so. The Foreign Minister pleaded for gasoline, but the State Department continued to doubt that it was needed for peaceful purposes. Its opinion was shaped by estimates provided by the British government of Spanish reserves and by the record of shipments during the previous year. True, the restrictions imposed on the use of oil within Spain were severe and ordinarily would have been taken to connote a genuine shortage. But the available facts suggested another meaning, that the restrictions were being used as a means of hoarding for war, or possibly even as a measure of deception.

The truth of the situation is still not easy to decipher. The opinion that Spanish stocks were excessive and that the need was not critical was in some measure valid. So were reports that certain shipments had been turned over to Italian and German ships. But the estimates of stocks which influenced decision were wrong. Spanish reserves were smaller than was thought. The exercise of tracing out the facts in detail is carried on further in a Supplementary Note.[2]

The next requests of the Minister of Foreign Affairs for oil were met by Weddell with the placid reply that the American government was waiting for a settlement of the telephone dispute. Our wish to wait for clearer proof of what lay ahead was strengthened by attacks in the controlled Spanish press, which grew more and more harsh. An evident attempt was being made by spirits hostile to us to prepare the minds of the Spanish people for entry into the war. At this juncture (August), Serrano Suñer, who controlled the press and radio, was doing his utmost to arouse the Spanish people against Britain and the United States. Hence he was glad of any quarrel, and ready to risk the loss of overseas supplies in the thought that Germany would take care of Spanish

Minister of the Interior have up until the last few days repeatedly pointed out the Spanish offer to me, so that it may be assumed that Spain even today will keep its promise made in June." *Documents Concerning Relations between the Spanish Government and the European Axis*, No. 1. Published by the State Department. They will hereinafter be cited as State Department Documents.

[2] See Supplementary Note No. II.

needs. The refusal of Germany to do so during the next three months was to prove one of the reasons why the drive for intervention finally failed.

Franco, we know now, was testing through Serrano Suñer what he could hope for from Germany. But with ever-present instinct to take from each day whatever might be had, he guarded himself against the loss of American products. On August 6th the Foreign Minister met Weddell at the door of his office and stated that the telephone matter was settled at last. Weddell, acting on orders in hand, then stated that the American government would permit Spain to obtain such quantities of oil as it could transport and the British would navicert.

Of the circumstances of this midsummer Spanish pivot we now know much more than the American government knew at the time. But we are still left to guess at the thoughts that made Franco's bargaining mind go around, made it give in to get oil. Was it foresight that Germany would refuse to supply his needs except on objectionable terms? Was it fear that the whole Spanish economy would collapse if he remained at odds with us? Spain might find itself deprived not only of oil but of fertilizers, cotton, and wheat. The Spanish government was about to pick up again the dropped request for a large credit to buy these products. Or was he afraid that the American government might welcome the growth of the quarrel as a pretext for attacking the Canary Islands?

Or was it because of a wish to preserve Spanish oil reserves while he waited the approach of his chance to inherit—by default or by arms—Gibraltar and Morocco? Had he not on July 17th publicly declared that:

"It is necessary to make a nation, to forge an empire. To do that our first task must be to strengthen the unity of Spain. There remain a duty and a mission, the command of Gibraltar, African expansion, and the permanence of a policy of unity."

As Hoare has written, these words were not merely rhetoric. Even after close scrutiny of the record (reviewed in later chapters) of the exchanges between Spain and Germany during this period, it is difficult to know what was in his mind. At all events, in conceding to us, he had given but little, and nothing that could not be taken back.

IX

BRITAIN'S LEAD (THE AUTUMN OF 1940)

Our Action Gives Britain Its Chance

THE cold and untrusting wind that blew across the Atlantic made good weather for British sailing. The American pinch upon the flow of oil to Spain gave the British government a prized chance to display its influence and usefulness. With quick insight Britain made the most of it. Shrewdly, seeing behind the posters that called for war at once, Hoare wrote home to Lord Beaverbrook about this time (August 7th):

"My own impression is that the Spaniards are sitting on the fence until they see how the invasion of England, and possibly Egypt, goes. They are convinced that they will get something for certain out of the war in Africa and an arrangement about Gibraltar. But they are terribly short of everything that is needed for fighting and on that account they would only come into the war if they were convinced that it was virtually over."

His conclusion, accepted by his government, was that

". . . to treat Spain as an enemy is playing into the hands of the Germans, who are determined to force the country into war against its wish." [1]

Britain in that summer was too close to mortal danger to choose its enemies or friends. Most of the Spanish people might be counted on, it thought, to be friends if not driven by injury or necessity; they had not been drilled or beaten into supine obedience. The government—even if it wished—could not ignore them. Thus Britain strove to maintain the flow of trade from the Empire

[1] Letter to Lord Hankey, July 27, 1940, printed in Hoare, ibid., page 23.

into Spain and to advertise the fact in all parts of the needy land. After the first gust of alarm in June, it quickly set about to make clear that it had no wish to see the Spanish economy collapse for lack of oil. Once assured that Spanish stocks were not excessive, British tongues would speak of Spanish needs, make sure they were not neglected.

Thus, while invasion talk filled the air, British representatives sat down with Spaniards to prepare a long-term program of supply that would take care of Spanish requirements but not permit the accumulation of great stocks. The American government gave assent. By September the schedules were approved; the oil question was, for the time being, settled.

At this time Spain could have had more oil had it wished. Britain offered more if the Spanish government would end the restrictions on consumption. How better, the British thought, to pamper the Spanish people in a season of shortage? But the offer was refused on the ground that Spain could not pay for more. The program envisaged an inflow equal to Spain's usual past imports, so scheduled as to enable Spain to maintain a safe level of stocks—two and a half months' supply but no more.

The American government, while (as it will be shortly related) refusing to lend Spain the dollars needed to pay for this oil, favored the operation of the agreement with Britain. We permitted American-owned tankers sailing under foreign flags to carry oil to Spain—after obtaining a promise from the British government that they would not be hauled within the combat zone. We raised no objections to American tankers sailing under British or Norwegian flags. We issued cargo licenses for Spain and the Spanish colonies.

These arrangements regulated, although not without some breaks in the schedule, the flow of oil to Spain and the Spanish colonies during the rest of 1940. They were maintained in the face of frequent and anxious rumors that Spain was about to enter the war. Each time that Serrano Suñer went abroad, to Berlin, Rome, Berchtesgaden, the regulating hands quivered. Each time a new report was received of the fueling of a German ship, they tightened in anger. But they continued to match our oil against German promises.

This policy was justified by events. After scrutiny of the secret record of Spanish negotiations with Germany these conclusions seem warranted: the opposite course, a refusal to permit Spain to secure oil, might quite possibly have caused the Spanish government to come to terms with Germany; and the continued receipt of food and oil from overseas nourished Spanish popular opposition to the Axis. Oil was a universal particle in the stream of Spanish life. It enabled the fishing boats to bring in their catches, the factories to operate, the railroad locomotives to make their runs, the buses to move through the city streets, the trucks to bring food to market. Britain was effective, despite the many forms of censorship, in making it known that it was the guardian of this particle.

Our interference had saved the American telephone company in Spain, ended diversion to the Axis, depleted the Spanish reserves (for whatever purpose accumulated), given Britain a chance to bring home its usefulness, and brought future supply under control. In all these ways it hindered the junction of Spanish and German policies.

The dialogue of difficulties between the Spanish and German leaders was soon to become routine. At each meeting the Spaniards argued that Spain could not properly prepare or start to fight unless supplied in advance with oil and food. The reply was always that Germany would provide enough when, and only when, Spain began to fight; it could not spare such essentials merely to earn goodwill. This difference was never spanned. Franco waited in the hope that military events would make it possible for him to gain his aim without a fight or in so short a one that he would need no outside help. In the meantime, while he refused to promise to remain at peace, he also refused to go to war except at a time of his own choosing. The oil supplies of the Western Hemisphere made it possible for him to assume that position; British resistance made it advisable for him to maintain it; German lust for power made it perilous for him to do otherwise. But of this, much more later.

During the autumn of 1940 the American attitude toward the war changed rapidly. We moved from stunned alarm toward determined action. The United States was becoming ready to see

England through the fight at no matter what risk. The State Department, free of the fear of punishment, moved along with the country. Sessions within the office of the Secretary of State ceased to be searches for tactics that would cover the movement with an invisible or reversible cloak.

X

FOOD OR EMPIRE; OR BOTH?

The Crisis of Decision (Autumn of 1940)

IN TELLING of the attempt to prevent Spain from accumulating an excess supply of oil, we have outdistanced the main story of American relations with Spain during the second half of 1940.

Franco and his Cabinet, it will be recalled, had in June met our offers of economic help with disdain. The State Department had correctly assumed that he was measuring the lures and risks of war. As the United States went forward with aid to Britain, it was hoped that our meaning would be understood in Spain. The summer of hushed waiting passed. The beam of invasion still pointed straight at the cliffs of Dover. The Italian assault toward the Suez Canal started. But the uneasy quiet over the western Mediterranean was unbroken. It might—the hope persisted—remain so for as long as Britain held a battle line; the future decided on distant battlefields and in the remote reaches of the sky. No matter what the ultimate turn, Britain was gaining that which the military governors of Gibraltar begged—time, time, more time.

Late summer reports from Madrid confirmed that the people in Spain wanted no part in the war. They remained dully unmoved by Fascist appeals, growing more hungry and troubled. The harvest was worse than expected. The Spanish government admitted that domestic wheat supplies would be 1.3 million tons less than minimum needs. This gap was one of the vital facts of the war. Spain had to find both the food and the means of paying for it. Supplies of many essential raw materials were similarly low. In the case of cotton, for example, there was only enough to permit some mills to work two days a week. The Spanish government, using both British facilities and the secret help of German banks, was arranging for small imports from Brazil and

Argentina, but the amount in sight was far from enough. There was not enough coal for the steel mills. The stocks of gasoline for which the Spanish government had laid out so much of its foreign exchange were being used up.

In summary, unless the Spanish government received help from somewhere, the coming winter was certain to be one of great distress, and possibly one of disorder. Would the help come from Germany or from the Allied world? Or could they both be induced to contribute? Would Spain have to go to war to obtain what it needed? Or would it have to renounce hopes of an empire?

The Spanish government, as already stated, had explained its plight to Germany as early as June. It had submitted schedules of its wants as a feature of a proposed joint program looking toward Spanish entry into the war. But Germany had sent nothing. It had not solicited Spain's help and showed no signs of willingness to pay for it. In late August Franco began to knock harder at the German door, to describe his needs to Hitler with greater fervor. But he must have gathered from Hitler's summer silence that Germany would measure his requests carefully and ask much in return. He dared not wait for the reply. He had to search for food at once, wherever it could be found. The British government was eagerly striving to provide whatever could be spared from its areas of supply, but that was not enough. The only country with enough, and to spare, was the United States. Leaving Serrano Suñer to explain to Ribbentrop that it was an act of expediency, the Spanish government resumed its attempt to secure aid from the United States. Now it reached for the chance it had renounced in June, when Franco had told Weddell and Hoare that Spain would need nothing from their countries.

On September 7th the Minister of Industry and Commerce advanced the idea that the American government should extend a credit of about 100 million dollars. Of this, he explained, Spain would like to use about 22 million to buy wheat, 20 million to buy gasoline, 20 to buy cotton, and the rest for machinery, rubber, scrap iron, and other materials. The Minister reviewed Spain's good record as a debtor and tried to show that the loan would be advantageous to the United States. Weddell recalled the snub of June. But he said that he would be glad to transmit the request to Washington. He added that he was sure that, as before, we would wish a clear view of the Spanish attitude toward the war.

Weddell urged Washington to give a favorable answer. The risks of rejection, he judged, were greater than those of acceptance. The Spanish course in the war was still fluid, he thought; the pessimism of June had given way to a half-hope. Therefore we would be wise to free the Spanish government of any need to yield to German pressure. Further, he warned that internal conditions in Spain were becoming dangerously bad; unless the people secured more food and other essentials, there might be riots or rebellions; in which event the Spanish government might choose or be compelled, as the price of obtaining German aid, to enter the war; while, in contrast, he thought that if the United States gave help, Spanish resistance to the Axis would grow stronger and firmer. Lastly he reported that the British government favored the grant of substantial help. Even if later it should enter the war, according to Hoare, the gamble would not have been entirely lost because the Spanish people would be on Britain's side.

The State Department did not find these judgments easy to appraise. Certainly the two Ambassadors should know better than anybody in Washington the struggle of forces and feelings in the Spanish government and among the Spanish people. But it was possible, even on the basis of their reports of the Spanish situation, to disagree with their strategy. It was plainly unwise to prevent Spain from securing food. It also seemed clear that Britain was well advised to keep import channels free and to give help in finding minimum amounts. But was it wise quickly and generously to relieve Spain's troubles? Franco's intention could not it was felt, be trusted. Certainly he would march if German troops landed in Britain, no matter what promise had been given. Would he not trifle with us as Mussolini had with Britain in April? Was not weakness—if not too desperate—more likely to keep him at peace than obligation? Was it not best therefore to permit Spanish troubles to protract themselves?

The Madrid version of probabilities was taken up in some sections of the State Department; the opposed version in other sections. The opposing lines of conjecture met in several agitated conferences. Both, in retrospect, seem partly spun out of feeling or fancy.

The Riddle of Necessity

Secretary Hull supervised the argument, in so far as he could in the midst of many other matters. Discussion was tinged with the knowledge of the general American loathing for the Spanish regime. When opinion seemed to be running too strong in one direction, it was subtly offset. When it seemed to be becoming too assertive, it was quenched by long pauses or oddments of anecdote.

The officers of the European Division stood staunchly behind Ambassador Weddell. They urged that we offer a loan, but in such a form that we would control its use during the period of expenditure. This was a clever combination of those two standard tools of diplomacy—the "carrot" and the "stick." But those of us concerned with economic matters were doubtful that the idea would work as conceived. It might cause a worse quarrel than refusal. Besides, their books seemed to show that financial measures seldom bought off evil intentions.

Norman Davis, then president of the American Red Cross, was close at Hull's side whenever the map of European diplomacy was under inspection. He proposed a way out. Instead of making a loan, he suggested, the President might use part of a special relief fund of 50 million dollars which Congress had voted. This would suffice as a first step to show our willingness to help the Spanish people. But it would not provide Spain with the means for supporting a war. And, hardly less in point, it could be done without a mean fight within the United States. The Secretary of State grasped the suggestion, but specified that the Spanish government should be asked for assurances that it intended to remain at peace.

The discussion had consumed almost a fortnight (September 7–19). When the draftsmen set about the task of conveying these thoughts to Madrid, they found themselves submerged in rumor, which seemed to make the instruction out of date before it was sent. British sources reported that Germany was about to occupy all of France. If Germany did so, it was probable that French Morocco would revolt, and that Spain with German help would try to seize that territory. Then, too, Serrano Suñer set off (on

September 12th) upon his quest in Berlin and Rome. Despite the denials of the Spanish Foreign Secretary, this mission seemed in Washington to have an ominous similarity to other special meetings of Axis leaders—before they threw their strength in battle. Who could doubt that Franco shared deeply in the wish to accomplish Britain's defeat?

Serrano Suñer's talks (September 16–27), we know now, etched clearly for the first time the differences between Franco's ideas of what Spain should give and receive, and Hitler's idea. They did not fit at all with each other. But the group of American officials who were drafting the reply to the Spanish loan request could not foresee that, or at all events did not. Thus caution grew with every revision.

As sent to Weddell on September 19th, the response authorized him merely to state that the American government was disposed to consider ways and means of helping, provided the Spanish government promised to stay at peace. The rest of the message sent was for Weddell's mind only; it explained that a large loan such as Spain asked could not be arranged in a hurry, that time seemed of the essence, and that therefore the State Department and the Red Cross were discussing the possible provision at once of a substantial amount of wheat and other products for relief. We were building a fire with the smoke of straws.

Weddell sent back word (on the 20th and 26th) that such a message could not have an effect on Spanish policy in the critical weeks ahead. For that, he said, the proffer of aid would have to be more concrete and the demand for assurances more flexible. Weddell was seeking some substantial counterproposal to those which Serrano Suñer was expected to bring back.

The current reports regarding Spain had grown so grim that the State Department would probably have refused even to discuss the idea of aid any further, had it not been for the affirmations of the Spanish Foreign Minister, Beigbeder. Every time others said Spain was going into the war, he said it was not. On September 26th he told Weddell that Serrano Suñer's current visit to Berlin had been made on his private initiative, inspired by vanity and a craving for publicity, and that it would not produce any change in the situation. The Foreign Minister's forecast turned out to be correct. But later knowledge shows that his version of Serrano

Suñer's mission was short of the fact.[1] Either he was misled by Franco or he felt justified in deceiving us for a benevolent purpose. The United States and Britain must not know, the Foreign Minister may be imagined to have said to himself, that the Caudillo is engaged in cold plots with Hitler; in the end I think that they will come to nothing; and they can be made to fail if the United States and Britain can be induced to help Spain now. Thus it may be possible to acquit him of double purpose. Certainly both Weddell and Hoare were impressed with his brave and buoyant support of the Allied cause.

Weddell compounded his pleas. So did Hoare. In doing so, in a letter written to Lord Halifax, the British Secretary of State for Foreign Affairs, on September 27th, he described the situation as follows:

"Colonel Beigbeder is convinced that we are on the brink of a turning point in Spanish policy. Hitherto, there have been two contending parties in the Government and the country, the party of the short war led by Serrano Suñer, and the party of the long war led by the Minister for Foreign Affairs. Serrano Suñer and the young men of the Falange have staked their fortunes upon the war ending this autumn and ending with a complete German victory. Colonel Beigbeder has equally staked his fortunes upon the war not ending quickly and not ending in a complete German victory. According to the Minister for Foreign Affairs there seems now an excellent chance of his own policy being confirmed and of Serrano Suñer's being discredited. . . ."[2]

We may pause for a note upon the ingratitudes of history. Serrano Suñer believed that a quick German victory was certain; he tried his utmost to govern Spanish policy in this belief; he was wrong; he failed in his effort; and he became the next Foreign Minister. Beigbeder believed that Britain would be able to sustain resistance; he tried his utmost to shape Spanish policy in that belief; he was right; he was effective; and he was dismissed from office. In a large sense Beigbeder made his own belief come true; for by deterring Spain's entry into the war in the autumn of 1940, he prevented it from being a short war. But this is a privileged sally into what was then the unknown future—an interruption of the narrative of American response to the Spanish request for a loan.

[1] See Chapters xiii and xiv.   [2] Hoare, ibid., pages 50-1.

XI

ON THE TRAIL OF ASSURANCE

Within Our Grasp

THE pleas from Weddell and Hoare did not cause Secretary Hull to become freer in his gestures. He replied that he could not just then define more clearly what might be done for Spain, and that he would await firm assurances before trying. Anyhow, Weddell was told, the American government would not be able to consider a loan in the amount asked.

Weddell—when he saw the Foreign Minister on September 30th—tried to make his lecture material sound like a substantial program. Beigbeder's answer was direct and quite free of the usual dust. The Foreign Minister, making it clear that he was speaking for his colleagues as well as himself, said that while it was impossible for political reasons for the Spanish government to make a public statement or sign an agreement defining its future policy, he could give official assurance that Spain would remain out of the European war until or unless attacked. He then asked Weddell to let Washington know that Spain would have to obtain at least 800,000 tons of cereals before the next crop in June. Unless shipments started at once, the bread ration would have to be promptly reduced by one third.

Weddell became more convinced that the tide was turning toward peace. Serrano Suñer's visit to Berlin had ended a few days before. Nothing had happened. There were no signs that Spain was about to send its Army into action. But there were rumors that Franco would soon meet Hitler. Weddell urged the State Department, on the basis of Beigbeder's statement, to supply the needed cereals on liberal credit terms at once, and then concern itself quickly with other Spanish needs. The British government also earnestly pleaded for a generous response. This was the hour, it said, to wear all ribbons and medals. A vigorous effort was begun, using every means of publicity, to let the Spanish people know of the help Britain was giving; to pass the knowledge through and over the German press and radio control. The Prime Minister took part in this campaign through a speech in the House of Commons. On October 8th Churchill said:

"There is no country in Europe that has more need of peace and food and the opportunities of prosperous trade than Spain. . . . Far be it from us to lap Spain and her own economic needs in the wide compass of our blockade. All we seek is that Spain will not become a channel of supply to our mortal foes. Subject to this essential condition, there is no problem of blockade that we will not study in the earnest desire to meet Spain's needs and aid her revival."

Before the State Department made up its mind how to act, still another and more pointed appeal was made by the Foreign Minister. On the 3rd of October he told Weddell, saying his words over slowly and solemnly, that President Roosevelt could change the policy of Spain and Europe by a telegram announcing that wheat will be supplied to Spain; that the psychological moment for such action had come.

Secretary Hull did not doubt that critical decisions were in the making. But he still doubted whether we could sway them by a show of friendship. He still found it hard to believe that Franco's Spain—once fed—would not strike at Britain if her defenses failed. Perjury was so common in Axis circles, with no fee to conscience or to the critics; why should it not be practiced for a loan?

The whole tenor of the American press showed that if this government granted a loan, and that if later Spain entered the war, those who made the mistake would not long remain in office. So caution continued to guide. Red Cross relief might be sent, to show American sympathy. But no firm promise of a loan until Franco gave conclusive proof of his intentions. This decision seemed dumb to the political officers in the State Department. They thought that Weddell's program deserved full faith and support.

On October 4th the Ambassador was told to inform Franco that President Roosevelt was ready to ask the Red Cross to ship a quantity of wheat for the urgent needs of Spanish civilians. The text of this paragraph, as sent across to the White House for approval, contained mention of a large specific amount (100,000 tons). When it came back, the figure was cut out. As for the credit that Spain asked, we would let Franco know later; we would watch him as he watched others.

Weddell told the Caudillo of the President's offer on October 8th. Franco accepted with thanks.[1] The Ambassador supplemented his report of the talk by a repetition of the advice that loan talks be started without further delay. For he thought the present Spanish government could be counted upon, if given real support, to resist Axis pressure up to threatened or actual invasion by Axis troops. It was wise to improve the chance.

This opinion was in one way wrong, in another right. Franco, during this whole period, was busy with a plan of participation in the war; or rather with a plan to join in the final phase of the assault if and when he was certain that Britain was beaten. He was offering Hitler a pledge to enter the war if given supplies, help, and rewards. But he was insisting on the right to select the time and conditions for action—which was equivalent to the right of deciding whether or not he acted at all. And he was indignantly becoming aware that Italy and Germany firmly intended to hold on to parts of the African lands to which he professed Spain to be entitled; in the event of victory her colonies would have new neighbors. Into this, however, we will enter more carefully later on, when the record of the secret Spanish-German talks is reviewed.

Weddell's views, supported by British sources, impressed. The President and the Secretary of State decided to act more boldly. On October 12th Weddell was advised that the American Red Cross would send its first wheat shipment at once. He was also told that he could inform Franco that the American government was ready to discuss a credit for Spain. But again on a conditioned basis—Franco was to be asked to confirm his intention of staying out of the war and of so using a loan that it would have a genuine and lasting economic result.

In framing this offer, ignorance was a handmaiden to hope. Had the American government known how far, by then, Franco

---

[1] He also accepted the various conditions attached: no export of wheat, Red Cross participation in the distribution of our gift, fair publicity. But the last two were not observed.

had gone in arranging with Hitler upon the means and measures for a campaign against Gibraltar and the Straits, it would not have made the effort. Lack of knowledge permitted a hopeful reading—and as it turned out in the end, a correct reading— of recent favorable signs. Among them were the repeated statements of Beigbeder and Franco's swift acceptance of our relief aid. It seemed unlikely that even Franco would take the gift and then at once turn against the giver.

Weddell hastened along the talks about the credit with the two members of the Cabinet who were on our side—the Minister of Foreign Affairs and the Minister of Industry and Commerce. Both were glad. They begged for further details and urged that we hurry with the public announcement. Even now it is not possible to be certain of their thoughts. But it is likely that, knowing of Franco's plan to meet with Hitler in the near future, they were seeking to prove that German help was not needed; and maybe beyond that, to whet resistance to any action that might end all chance of food and peaceful work.

Weddell on October 16th echoed both their requests for details regarding the amounts and terms of the possible loan, and their sense of the need for speed. He urged that we begin to discuss these matters at once and let the action be known; our conditions could be made plain in the course of the talks. Serrano Suñer, then, would have to do battle against our offer. It is doubtful whether the Secretary of State would have adopted this strategy in any case. He could not have explained it to an opposed public. The assurances asked of Franco were both his aim and his safeguard. Without them criticism strong enough to defeat the loan was likely; even with them it would be great. A draft maintaining the previous instruction was in the typewriter when news arrived that ended all thought of haste.

And Out Again; Serrano Suñer is Made Foreign Minister

Beigbeder was dismissed from office. He had spent the evening of the 15th in first-name talk with the Caudillo, which had touched upon the need to secure oil, cotton, and wheat from the United States. Franco had found no fault with his conception of Spanish independence. Beigbeder had taken his hat with no sense that the talk had been held under the ax. The morning newspapers of the 17th first let him know otherwise. Neither Weddell nor Hoare had foreknowledge of the action.

Beigbeder had been the guardian of Spanish neutrality and an outspoken advocate of the opinion that Britain would in the end win. Now he was gone, dropped without regard for the effect in Allied circles. Nor was that the worst of it. Serrano Suñer, fresh from his secret talks in Berlin and Rome, was put in his place. Hereafter we would have to deal with that scheming and twisted associate of the crews that met at Nuernberg, and saluted under the Swastika. Nor was that the whole of it. The Minister of Industry and Commerce, Luis Alarcón de la Lasta, was also removed from his office. He was a moderate and peaceful man, a merchant of Seville. His successor, Demetrio Carceller, was reputed to be a tough and active Falangist. A capable, self-made man of business, whose affairs had flourished under Franco; director of the oil monopoly in the Canary Islands. He had gone to Berlin along with Serrano Suñer, in charge of the talks on economic matters. The changes were generally taken to mean, at best, that the Spanish Cabinet would thereafter be ruled by men with an eager will to work with, or under, Germany and Italy. At worst, that Franco had agreed to enter the war (as in a conditional way he had) and these men were selected to carry out the final steps.

A shiver ran down the spine of all who studied the map of the western Mediterranean in this October 1940. It interrupted the frail chain of discussion regarding a possible credit from the United States. But there was one feature of the change within the government that somewhat allayed anxiety, and suggested another meaning. Franco took over from Serrano Suñer the control of the Junta Política of the Falange Party. Perhaps—the idea was not to be dismissed until tested—the shift would turn out to be a move by Franco to "appease" Germany for failure to satisfy its wishes. He had once before dissembled his love by kicking a Foreign Minister downstairs. Jordana had been dropped in the summer of 1939, after the refusal to link Spain inseparably with Germany and Italy.

Hoare was inclined to interpret the event in this way. Accordingly he advised that the talks under way about relief and loans be merely suspended, not put out of mind. Weddell gave the same counsel. The political officers of the State Department supported their line of belief: that the battle was not lost; that Franco, even if he wished, would not dare take the final plunge until the war was all but over; and that a continuation of our talks might still serve a useful purpose—to show that Spain need not have recourse to Germany. Secretary Hull was doubtful whether anything could be gained by going on with associations so disliked at home. It was decided to ask Weddell to tell Franco directly that our decisions in regard to relief and credit would depend upon our conclusions about his intentions. The language of the cables to Weddell, so instructing him, had a firmness of tone that came from the White House. Unlike most previous messages, they were tinged with a sense of our power rather than our helplessness.

But Franco and Serrano Suñer were not disposed at that moment to discuss their intentions. What could they say that they might not wish to change? Would they say the same to Hitler a few days hence, when they talked with Hitler? For the meeting at Hendaye was only a few days off (the 23rd). Were they to admit that they had not made up their minds? That they were waiting to see how the battles of Britain and the Suez Canal ended, waiting to hear what Germany bid and asked? Such plain speech would butter no bread.

To get through the turnstile of circumstance Franco used his gift for language that could mean several things. Hoare saw him before his departure for Hendaye and Weddell relayed the substance of their talk. He said that the Cabinet changes did not connote any change in the foreign policy of Spain—leaving Hoare to form his own notion of what that was. For he also expressed great wonder that Britain should continue so exhausting a war in which it could have no hope of victory. Serrano Suñer echoed Franco's statement regarding Spanish foreign policy, adding that its aim and will was to be independent. He had then entered into bitter complaints about the effect of the British blockade system on the Spanish economy.

The State Department and the White House waited to see what message would emerge from the parlor car standing near the little railroad station of Hendaye. Along the platform there the diplomats of the world had so often walked on their way to their holidays. It was a place-name that reminded of days of sunny pleasure. Was it hereafter to be remembered for another reason: as a point of surrender to Hitler—Vienna, Munich, Berchtesgaden, Bordeaux, Compiègne?

Only now are we gaining real knowledge of the earlier dealings between the men that met at Hendaye on October 23rd. They form a strange and eventful tale, hidden from the American government at the time. It has become possible to compare the picture and ideas that guided American policy as reported thus far with what actually went on. Possible too, in part, to judge the reasoning behind our policy.

Thus before going on with this narrative of American diplomatic action, it is well to peer backward into the other side of the mirror of events.

XII

THE OTHER WING OF THE MIRROR

June among the Dictators

THE American government had little sure knowledge of the Spanish-Axis relations. It knew this. All attempts to learn ended only in nervous impressions, not calm conclusions. These had only overnight value.

Learning was the harder because the only really open door in the official mansions of Madrid was the Foreign Office. Though this department formally managed Spanish foreign policy, it often did not govern decision. Or at times even know of it; the Foreign Minister seemed to learn of certain steps only after they had been taken. Vital affairs between Franco and the Axis were conducted outside the purview of the Foreign Office, perhaps even of the Cabinet. The dictators mistrusted their professional diplomatic staffs. Trained in suppleness the professional might be, but averse to planned betrayal. Many of them were, by taste or training, on Britain's side. Franco, like Hitler, found it more satisfactory to use men who accepted duplicity as a natural weapon, who practiced it with ardor; and so he consigned secret business to chosen party and military leaders. While leaving the Foreign Office to deal with Allied countries, he sluiced his talks with the Axis through special agents—such as Serrano Suñer and General Vigón.

Thus, American decisions about Spanish matters were haunted by an awareness of ignorance, a fear of being trumped. They were conceived in a haze of surmise in which even the rainbows were suspect. Basically they rested (during this period) on the British will to believe that Franco would not go to war as long as there was any kind of peril in doing so. This belief turned out to be correct.

The accords between Franco, Hitler, and Mussolini were made and kept in secrecy. Such thorough secrecy that the full text of the most important one has not yet turned up in the mounds of German and Italian diplomatic records now, like the seven cities of Troy, under excavation. They were buried in the deepest level. For Franco the secrecy must have seemed useful no matter what turn future Spanish policy might take. On the one hand, it made it possible to avoid trouble with the Allies and the United States while seeking their help for Spain; on the other hand, it left him freer to squirm out of these accords—should he ever wish to do so. Hitler and Mussolini had equally strong reasons for concealment. First among them was the wish for military surprise. But the silence in which the liaison was shrouded made it easier for Spain to detach itself when the attraction passed. It was a method of managing that in the end left the Axis with only a discarded plan, a bitter reflection.

The Spanish government during its enforced trial of neutrality had restlessly scanned the horizon of opportunity. Who knew, at a time when old empires fought, what fragments might not fall a prize for the deserving and the adroit? In June 1940 Franco wrote out vows of fealty to the apparent victors. Thus he put Spain in the line of deserving heirs. He edged nearer the battle but with care not to come too close. The country was still miserable; the people were still opposed to war; the Army was not equipped to fight; the administrative machine of government was failing; and there were many discontented elements.

On June 3rd Franco wrote Hitler a note. In this he reviewed the hindrances that had compelled Spain thus far to adopt an official policy of neutrality and constant watchfulness. But, he hinted, he might soon be free to act. In closing he wrote that he felt he need not assure Hitler of the sincerity of his wish not to be aloof from Hitler's needs and how greatly it would please him to perform at that moment the services that Hitler esteemed the most.

The letter was followed up by messenger and by memorandum. General Vigón (about to be made Chief of the Spanish Air Ministry) went to talk with Hitler and Ribbentrop on June 16th at Castle Acoz. He informed them that Spain intended to attack Gibraltar and received the Fuehrer's approval. But, Vigón made clear, there were difficulties in the way of turning intention into action; that Spain could not live without the food supplies due to arrive from the Western Hemisphere; and Franco was afraid of an American landing in Morocco or Portugal. Hitler tried to dispose of these reasons for hesitation by saying that Spain could count on Germany's utmost aid. But he avoided discussion of Spanish claims in Africa, suggesting that they should be talked out with Mussolini first. Germany, Ribbentrop added, had no interest whatsoever in the Mediterranean; an attitude which, it will be seen, did not last long.

But military events went too fast for the paces of diplomacy. Pétain asked for an armistice the very next day (June 17th). Decisions might soon be taken that would settle Spanish claims once and for all. Franco moved swiftly to endow them with formal standing. Through the Spanish Ambassador in Berlin, he put before the German government a statement of his position, needs, and claims.[1]

"The Spanish government" declared itself "ready, under certain conditions, to give up its position as a 'non-belligerent' state and to enter the war on the side of Germany and Italy."

The conditions were: First, that Spain be promised satisfaction of a set of territorial demands, to wit:

". . . Gibraltar, French Morocco, that part of Algeria colonized and predominantly inhabited by Spaniards (Oran), and further the enlargement of Rio de Oro and of the colonies in the Gulf of Guinea. . . ."

Second, that Germany and Italy provide the military and economic supplies that Spain needed for carrying on a war. Important among the needs were large amounts of wheat and oil. At this very time, it will be recalled, Franco was showing indifference to American and British offers to assist Spain to obtain these products. Weddell and Hoare had not even been given the chance to spell them out; no doubt the Caudillo perceived that the

[1] This probably was presented on June 19th, though it may have been the day before or the day after. Its main features are explicitly mentioned in the memorandum prepared by the German Ambassador to Spain, Stohrer, on August 8, 1940, already cited.

United States, anyway, would seek to pledge him to continued neutrality and peace.

Franco must have been confident that Hitler would send a quick and favorable answer to his proposals. But he did not. The papers were sent to the experts for study and reflection. For Hitler's hope and wish in the weeks ahead was "to act quickly to end it all." As he walked up the steps of the Madeleine, what need could he feel for costly Spanish help? What reason was there then to hurry to promise Spain rich lands in Africa and the means to occupy them? Spain could wait while he took the last steps to mastery, completed his arrangements with France, and arrived at a settlement with England—by treaty or by arms. When these matters were clearer, there would be time to reckon what place and space Spain should have in the New Order.

The waiting was disturbing to Franco and Serrano Suñer. No two men were more sure that Germany had won the war. It is safe to credit them with the thought that the nearer the actual end drew, the smaller the value that would be attached to Spanish action. Further, as they waited, Spain grew weaker, less able to endure even a short military action by itself. The import of grain from the Western Hemisphere had come almost to a halt for lack of funds. The United States was reducing oil shipments. The people would soon be short of food, and industry of oil. If these could not be obtained as premium for a promise to enter the war—as essential to make the promise good—the Spanish government would have to deal elsewhere. Then who would get Gibraltar, who Morocco, who Oran?

Thus the Spanish government besought an answer. Serrano Suñer (and Beigbeder, too, according to the German Ambassador in Madrid) during the summer repeatedly called the Spanish proposal to German attention.[2] General Vigón supplied his German associates with details as regards military needs. Other Spanish officials did the same for economic needs. Franco solicited Mussolini's assent and favor. On August 5th he sent a letter from Madrid, parts of which read:

"Since the beginning of the present conflict, it has been our intention to make the greatest efforts in our preparations, in order to enter the

[2] State Department Document No. 1, already cited.

foreign war at a favorable opportunity in proportion to the means at our disposal. . . .

"The rapid and devastating victories in Flanders altered the situation; the defeat of France liberated our frontiers, lessening the grave tension which we along with our Moroccans have been bearing since our Civil War.

"From this moment, our horizon became brighter, our operation became possible and could become very effective, once the difficulties of provisioning have been removed. . . .

"The consequences which the conquest of France is to have for the reorganization of the North African territories have made it advisable for me, now that the time has come, to charge my Ambassador in Rome with transmitting to your Excellency the Spanish aspirations and claims traditionally maintained throughout our history. . . .

"In this sense, we have requested from Germany the necessities for action, while we push forward the preparations and make every effort to better the provisioning situation as far as possible.

"For all these reasons, you will understand the urgency of writing you, to ask your solidarity in these aspirations for the achievement of our security and greatness, while I at the same time assure you of our unconditional support for your expansion and your future." [3]

This letter was probably sealed with genuine hope that Mussolini would cause the Germans to warm up. Franco attributed to Mussolini a certain grandeur of view and generosity of nature to which he could appeal. But the note was flicked with concern lest Italy would demand part of the French territories for which he longed—if Germany would turn them over to their last-minute soldiers. There were points of conflict in the scheme of division which Ciano had sketched out in his Diary on June 14, 1939:

"The Duce desires that we begin to define with Spain the future program for the western Mediterranean: Morocco would go completely to Spain; Tunisia and Algeria would go to us. An agreement with Spain should insure our permanent outlet to the Atlantic Ocean through Morocco."

Franco had, more likely than not, become aware of these Italian ideas. Ciano had explained them to Ribbentrop some weeks before—pleading the primacy of Italian strategic and political interests over Spanish. Ribbentrop had responded merely by observing how strong a combination Germany, Italy, and a "satisfied" Spain would be, how able to guard their joint conquests. Germany, he mentioned before leaving the subject for another day, also had historic aspirations in Morocco. Hitler and Hitler alone would have the power to decide who might get what. He was going to try to postpone the decision until the war against Britain was won; to plead with both to fight first and divide the gains later. In the meantime his Naval Staff advised him not to permit Italy to assume first place in French Africa and to act as "impartial guardian" of Spanish and Italian claims.[4]

Mussolini replied to Franco's letter on August 25th. His bland phrases made it clear that Franco would have to fight his own battle. Mussolini said that he was certain that events would not permit Spain to choose its own time to enter the war; and if Spain did not enter the war, it could hardly expect satisfaction. The main paragraph must have left the author of the plea with the sense he had wasted his time:

"I should like to say to you, dear Franco, that I, with these my practical considerations, do not wish to hasten you in the least in the decision that you have to make, for I am sure that in your decisions you will proceed on the basis of the protection of the vital interests of your people and I am just as certain that you will not let this opportunity go by of giving Spain her African Lebensraum."[5]

All the phrases of brotherly salutation in this message did not blur its clear meaning. The German and Italian governments would measure their treatment of Spain by the need for, and value of, Spanish help; and they intended to ask a return for anything they gave.

While Mussolini was composing this reply, the German authorities in Berlin continued to scrutinize the Spanish proposal. Whether on his own or by request, Stohrer, the German Ambassador in Madrid, on August 8th drew up for Hitler and Ribbentrop a strictly secret note on the subject. This weighed the advantages against the costs and risks. The final section of his analysis, summarizing the strategy to be followed if Germany decided to enlist Spain, throws much light on later events:

[4] "Fuehrer Conferences," a collection of records of meetings between Hitler and the heads of the German Navy, published by the U.S. Navy Department. Papers for the year 1940, Vol. I, page 27.

[5] State Department Document No. 3, Letter Mussolini to Franco, August 25, 1940.

"If the operation is undertaken, it is in any case necessary:

"1. To have the preparations go forward in as camouflaged a manner as possible, to make available in Spain supplies of gasoline and war materials (ammunition, bombs) which can be unobtrusively transported by railroad and truck, and, not until the last moment, to bring the heavy guns collected in the south of France across the border by fast transit and into the prepared emplacements, while the air arm is absolutely not to make its appearance until the operation begins in earnest.

"2. The moment for initiating the preparations and the operation itself must be adjusted to the expected development of things in England itself, in order to avoid a too early entry of Spain into the war, that is to say, a period of war unendurable for Spain, and thus under certain circumstances the beginning of a source of danger for us." [6]

While this memorandum went round the circuit of the German ministries, the Spanish government continued to explore how, and how far, it would attain its aims. The Spanish Foreign Minister on August 20th again sought a reply from Berlin in terms that led Stohrer to inform the German Foreign Office that he had the definite impression that the Minister considered Spain's participation in the war an absolute certainty.[7]

This was quite contrary to the impression that Beigbeder was giving Weddell and Hoare; and it is most doubtful that the German Ambassador had valid grounds for it. General Vigón reviewed further with Admiral Canaris (Chief of the German Military Intelligence) the Spanish estimates of the military aid and supplies that were needed. Serrano Suñer contrived through Stohrer to be asked to visit Germany to discuss the conditions of Spain's entry. Then he sought Franco's backing for his mission. The available documents contain a hint that Franco was hesitant to sponsor that errand which his ardent brother-in-law arranged. But he did so—giving orders, later events seem to prove, to stick stubbornly and strictly to the terms contained in the Spanish memorandum just cited. On August 26th the German

[6] State Department Document No. 1, already cited.

[7] Stohrer added that the extent to which the Spanish government was calculating on its participation in the war was shown in the highly confidential information given to him by the Minister of Foreign Affairs that at the signing of the Spanish-Portuguese agreement supplemental to the Non-Aggression Pact, it was orally and secretly agreed that Portugal would give Spain an entirely free hand in the event of an attack on Gibraltar.

government extended an official invitation to Serrano Suñer to come to Berlin for the purpose that he so ardently longed to serve.

Between this date and the meetings in Berlin three weeks later, it became clear that Britain would not negotiate a peace. Churchill convinced the world that Britain would fight on. The noise and sight of planes falling over England began to show that it would. If a careless risk was taken, Spain, or its islands, might be caught in a long war. Hoare, and Weddell, as recounted, did their utmost to impress that danger. The people of Spain read of Serrano Suñer's travels in Germany with uneasiness—which gradually turned to hate.

Franco, without waiting for Serrano Suñer to go and return with a promise of the food and raw materials, put before the American government (on September 7th) the loan request, the reception of which has been described in the earlier chapters on the Washington scene.

XIII

THE OTHER WING OF THE MIRROR: FURTHER SCENES

The September of Dissension

THE German government, awaiting Serrano Suñer, put its ideas about Spain in order. These were not at all the same as the notions that Franco and the Falange had been pasting on the minds of their followers. Berlin planned to create a system of authority reaching over Europe and Africa, every part of which would be subject to German will and serve German advantage. In this scheme Spain would be a useful particle.

The Foreign Office sketched out possible German offers. Spain might be promised Gibraltar, the district of Oran, and much of French Morocco. But within the expanded Moroccan territory Germany should retain two main ports and their adjacent regions; also control over large Moroccan mining and other enterprises. Within Spain itself Germany should acquire the French and English properties and be granted special economic rights. Thus the new Spanish colonial lands would be fitted into the German "raw-material empire," and Spanish production and trade would enrich Germany.

There was still another item of German desire on the list, one that turned out to be more troubling to Spain than any other; Germany wished Spain to cede one of the Atlantic islands.

"The Fuehrer," read the minutes of his meeting with Raeder, Commander in Chief of the Navy, on July 17th, "would like to acquire one of the Canary Islands in exchange for French Morocco. The Navy is to establish which of the islands is the most suitable, aside from the two main islands." [1]

[1] Conference July 11, 1940, Hitler, Raeder, and Jodl. "Fuehrer Conferences," 1940, Vol. I, page 69.

Opinion in the United States was waking up to the meaning of Axis control of the north and west African coasts. German staff memos began to show serious concern over the possibility that we would seize the Azores and Canary Islands—particularly if Spain or Portugal were drawn into the war. It was deemed imperative to act first, as Germany always had.[2] Spain should be asked to permit Germany to protect itself against these mischances.

As regards supplies for civilians and soldiers both, German ideas diverged just as much from Spanish proposals. The lists forwarded from Madrid were torn apart by experts in sparse living for others. The amounts of military material asked were deemed far too great. The German Army expressed itself as convinced that it would be more effective to supply complete German military units than to send great stores of German weapons. The quantities asked of such products as oil and wheat were judged to be hugely overstated. Spain wrote large and carelessly.[3]

Germany was not inclined to indulge lavish wishes. Any products sent to Spain would be drawn from stores too small to suit the managers of the German economic and military programs. To supply even a substantial part of what Spain asked would spoil other plans, both the Economic Ministry and the Ministry for War advised Hitler.[4]

[2] The subject was discussed at length at a meeting of Hitler, Raeder, and Jodl on September 6th. "The danger," the record of this discussion concludes, "of a British or American occupation of the Azores and Canary Islands is particularly great in the event that Spain or Portugal enters the war. The Fuehrer therefore considers occupation of the Canary Islands by the Air Force both expedient and feasible." "Fuehrer Conferences," 1940, Vol. II, page 19.

[3] For example, it asked for about 800,000 tons of oil products (which was far greater than normal), about 800,000 tons of wheat, 100,000 tons of cotton, 25,000 tons of rubber, 625,000 tons of phosphates and other fertilizers.

[4] The tightness of the oil situation before the fall of France gives rise to wonder as to how Germany would have continued to manage had the assault in the west failed. At a conference held on March 29, 1940 between Hitler, Raeder, and Generals Keitel and Jodl, Raeder reported that Goering stated that "Army and non-military supplies will be at an end in May, and those of the Air Force by July. The Navy must help to ease the situation from its large supplies of Diesel oil." Raeder said that the Navy was ready to do so but would surrender oil only on special orders from Hitler. "The Commander in Chief Navy," the record of the conference continues, "reports on the incorrect procedure followed by the Ministry of Economics. In peace-

Exports to Russia under the Soviet-German economic agreement of February 11, 1940 had been held back by Germany in order to retard Russian production of war materials. Russia had sent notice it would end its shipments unless Germany corrected the situation. But it could not, according to the experts in the Economic Ministry and the Ministry of War, be corrected soon enough without scanting the Fuehrer's armament program. The prospect was, therefore, that Russian deliveries would soon fail. This meant:

"that the large imports [into Germany] of raw materials, especially of grain, mineral oil, cotton, rare metals and non-ferrous metals, phosphates, will at least temporarily cease and at best will be resumed later upon a much lower scale and with great sacrifices in German deliveries. In the opinion of the Reich Food Ministry this would be especially serious in the case of the grain supply. . . . The Reich Food Ministry points to the fact that the national grain reserve will be used up during this grain production year so that we would start the next grain year without such a reserve." [5]

The supply of other products was short of what eager minds wanted for their many projects. They were running a strict rationing system, not a banquet table. The Spanish seemed to regard themselves not as holders of ration books, but as esteemed guests.

To adjust so large a spread in political vision and to agree upon the sharing of goods so greedily sought, a deep sense of mutuality would have been needed. This did not—in September 1940—exist. Hitler in exultant mood was not kind to the pretensions of others; nor was he given to the art of gentle deflation. As for Ribbentrop, only vain bluster came out of that loose mouth. Serrano Suñer was too flawed and driven a man to win from that pair respectful regard for the great claims he was about to present. He was of their own impudent scheming breed.

He set out for Berlin on September 12th. Among his working staff was Demetrio Carceller, of whom notice has already been

time they permitted themselves to become completely dependent on Shell and Standard. . . . The result is that the Ministry of Economics has neglected to provide oil supplies for industry." "Fuehrer Conferences," 1940, Vol. I, page 28.

[5] This secret memorandum, dated September 28, 1940, explaining the situation is to be found on pages 276-7, Volume VI, *Nazi Conspiracy and Aggression*, Document No. 3579–PS.

taken. While Serrano Suñer spent his time upon military and political topics, Carceller guided the discussions of economic matters.

It will be recalled that reports of Serrano Suñer's trip had caused the American government to hesitate over its response to the Spanish loan request of September 7th. The Foreign Minister, as has been noted, tried to ward off any adverse effect on his attempts to secure overseas supplies; he gave Weddell and Hoare to understand that the mission had no serious official sponsorship. This was not so. Serrano Suñer had, in truth, thrust himself forward. In truth, also, he lacked the support of many groups in the Spanish government and Army for the program that he advocated in Berlin. But once on his way, he was authorized by Franco to advance that program, and to obligate Spain in Franco's name.

Serrano Suñer in the first talk with Ribbentrop on September 16th described himself, not as a diplomat, but as a representative of the Spanish government sent by Generalissimo Franco as his personal confidential representative and charged with a specific mission. The correctness of this designation is shown by a letter sent by Franco to Hitler on September 22nd in which Serrano Suñer was described as "my envoy." [6] Later on, when recounting to Mussolini at Bordighera what had occurred, Franco said that Serrano Suñer, like a good envoy, had kept him informed from day to day.

Serrano Suñer entered the talk on the first day (September 16th) full of good graces, which gradually slipped away. He began as Franco had before him: Spain had wished to enter the war from the beginning and had only been constrained by economic wants and a lack of weapons with which to defend itself. Now it wished to participate if it could be supplied with the necessary requirements. There was in Spain even a certain disagreeable surprise, he went on to remark, because the material necessary to wage war, especially artillery, had not yet arrived from Germany.

A pilgrim he was. But no Don Quixote, it soon appeared, madly bent on serving a noble cause. Carefulness—defined in Madrid—enclosed every side of the Spanish position. No door was

[6] State Department Document No. 5. Letter from Franco to Hitler, September 22, 1940. This letter was not delivered until September 27th.

to be left open to the drafts of danger or failure. It was essential, he said, that Spain should be able to prevent or defeat possible attack anywhere in its domains, upon the Atlantic islands or the African coastal colonies, or upon the Cantabrian coast where the rebellious elements were strong. All these vulnerable points must be so well defended before Spain moved that enemies would not be likely to dare an assault; and if they did, that the attempt would fail. The requests for arms were drawn up to provide that certainty. Besides there must be adequate supplies for the Spanish people before the action was begun. These, and a firm promise of the areas that Franco had already named, were Spain's terms for entering the war. In return, it would grant Germany certain special and valuable economic privileges both in Spain and in the lands to be ceded. The Spanish proposals were the dream of any soldier: no uncalculated risks, the chance to select the time for action, and assured rewards for victory. Could Franco have really believed that Germany, in its most victorious season, would accord these terms for Spanish aid or to cement the Spanish connection? It is hard to believe. But he is, as Sir Samuel Hoare and others found him, a complacent man.

Ribbentrop tried to correct the Spanish perspective. He thought the Spanish reckonings of danger unreal and the Spanish demands —political and economic—excessive. The situation, he deftly pointed out, was wholly different from what it had been at the start of the war. German armies had destroyed France; England would be thoroughly beaten—London would soon be only ashes and rubble. German and Italian victory was sure. Still he did not spurn Spain's wish to join them nor challenge Franco's wish to choose his own time.

As for Spain's territorial demands, they were, he said, "in principle" acceptable. But the details would have to be adjusted. Germany planned to acquire for itself middle Africa, and the contour of German aims would have to be taken into account. Spain could fairly be asked to complete the German scheme by yielding the points that would make the great new German Empire immune to any and all possible future attacks. Defined, these were two. First, Germany wished to have two Moroccan ports as bases, and the regions around them. Such an arrangement, Ribbentrop, being the geopolitician, said, would bring Germany,

Italy, and Spain together in a three-headed control of the destinies of Europe and Africa. Second, Germany wanted Spain to cede one of the Canary Islands as an outlying base against distant enemies.[7]

Serrano Suñer argued on many points—and upon one with rough fervor. Throughout the conversation he firmly refused to discuss the possible cession of one of the Canary Islands. There is no need further to trace the other veins of differences that were revealed.

This first talk between Serrano Suñer and Ribbentrop—and the further talks with Hitler and Ribbentrop that followed—showed how far apart were German and Spanish terms. But more than that, it signified that Franco's ideal was out of grasp, no matter how complete the victory over the Allies. For the German will to hold the uppermost place in all parts of the European world was made plain. Thenceforward it would have been strange had there not been somewhere in Franco's mind fear of any deal with a triumphant Germany.

Ribbentrop and Serrano Suñer had brushed the ground for Hitler; the next day (the 17th) he walked over it. They had discussed the terms and conditions of action; it was the plan of action itself that engaged Hitler. The basic elements of his argument were simple; they were the same that had guided him in his ascent and trumphs, the same that were to take him and Germany to ruin. They were, in short, though he never stated them in short, that if the will to action existed, the means were sufficient; that if the direction of the action was bold, victory was certain; and that success in action would be sure to yield enough advantage to satisfy all partners. The conclusion was pointed; there was no need to settle in advance what each should get. In these ideas he led Germany, in them he sought to lead the whole Axis-ruled world. Spain could join, take its place, and accept its allotted share, or stay out and remain poor and weak. But this is

[7] This was in accord with the recommendations that had been submitted by the Naval Staff (June 20, 1940), "On the Policy of Bases—the creation of a large united German Colonial Empire in Central Africa (from French Guinea and Sierra Leone via Togo, Nigeria, the Cameroons, the French Congo, the Belgian Congo, to German East Africa), which is necessary for national and economic reasons, necessitates bases on the coast of the colonial territory." "Fuehrer Conferences," 1940 Vol. I, page 65.

an interpretative summary of Hitler's position—as revealed in this and later talks with the Spanish leaders—not a decalcomania of what he actually said on this occasion to Serrano Suñer.

On the military problems Hitler was precise and dogmatic. First he devoted himself to proving that the conquest of Gibraltar and the Straits was easy. Spain would, therefore, not need as much military strength or equipment as suggested or of the types that Spain most seemed to want. This, Hitler said, was the view of his most expert and experienced officers. His discourse went into all points of the combat operation. He dismissed the fear of a successful British landing anywhere on the continent as an absolute chimera; German dive bombers would ruin any attempted landing in Spain or Portugal. Further, by the same machines, the harbor of Gibraltar could quickly be made useless and the English fleet driven away from Gibraltar and the entire vicinity. Spanish plans for the conquest of the fortress of Gibraltar rested mainly on the use of heavy artillery for bombardment. The fortress could best and most quickly be taken by an attack from the air and by specialist troops particularly trained and equipped—like those who had taken Fort Eben-Emael. Apparently assuming that this would create no misgiving, Hitler promised that Germany would provide the air force for the attack on the Rock and the expulsion of enemy ships from the Straits; it would also make available the specialist troop formations.[8] This exposition impressed Serrano Suñer. He asked to have it written out for Franco.

At the end, Hitler switched to the politics of conquest. He painted the great colonial raw-material empire that Germany planned to create for its permanent security. Like Picasso's later works, the eyes looked in all directions. One rested on the Spanish islands in the Atlantic. These must be under the protection of a strong power which could frighten off or defeat any other imperial tendencies—such as those which were coming to the fore in the United States.

Serrano Suñer's rejection of this suggestion the day before had not sufficed. In a final talk with Ribbentrop he made it rudely plain that Spain would not agree. Before doing so it is probable

[8] State Department Document No. 4. Talk between Hitler and Serrano Suñer, September 17, 1940.

that he had spoken with Franco on the telephone. Serrano Suñer said that it was absolutely impossible for Spain to cede islands that historically belonged to and formed part of Spain. But he advanced a substitute, that Germany seize instead the Portuguese island of Madeira. As for the German wish, Serrano Suñer added, to retain two large areas within Morocco, as well as control over the most important sources of raw material, if Spain gave these up, Morocco would be nothing more than an empty shell.

Serrano Suñer could not resolve issues such as these. The claims he had brought were those of an equal in an association of conquerors; the answers he had been given were fit for a minor dependent. Spain's hopes were drawn out of Spain's past, which was real only to Spain. They were out of accord with the division of power illustrated by the presence of German troops at the Pyrenees. Thus gloomily he set off upon a tour of France and Belgium while Ribbentrop went to Rome to see Mussolini. Hitler promptly sent a summary of his ideas by courier to Franco, a summary written with easy assumption of mastery of military matters. His genius shone in the sky and Franco, like his own military staff, would, he was sure, come to admit it. His letter was one of instruction rather than command, for he still did not attach great importance to the Spanish decision.

On economic matters, it should be noted, the Serrano Suñer mission had failed as completely to reach accord with their German colleagues. Spain wanted Germany to send foodstuffs and raw materials at once, to scatter this bread upon the Spanish waters. The Germans, found the request almost absurd. They were not willing to dispense their hoards carelessly or in return for a vague promise. They wanted payment in the future for what could not be paid in the present. Their view is shown by the text of one of the draft proposals that they placed before the Spanish government. In this the Spanish government was asked to grant Germany the dominant position in Spain's economic life with the exception of possible agreements still to be reached with Italy. It was asked also to promise primarily to use German co-operation in the reconstruction and expansion of Spanish industry, agriculture, mining, transport, and finance, and particularly to consider German supply needs for raw materials and keep open possibilities for German exports. Regarding participation in the exploitation of any raw-material sources Germany was to get first priority.

The basic split in attitude that emerged is displayed in the sulky exchange between the senior Spanish and German representatives on September 19th. The Spaniard remarked that for Spain the objective of this war would be the elimination of foreign rule, and that it would not make a good impression if Germany should take the place of England. According to the German proposition, he said, Spain would have to bear the entire expenditure of the administration of Morocco, but would not secure the benefits. The joy over the heritage would be considerably decreased and could even change suddenly into the opposite. If Germany, he concluded, should insist on her severe demand, it would be better if she kept Morocco for herself. To which the German representative replied that nobody in Germany or the world would understand if Germany waged a war of life and death with two major powers and did not secure her raw-material requirements after victory.

Here was the proof of what Weddell and Hoare so often told Spanish officials; that if Germany won, Spain would become a German province. The remark had always been rebuked. But the mind is left to wonder whether, after reading such texts as these, the Spaniards did not admit to themselves that it was true. Such demands must have made it clear that while American and British offers would not make Spain great, they would leave her free. Carceller, in particular, seems to have returned from Berlin with changed ideas. He seems to have concluded that German and Spanish claims would not be reconciled, and thereupon became an active seeker of American help.[9]

The Germans went over the Spanish statement of needs with a scythe. The Spaniards had reckoned them with a free hand. To be sure of enough, to bargain, or possibly to make a bargain impossible? The riddle remains. But the first guess is the best. Some of the Spanish requests, as for rubber, could not be met at all. Others, such as that for oil and wheat, the Germans offered to meet only in part.

Despite the deep differences in desire, the German and Spanish economic experts did not wish to part without leaving some

[9] See Chapter xxi.

basis for further discussions. They therefore presently subscribed to a series of gaping texts. These dealt with the provisioning of Spain for war, the exchange of goods during and after the war, and the economic privileges to be granted Germany in Spanish domains. But they turned out to be only the raw material for further argument.

Such was the outcome of Serrano Suñer's first excursion to Berlin. Spain was offered the scant minimum necessary for a military campaign modeled after the lightning-like German successes. The planned German military action would be powerful enough to win. But by the same token, as Franco was shrewd enough to perceive, the German Army would have to be given, or would take, charge of the combat operations. If the campaign should lag, Spain would be dependent upon continued German help; and with it German control over Spanish life. Then, even if victory were won and Spain secured Gibraltar and territory in Africa, Germany would retain in the center of Morocco two great bases and many special economic privileges. In Spain itself, clawlike German economic enterprises would have been promised full freedom. And lastly, even if Germany did not insist upon the permanent cession of one of the Canary Islands. who could know when its soldiers, ships, and airmen would leave them?

It is not hard to understand Franco's wish to bargain longer and firmly. Nor to understand why the Spanish government showed so much patience, during the fall months, in its negotiations with Britain and the United States about oil, food, and other raw materials. Germany would be taught that Spain had a choice. Spain's needs would be met. If only it did not prove necessary, in order to get what was wanted, to cast away the chance to join in the war—if and when that could be done safely!

Franco showed himself a master of the alphabet of hesitation. The condition of Spain supplied the first letters. The failure of Germany to invade Britain and of Italy to rout the British in the east supplied the middle group. German proposals supplied the end letters. The combination of British and American policies during the summer and early autumn of 1940 fostered the hesitation. They furnished Spain with enough of such essentials as oil, coal, and food to struggle along, but not enough to carry it through a war without becoming vitally dependent on Germany. They held open a prospect of plenty if Spain stayed at peace. Thus they served as an incentive to be wary and independent in the next stage of argument with Germany about what Spain was to get and do.

XIV

THE OTHER WING OF THE MIRROR: STILL FURTHER SCENES

The Worth of Spanish Friendship

IN THE middle of September Franco was not ready to commit himself either to the Allies or to Germany. With skill he would keep Spain safe and draw advantages from each side while watching the outcome of their battles. Thus, as recounted, he permitted Beigbeder, the Foreign Minister, to continue to assure us and Britain that Spain would stay out of the war. Thereby he preserved the chance to obtain grain and oil, fertilizers, cotton and rubber. But despite Serrano Suñer's reports of difficulty, the hope of gaining an empire gleamed. Britain's downfall might yet be brought about in one fortnight of clear weather and calm seas. It would be folly to cast away the chance to gather for Spain the African lands just across the narrow sea. A victory of the Axis in which Spain did not share might be more unhappy for Spain than its defeat. Italy and Germany would be fearsome as close colonial neighbors.

So he took over from Serrano Suñer the task of winning the right of admission to victory without paying too high a price. But the Germans then (and later) were sure that he would pay what was asked. Ribbentrop, on his way to see Mussolini after his talks with Serrano Suñer, had no doubt that fortune was smiling on Germany everywhere, and that Franco would decide to place himself within the orbit of success. Ciano has recoorded the mood with which he entered this new series of talks:

"In the car Ribbentrop speaks at once of the surprise in his bag: a military alliance with Japan, to be signed within the next few days at Berlin. . . . He thinks that such a move will have a double advantage: against Russia and against America. . . . As for England . . . the weather has been very bad and the clouds even more than RAF have prevented final success. However . . . the invasion will take place anyway as soon as there are a few days of fine weather. The landing is ready and possible. English territorial defense is non-existent. A single German division will suffice to bring about a complete collapse." [1]

With bubbling candor Ribbentrop related to Il Duce the talks with the Spaniards in Berlin and Hitler's ideas concerning the conquest of Gibraltar. The Spaniards, he said, wanted to conquer Gibraltar themselves. But in order to prevent any failure, Germany would provide Spain with special troops equipped with special weapons and a few squadrons of planes. With these the Fuehrer was convinced that the conquest of the Rock was "absolutely possible." He then explained the Spanish territorial demands. According to the German record of this talk, Mussolini said that the Spanish wishes did not clash with the Italian. Had he decided to renounce his conflicting claims with Spain? Did he hope thereby to ensure acceptance of his greater claims on France? The answer is obscure.

Then Ribbentrop informed Mussolini that upon his return to Berlin, where Serrano Suñer would be waiting, he intended to sign a secret protocol dealing with Spanish entry into the war and its requisites. The time of entry would be left for Spain to decide —on the understanding that it would be as soon as preparations were complete, and particularly as soon as German special weapons, troops, and planes had arrived in Spain. [2]

Ribbentrop's optimism was catching, for Ciano wrote in his Diary on the date of September 20th:

"A second conversation with Ribbentrop. It has to deal principally with Spanish intervention, which now seems to be assured and imminent."

The wheels of Axis diplomacy did seem to speed up toward a junction of the German and Spanish programs. On September 22nd Franco sent a reply to the plan of military strategy that Hitler, at Serrano Suñer's request, had transmitted. This letter

---

[1] Entry in Ciano Diaries, September 19, 1940.

[2] This summary is drawn from the incomplete record of the conversation of September 19, 1940, printed in *Nazi Conspiracy and Aggression*, Vol. IV, page 477.

was not delivered until the 27th. In the interval Serrano Suñer had resumed his talks in Berlin. Together the letter and the talks must have seemed to travel far toward decision.

Franco's letter warmly endorsed Hitler's ideas as regards the best way to capture Gibraltar. Later, it may be noted, he was again to change his mind on this matter. Even estimates of military situations may be affected by sentiments; Gibraltar could be easy to take on the day one was assured and pleased, it could be very hard to take on the day one was not. But for the day, Franco agreed that the attack could be safely and quickly carried out with the type of military help that Germany was ready to promise. In so saying, he added:

"For our part, we have been preparing the operation in secret for a long time. . . ."

The other features of Hitler's program, however, Franco firmly refused. While agreeing to the use of German dive bombers and destroyer planes for the defense of the Canary Islands, he wrote that he would not turn over one of the Canary Islands to Germany as a base. He also rebuffed the German request for military locations within Morocco as

"Unnecessary in peacetime and superfluous in wartime."

He evaded the German request for special economic privileges. He put aside suggestions for future economic arrangements as a deviation from the main subject.

Thus trying to dodge through the barbed-wire fence of German wishes, he sought to reach his own points of desire. He closed the letter with the hope that he would

"be able to renew the old bonds of comradeship between our armies" [3]

in the cause for which Hitler fought.

While this letter was in course of delivery (September 22–7), Serrano Suñer was leading even the Germans in zeal to sign some accord, even though it had blanks and obscurities. It would at least, he said, prove Spain's firm wish to enter the war and dispel rumors. His inner thought is traceable; if Franco entered into a

[3] The preceding summary is taken from the text of the letter as printed in State Department Document No. 5.

treaty that pledged Spain to enter the war, no matter how guarded, his struggle for mastery in Madrid would be won. He, Serrano Suñer, would be the keeper of Franco's word. Beigbeder would be the resister, the rebel.

But the design did not affect his efforts to secure for Spain unclouded and individual title to the whole domain of desire— the Africa that lay across the Straits. Serrano Suñer, in talks with Ribbentrop on the 26th and with Hitler on the 27th, drummed on Spanish needs and whistled when German claims were being sung. Why, it may be imagined the Germans asked themselves, had this man proposed himself for this mission if he was unwilling or unable to give in to them? They lost patience and became rudely abrupt—as when Ribbentrop dismissed Spanish objections to German claims in Morocco by saying that there was no point in talking about the mistrust caused by German claims for bases in Africa. If Germany wanted them, he rubbed in, she would get them since she wanted to establish a great colonial empire in central Africa. Furthermore, he added, defense against America required bases in Morocco and one of the Canary Islands.

These talks brought Serrano Suñer's long mission in Germany to an end. They had settled nothing. Even on supply matters the gap had been sealed only with foam. On the 27th, the same day that Hitler received Franco's letter, a senior German interdepartmental committee completed its study of this field. It found almost all the Spanish requests excessive, and it reported that Germany could not meet them—particularly the demand for oil. The conclusion was that Spain must be ready herself to promise Germany the delivery of everything possible, while Germany could not supply the quantities that Spain had asked.

The Allies need not have been as worried as they were about the offers that Serrano Suñer would bring back from Berlin.[4]

Ciano was in Berlin to take part in the ceremonies of Japanese entrance into the Tripartite Pact. The note in his Diary for the day on which the talks ended (September 27th) records without anguish the German disenchantment:

"He [Hitler] spoke ... of Spanish intervention, to which he was opposed because it would cost more than it was worth. ... Toward

4 See page 58.

us Italians the Germans are impeccably courteous . . . with the Spaniards on the other hand, the Germans are less courteous. Generally speaking, Serrano Suñer's mission was not successful, and the man himself did not and could not please the Germans."

Hitler on the next day (the 28th) summed up his thoughts on the situation for Ciano. After telling of the long list of Spanish requests, he remarked:

"Spain is to promise to Germany, in return, her friendship. One must," he continued, "think it over thoroughly if one intends to enter into such obligations and if one is to bar other possibilities from oneself." [5]

To make Ciano understand how painful the whole discussion had been, he said:

". . . and as a German one feels toward the Spanish almost like a Jew who wants to make business out of the holiest possessions of mankind." [6]

The "other possibility" in Hitler's mind was France. He had not managed to secure control over the French fleet or the French Empire in Africa. Now he was growing aware of how much difference they might make. If they went over to Britain, the war would be greatly prolonged. If he could win them over, Britain would be defeated even without invasion. It would be reckless, certainly, to fling them into the arms of Britain by promising Franco what he asked. Spanish help, as he said, was not worth it—certainly not till he knew more of the outcome of his attempt to subdue Britain from the air. Among the notes on Hitler's talk in Ciano's Diary on September 27th there is to be found:

"No more invasion of England. No more blitz destruction of England. From Hitler's speech there now emerges worry about a long war." [7]

[5] The Navy was urgently advocating the seizure of Gibraltar as soon as possible. Hitler agreed that it was highly important to clear up the Mediterranean question but showed reserve in his talk with Raeder at this time. "He will have to decide," he said, "whether co-operation with France or with Spain is the more profitable; probably with France since Spain demands a great deal (French Morocco) but offers little." Meeting Hitler-Raeder, September 26, "Fuehrer Conferences," 1940, Vol. II, page 24.

[6] Interview between Hitler and Ciano, Berlin, September 28, 1940. State Department Document No. 6.

[7] On August 1st Hitler had ordered that an attempt be made to be ready for the invasion by September 15th. The decision whether the operation was to be begun then or delayed till the spring was to be made after the Air Force had concentrated its attack on England for a week. On the 14th of

During the first twenty-six days of the battle above England (according to the current British communiqués) the Germans had lost 1,008 planes and 2,927 airmen, while Britain had lost 286 planes and 135 pilots.[8] The defenses of central London had proved so good that the bulk of German raiders were being driven out to the suburbs. Both Germany and Spain had been, no doubt, keeping the score of this battle while they talked to one another.

Serrano Suñer, before going home, went to Rome to see what help might be had from Mussolini. He had recovered his blitheness. Once again he avowed that despite all the difficulties he was convinced that war would unite all factions of Spain in a single group because the objectives—Gibraltar and Morocco—were so deeply felt by all and especially the young. Mussolini contented himself by repeating what he had already written—that he was convinced that Spain would be drawn into the struggle by its vital interests. Italy could spare no grain, but its Air Force would help make the battle for the western Mediterranean short and the outcome certain.

Hitler seems to have been both puzzled and balked at the Spanish refusal to see that he could not meet their wishes. When he met with Mussolini at the Brenner Pass on October 4th, he reverted to the Spanish problem with turgid intensity. Again he stressed his deep concern lest the remaining fighting forces of France go over to Britain. He was, he explained, reaching for an accord with Vichy and a compromise with Spain which would permit the formation of a coalition against Britain. Mussolini was undisturbed by this account of the trouble with Spain, but annoyed at the portended deal between Germany and Vichy.[9]

September the decision was deferred until October, and then repeatedly postponed again, until finally Hitler, on the urgent advice of his Army and Navy commanders, ordered that the preparations be stopped so that the assembled resources could be put to other uses. The record of discussions of the state of the enterprise between Hitler and Raeder, published in "Fuehrer Conferences," 1940, Vol. II, reveals the main stages of decision. The Navy opposed the operation except as a last resort if Britain could not be made to sue for peace in any other way.

[8] *New York Times*, September 29, 1940.

[9] This annoyance became stronger after Hitler began his talks with Laval and Pétain—shortly after which Ciano remarked in his Diary that he hoped "that Hitler will not offer us a cup of hemlock because of our claims against France." Ciano Diaries, entry October 25, 1940.

Nothing could have incensed Serrano Suñer more than the signs that Hitler was turning to France. He hated that land beyond measure. He was sure—and this conviction he shared with Franco —that, no matter what deals were made, it would in the end be Spain's enemy. But he did not retreat with injured anger. His job was still to get out of the situation all that he could, no matter how it turned. Thus, on the surface, he posed as faithful as before to the Axis connection. Down deep, however, he probably felt Spain released from faithfulness; now justified in betraying not only one side but both. He had arrived at the "independence" of the disillusioned crook.

In this spirit, it may be surmised, the arrangements for the meeting between Hitler and Franco at Hendaye were completed. Serrano Suñer sent buoyant messages to Ribbentrop promising complete counterproposals, including one for a ten-year military alliance with Germany and Italy. These were to be kept from the knowledge of the American and British governments, so that they would not cut off Spain's supplies.

"We believe," he wrote, "that all of these should be negotiated with the utmost secrecy in order not to jeopardize the several shipments of Argentine and Canadian wheat which we are endeavoring—with great difficulty—to acquire. All of this is for the good of the common cause. This will be done in such a way that when the rank and file of our diplomatic service, while they continue keeping the balance in order to obtain the greatest possible quantities of wheat and gasoline, our negotiations will be carried on through our personal contacts and through secret correspondence between the Fuehrer and the Caudillo." [10]

At this point both lines of this dual strategy were put in his hands, or so it seemed. As already told, on October 17th Beigbeder, who had stood out against him, was dismissed. Serrano Suñer was made Secretary of State for Foreign Affairs. The American government, as already recounted, abruptly paused in discussions of a possible loan. Serrano Suñer was glad rather than disappointed.

[10] Letter from Serrano Suñer to Ribbentrop, October 19, 1940. No. 7, State Department Documents.

XV

THE OTHER WING OF THE MIRROR: STILL FURTHER SCENES

Hitler and Franco Sign a Pact—to Seal a Vacuum

FOR Hitler the meeting at Hendaye was only one step in a quest for a coalition against England. He was seeking to draw France, Spain, and Italy together in a joint program for attack against England under his leadership. To Mussolini and Franco he would offer parts of Africa, but ask that map-making await victory. For what might be taken from France, he would offer Pétain compensation at Britain's expense. All were to trust his wisdom and fairness. He held the power to support or crush any of them. They would, he assured himself, fall into line. The main source of his error was in failing to see that they could not, even if they chose, compel their people to accept his leadership.

The first quick talk he held with Laval on the 22nd, just before meeting Franco, encouraged his belief that the French would be subservient. He was ready to offer Vichy a sharing partnership in the new Europe, a promise that France would retain a colonial empire equivalent to its present one.[1] Later on, when victory was won, he could undeceive France, if necessary. But he must not throw away the chance to deceive. Therefore he could not at that moment give a pledge in black and white to transfer to Spain large sections of the French colonial empire. If it became known, his plan would fail; the French forces in Morocco and elsewhere might even rebel and join England.

All this meant that Franco's claims would have to be reduced or deferred. Hitler was less ready to accede to them than he had

[1] William L. Langer: *Our Vichy Gamble*, pages 89 et seq., gives an interesting account of the meetings with Laval and Pétain and important extracts from the official record of the talk at Montoire on October 24th.

been the month before in Berlin. But he still tried at this Hendaye meeting to fix the Spanish decision to enter the war, or at least to sanction a German attack upon Gibraltar and the Straits.

The meeting was held in Hitler's spacious parlor car near the little railroad station. Their talk was a curtain of discourse behind which their assistants sewed upon the seams of various secret agreements.[2] Ribbentrop had brought along new texts dealing with the diplomatic, military, supply, and economic elements of the proposed greater alliance (for it was to include Italy). These he and Serrano Suñer worked upon while and after the two dictators explored each other's minds. Franco was not afraid. He had not come to capitulate but to bargain and to preserve his freedom to act as best suited his own purposes.

He, the official record seems to show, took the lead in the talk by plunging into a review of the difficulties he faced in placing Spain on Germany's side in the war—a review as long as those which left his Cabinet blinking and bored. Hitler tried to convince him that they were manageable, that Spain's needs would be taken care of if it entered the war, that the time had come to do so, and that victory would be quick and sure. But he made it clear that he regarded Spanish entry as an opportunity for Spain, not as a relief measure for the Axis. He went into details with regard to the great strength of Germany. He sought to dispel any mistaken impression Franco might have that England had not been wiped out on schedule. Germany would not begin the offensive against Britain until satisfied regarding the weather; he had waited for the weather he wanted before attacking France; the result was known; so now he would wait for the weather that would permit him to make the great attack upon England with certainty of success. In the meanwhile he assured Franco, as he had Serrano Suñer the month before, that Britain was being shattered by his planes and isolated by his submarines.

Yet, he went on, it would be foolish to disregard French feelings. His long address on this point was, in substance, a plea that Franco act without waiting for a clear delineation of the lands to be given to Spain. This was not the moment to settle the changes that would be made. It was the time to form a union

<hr />

[2] State Department Documents No. 8.

for the quick defeat of Engand, after which all partners would gain much. The dialogue reminds one of Don Quixote's effort to quiet Sancho Panza's wish for details about the kingdom that would be his at the end of his loyal services:

"I have already said to thee, Sancho, that thee shouldst not trouble thyself in any wise about this affair; for if an island were wanting, we have then the kingdom of Denmark, or that of Sobradisa, which will come as fit for thy purpose as a ring to thy finger."

On and on went the talk for nine hours—each entranced talker explaining himself in heedless stretches, recognizing no interruption or answer. Late in the night Franco broke off on the plea of fatigue. But his lava-like outpouring of talk left its mark upon Hitler. When a few days later, in Florence, Hitler told Mussolini of the pact that had been completed, he said that the exertion of reaching a conclusion had been so great that rather than have the conversation over again, he would prefer to have three or four teeth pulled out. Franco's subordinates could have warned him.

The Germans had thought that the talk would be resumed the next day, between Ribbentrop, Franco, and Serrano Suñer— for Hitler was off to meet Pétain. But when morning came, the Spaniards did not appear at Hendaye. A German searcher found them in San Sebastián, still tired and disgruntled. Franco left for Madrid.

So the dictators parted, leaving the chilled professions of their mutual esteem behind them. Franco had agreed to enter into an accord that would seal the unity of Spain, Germany, and Italy. But one that could be kept in storage as long as he wished. Serrano Suñer stayed behind to watch over the terminal work on the drafts. It was agreed that publication of the pact must be postponed until the actual Spanish entry into the war. Spain, Serrano Suñer observed, had an even greater interest than Germany in maintaining secrecy, for if the existence of this pact became known, England would prevent the delivery of 100,000 tons of corn and 150,000 tons of wheat for which Spain had already signed contracts with Canada.

To the last moment Serrano Suñer tried to get an exact definition of what was to be given Spain, but failed. Spanish demands had grown under the moon which guided British bombers to Berlin. He was now asking, according to what Hitler soon afterwards told Mussolini, for boundary changes along the Pyrenees and laying claim to French Catalonia.

The text of the so-called Protocol of Hendaye has not become available. But without too great risk of vital error a summary of its main features and parts may be identified. Its basic section contained some kind of political and military alliance between Spain, Italy, and Germany. Mussolini, on first reading the text, remarked that it represented the secret adhesion of Spain to the Tripartite Pact.

This accord was to be made public when Spain's preparations were complete and it was ready to enter the war. In his jubilance at having accomplished his task of persuasion, Hitler proposed to Mussolini that on that day the three of them meet in Florence —and together announce the pact as a signal for the assault on Gibraltar and the Straits. But when would that day be? The text did not state; no year, no month, no day, or any well-defined mark of circumstance.

The other sections of the pact dealt with preparations for Spanish participation and the terms of settlement after victory. They concerned: first, the plan for combining Spanish and German military preparations and operations; second, the provision by Germany of war matériel and supplies; third, German rights in certain of the economic resources of Morocco and the French and British properties in Spain; and fourth, the Spanish claims for territory in Africa.[3]

Of the section dealing with the last point, the language is known, along with evidence of the objection with which it was blotted. The Axis powers declared their consent to the reincorporation of Gibraltar within Spain, and their readiness in concluding peace after the defeat of England, to effect the transfer to

[3] It is not clear whether all these subjects were dealt with in the one instrument of agreement, named "The Protocol of Hendaye," which appears to have been an instrument of some seven or eight paragraphs. The detailed arrangements for military co-operation, supplies, and economic rights were relegated to supplementary accords or annexes, which were to have been completed later.

Spain of certain parts of Africa—in the measure that France could be compensated by grants of other African territories of equal value. German claims on France, it was specified, were to remain unaffected by this promise.

The honor of signing this pact was passed on by Serrano Suñer to the Spanish Ambassador in Berlin, de los Monteros. Ribbentrop tried to have Serrano Suñer include its text in the formal covering letters that they exchanged. Serrano Suñer chose not to. But he had ink for a postscript. In this he wrote that he should not like to refrain from letting Ribbentrop know that both Franco and himself felt bitter because, despite friendship, the trifling changes that they had sought were rejected—changes that would have caused Spain to feel more assured without changing substance or lessening Hitler's freedom of action.

The Germans were not worried by this reproach. Ribbentrop, during a stop on the railway trip home, telephoned to let Ciano know what happened. He was, he said,

"On the whole satisfied with the results achieved . . . the program of collaboration is heading towards concrete results." [4]

To the German Ambassador in Rome he wired that Spain had shown itself well disposed in general but difficult in regard to particulars; and that as for France, Pétain and Laval would co-operate with Germany.

A pact existed. That its authors wished it to come into effect, there can hardly be a doubt. But they remained free to hurry or to tarry, and in the end to act or not to act. The bridge of decision was not really crossed.

Franco waited and talked, measuring the risks of the bargain. Germany was offering supplies for action; Britain, with the United States alongside of it, was offering supplies to delay or prevent action. Franco tried to collect both premiums at the same time. The Allied supply program enabled him to do so while counting his fears. There were many. There was fear that the British might be able to seize the Atlantic islands or even land on the Peninsula. Hitler might tell him they could not, but how often they had before! The bones of British sailors buried in Spain rattled. There

4 Entry in the Ciano Diaries, October 24, 1940.

was fear that in a real campaign a hungry and angry people would turn against him; fear that he would be cheated of the African territories he wanted; and, though Spanish officials always denied it, fear that victory would turn out to be a German, not a Spanish one; if he had to use German forces to fight his own people it would certainly be so.

The pattern of negotiations between Franco, Hitler, and Mussolini that has been traced was to repeat itself with rising intensity during November and December. As it did, all Franco's fears became stronger. He formally endorsed the pact to join the Axis and make war on Britain. But even as he did so, he appears to have grown more determined not to be pushed into a decision. He began to reach and plan for some independent Spanish action —if ever a wholly safe moment should arrive. But an account of this evolution in Spanish policy must be postponed while the narrative reverts to the American and British wing of the mirror.

XVI

WASHINGTON AGAIN: AFTER THE HENDAYE CONFERENCE

A Penny for Franco's Thoughts

THE American government learned little about the outcome of the Hendaye Conference. No word leaked out of the accord that had been signed. The comment that traveled through the government offices in Madrid after Franco's return hinted that there were still barriers to Spanish action—as indeed there were. But how strong and durable were they? Had Franco refused to engage himself to act, or had the conspirators merely agreed that Spain should take further time to get ready?

Weddell and the British government, from high to low, concluded that the situation was unchanged and that the reasons for helping Spain were as good as ever. But the Secretary of State had never found these without flaw. If the shadow of hunger and revolt was lifted, would not Franco be freer to be bold? Would not Franco find excuses to betray the giver if the fortunes of war turned against Britain? Further, popular dislike and mistrust of Franco was still keen; large sections of the American press loathed the notion of trying to buy him off and were certain that he would not stay bought.

Between the inside whispers and outside shouts, Secretary Hull continued to waver. But we did not interfere with the purposeful expansion of Britain's aid. In fact, we quietly sustained British measures to help Spain obtain food from the Argentine and Canada, and oil from the United States and the Caribbean.

Weddell, it will be recalled, had been instructed after the discharge of Beigbeder to reserve any mention of American aid until we could judge the meaning of the event. He had his first serious talk with the new Foreign Minister on October 31st, a week after the meeting at Hendaye. Serrano Suñer evaded all queries as to what had taken place at that spot or after. But he made use of the turn in the talk to remark that he could assure us that there had been no pressure or even hint by Hitler or Mussolini that Spain should enter the war. This statement Weddell caused him to repeat thrice. Was it true? What did it mean? To make the riddle worse, the Foreign Minister proceeded to state that he could assure the American government of the political solidarity of Spain, Germany, and Italy. Murk within murk; half truths twisted around a bent branch of fact. Before the meeting ended, Serrano Suñer, probably with an inner smirk, said that the Caudillo had expressed extreme surprise that the shipments of wheat that we had promised had not yet arrived.

Weddell suspected that he was not being told all. But he did not guess how craftily phrased had been that aspect of the truth which he had been told. In any case, he remained of the opinion that, no matter what Serrano Suñer said, our ends would best be served by making a show of helping Spain. Thus he proposed: first, that if Franco agreed to the pertinent conditions that had been attached to Red Cross aid, news of the first wheat shipment should be announced at once; second, that we should discuss a possible credit for other supplies freely, with the realization that they might not be shipped. His thought was that we also might play a bit with open promises.

But Washington reached the sterner conclusion—for the moment it would frown, not tease or tempt. The White House had observed the jewel that Serrano Suñer had proudly pasted upon his chest, the sparkling declaration of solidarity with the Axis. Thus, on November 5th, Weddell was told not to resume his attempts to talk with Franco. If an interview was granted in response to previous requests, he was to make it bluntly clear that the American government paid for the Red Cross supplies; that our offer had been based on the notion that Spain would follow an absolutely neutral policy; and that if the conception of political solidarity meant that Spain planned to aid Germany in any way, we could not use public funds to help Spain.

Weddell's quick and agitated replies (of November 6th and 7th) to this message showed that he thought a mistake was being made, caused by a misreading of his report. He hastened to make clear that he thought Serrano Suñer's assurances went as far as could be expected then, and that despite Serrano Suñer's vain statement, no change in Spain's status was in sight. He found support for this opinion in a statement made on November 8th by Franco to Hoare—that if German troops crossed the frontier, force would be met by force. The Secretary of State did not know that a courier was then en route from Berlin to Madrid with the formal text of the pact joining Spain to the Axis, already signed by Ribbentrop and Ciano; a pact based on the anticipation that German and Spanish troops would march together, at a time of Franco's choosing. But he was tired of riddles and antics. The thinly carved phrases that were served did not satisfy. Nor did they seem to rhyme with the rest of the Spanish conduct. Only a few days before, it had expelled, without apology, the international administration of the Tangier Zone.

Welles, on November 8th, sent a message to Weddell even more blunt than the previous one. Franco was to be told that the American government could not justify any aid, even Red Cross relief, unless he made it *publicly* known that Spain would not help Germany in the war. Further, if Weddell could find an expedient way, he was to tell Franco that American opinion was deeply aroused over recent political executions, and that we hoped he would show mercy to political prisoners and refugees. For the first time since the war started, a cable went out to Madrid that was not tinged with fear. It contained some hint of the feeling that Serrano Suñer should be swept off the boards. But who was to do the sweeping? Britain was doing the fighting. If our directness was a mistake, it was Britain who would pay first.

The British government knew that full well. It reacted swiftly. As soon as Hoare learned of this message—and he learned of it very quickly through Washington—he sounded a loud alarm. Twice (on November 9th and 11th) before Weddell could act, the British Embassy in Washington begged the State Department to reconsider. For, in its views, Franco was sincere in the statement that he had made to Hoare about Spanish policy. While, on the other hand, the British thought it of little use to delay offers of aid in the pursuit of verbal assurances of uncertain value. For famine was imminent; and the British government was afraid that if we refused to give help unless the Spanish government openly separated itself from Germany, it would be driven into German arms. Why or by whom the British argument did not make clear. But it urged the State Department to hurry the relief and the credit talks. The British government was about to show its faith by opening negotiations at once with Spain for another loan of two million pounds.

The State Department was swayed by British anxiety, but still unconvinced that help was a better guarantee of Spanish neutrality than need. Therefore it took its time to reply. Weddell, while waiting to see Franco, tried out his orders upon the new Minister of Foreign Affairs (November 12th) and the new Minister of Commerce and Industry (November 19th). Serrano Suñer showed again how well he could mislead without telling an outright lie; or can he be said this time to have flatly lied? He described Spain's situation vis-à-vis Germany as being identical with America's relations to Britain, except that Spain had nothing to give the Axis. When Weddell asked whether, if German or Italian troops crossed the frontier, Spain would resist by force, he said it would—to the last man. Again a chosen phrase spoken out of the side of the mouth. A few days before (November 11th), he had signed the pact of alliance with Germany and Italy; and certainly *he* regarded it as a compact for war, to be begun quickly.

By means of such responses Serrano Suñer managed to give Weddell the impression that his taunting remark about political solidarity was a matter of mind and sentiment—hardly convertible into Axis aid. Having done this, he hurried off to talk again with Hitler at Berchtesgaden, leaving Weddell's request for an interview with Franco to await his return.

Carceller took up the task of maintaining the twisting trail. His talks in Berlin had brought him no gifts of supplies, no promises of aid until Spain went to war. He told Weddell on the 19th, with an air of objectivity, that it was an error to suppose that Spain saw eye to eye with the Axis in all respects. Some of its ambitions were, he said, clearly contrary to those of Germany and Italy. But, he added, any such public declaration as the American government sought was out of the question; we were forgetting the powerful German Army along the Spanish frontier. The Army was certainly there; in fact, certain of its units were there in accord with the tactical plans devised by the Spanish and German military staffs being trained for an assault on Gibraltar and the Straits. Carceller ended by saying that Franco knew of our proposals and that he was not pleased. Presumably we were to make a further study of how to please him, how to ease his way.

In these two talks Weddell stood on the letter of his instructions. But in his reports to the State Department he urged that the request for a public declaration be given up. Equivalent private and personal assurance might, he thought, be obtained. He warned that the food situation was becoming worse; that a crisis of hunger might bring internal trouble; and that if the present Spanish regime were threatened, German forces would move into Spain. At the same time the British government resumed its pleading. It was most worried lest by asking Franco to put his hands on the top of the table, we should incline or force him into the arms of Germany. Was he or was he not already there?

XVII

THE WINTER OF INDECISION (1940–1)

Franco Refuses to Foretell the Future

THE President, besieged by this advice, agreed to drop the attempt to secure a public assurance. Weddell was told that he need not insist upon one. We would accept words spoken in private if they were formal and clear. The message, of course, expressed our ignorance of the pledge that Franco had already permitted his Foreign Minister to sign.

Meanwhile Serrano Suñer had gone to Berchtesgaden in response to Hitler's summons. There he had squirmed and pleaded for delay, giving Spanish hunger as a main reason. On quitting Ribbentrop he had told him that, in order to obtain supplies, he would foster the illusion that Spain would not enter the war. Upon his return to Madrid (on November 22nd) he made merely the cryptic remark to Weddell that Spain would secure wheat wherever it could be found. A few days later (November 26th) he followed up this remark by stating that Franco was convinced that the United States had no real wish to help Spain; that in fact, it wished Spain to starve.

These comments seemed an ominous overture to Weddell's talks with Franco, which finally took place on November 29th. To Weddell's surprise, he was received with warmth, almost with cordiality. Who, at the moment, could know why? Was it merely to lure the food and oil wanted? Was it fear that the United States might seize the Atlantic islands? Was it because Franco had decided to resist the German bidding, at least till the Spanish people were no longer hungry and all risk was past?

Weddell lost no time in stating that his government wanted light upon Spain's relations with the Axis before going forward with gift shipments of wheat or considering a possible credit. Franco volunteered only bits and pieces about his recent contacts with Hitler. Then he appended to them the straightforward remark that no one could foretell the future.

Weddell seems to have tried to place words in Franco's mouth —hoping, no doubt, that they would take root there. He asked whether he might report to Washington that Spain did not envisage any departure from its present international attitude, or the extension of any aid to the Axis. Franco assented. But at once added that Spain could not help the Axis if it wished, and repeated that no one could foresee what the future might bring forth.

Weddell reported to Washington all these remarks dutifully. He stated that there was no use in trying to get Franco to declare himself more conclusively. He urged us to proceed with faith. Neither the President nor the Secretary of State knew of the way in which Franco had associated Spain with the Axis—on paper— for the conquest of the Mediterranean. But they did not trust him, or their power to attract him toward a faithful neutrality. They let the days go by despite the rapid flow of cables from Madrid that called upon the fear of internal trouble and German invasion. The Secretary turned aside another British plea by suggesting that Britain might arrange to ship wheat from Canada. He made no comment on the news of further British efforts to feed hungry Spain. Thus passed the first fortnight of December.

During this period we now know that Franco refused, with set will and an infinity of excuses, to fix a date for the start of operations against Gibraltar. Only six months before, he had written Hitler that he was eager to serve the Axis cause at the time when his help might be most wanted; the time had come; the request had been made, and Franco said that he could and would not enter the war. The decision was, he vowed, against his deepest wish; and whether this was so or not, the result was the same. Britain was spared a vital engagement—with odds against her. Gibraltar, the Straits, the Mediterranean, and North Africa remained open grounds for Allied operations.

Serrano Suñer's conduct began to reflect this decision, though, of course, that was not understood at the time. He hustled to put into form a suitable public announcement about the Red Cross help. His pleas to Weddell for food and oil ceased to carry a note of boastful disdain. They sounded almost like a whimper. But, as Welles had pointed out to the Spanish Ambassador on December 2nd, the Press and Propaganda Services of the Spanish government were sending scandalously false stories about the United States throughout Latin America.

Weddell's agitation over our coldness sprouted again. The European Division of the State Department took fright at the vision of trouble brewing in Spain—which might bring in the Germans. Once again it proposed that we throw out a line to Spain, but hold it loosely, so that we could drop it quickly if it began to burn our hands. The Secretary of State nodded and the President approved. A new offer was cabled to Weddell on December 19th.

This was to make our first Red Cross shipment as soon as Britain announced its arrangements for sending wheat from Canada and the Argentine. Britain—it turned out only for a brief spell—had suspended aid till Spain should promise not to fortify the coasts of the seized Tangier Zone.[1] Then, the State Department's message continued, Weddell might also inform the Spanish government that we were ready to discuss a possible credit, and we would so state publicly. Our statement would—with Spanish consent—make clear that we felt that our purpose in making the loan would only be achieved if Spain remained out of the war.

Subtlety of subtleties; we were to say for Spain what its government would not or dare not say. Thus we would let the Spanish people know we wanted to help, and also outwit opposition in the United States. In good conscience, for in the course of discussing the credit it was intended to ask satisfaction of·many·wishes. These included assurances that Spain would remain out of the war and did not intend to aid the Axis, and a promise that Spain would cease its press attacks upon the United States, not only in Spain but throughout the American hemisphere. These conditions were correctly called, by the Secretary of State in talk with his staff, "mountainous."

---

[1] As well as the restoration of various British rights within the zone. For an account of this important episode, see Hoare, op. cit., pages 64-5.

Franco is Left to Make up His Mind

This brightly conceived plan of December 19th was never acted upon. Doubts and objections sprang up from many directions. Weddell did not think it wise to wait on the British. Some of Secretary Hull's staff were against even the feint of a loan to Spain, and were not sure it was a feint. Norman Davis was unhappy at the thought that if we went forward with the relief shipment and hedged on the loan, the Red Cross might suffer from American dislike of the operation. Lastly, the willingness to brave criticism was weakened by twisted stories in the press concerning "inside" events connected with the Spanish loan request. Feelings were hurt, suspicions were sown within the government. For the time being, it became too troublesome to help Spain, for no matter what reason.[2] The school of thought that counted on Franco's weakness rather than his appreciation prevailed.

The State Department scrambled back. Secretary Hull reverted (December 23–30) to his earlier position that we could not justify any offer of a loan unless we knew first that Spain would remain at peace. He also decided that any action on our part must await action by Britain.

Messages to that effect were drafted with dejection. For each day's assortment of cables contained reports that unless we found a way to prevent it, Germany would soon enter the western Mediterranean. The Vichy government, so well-sponsored rumor went, was about to permit the Germans to go to Tunis, while Franco would permit them to march toward Gibraltar and Morocco.[3] The momentum toward association in such a program

[2] These stories, which appeared in the greatest of detail in a column edited by Drew Pearson and Robert Allen called the "Washington Merry-Go-Round," dramatized a supposititious conflict over Spanish policy between the Secretary and the Under Secretary in a way that damaged their relations.

[3] On December 14th Admiral Darlan in talking with H. Freeman Matthews of the American Embassy at Vichy, after renewing assurances regarding the French fleet and bases, remarked that if the British blockaded France, "we may attack Gibraltar and with Spanish and German help the Rock wouldn't hold out long." Langer, op. cit., page 117. Chapter iv of this book, called "Alarums and Excursions," is an animated and detailed record of the fright-

seemed in Washington at the time almost irresistible. Only since have we learned of the clefts between. As will shortly be recounted, while we wavered, the Spanish government was sliding out of the liens granted in earlier days. Franco had made up his mind; he would not throw open the road to Gibraltar and Morocco to the German forces. He refused to risk disaster for a victory that might leave Spain in the thrall of Germany. It is even possible to imagine that he did not think our conduct at this time strange, since he knew better than anyone else how much past cause he had given for it.

The State Department on January 7, 1941, in a gesture that had by then lost importance, agreed to have the first shipment of Red Cross wheat move forward. Serrano Suñer made another effort to frighten us into doing something more. On January 11th, talking to the National Council of the Feminine Section of the Falange, he said:

"However, the problem must be solved now. We need bread that the people may eat, we need raw material that the people may work, not one day or two days, but every day! And if to these needs persons should remain insensible, and if to our requests they should deny us bread or make it impossible for the Spanish people to work, or should they require our honor as the price, then, Comrades of the Falange, what risk, what suffering, even what death! . . ."

The Spanish press gave first place to this menacing discourse. It came, we now know, out of a spasm of disappointed desire. Hitler had refused to supply the needed food and raw materials unless the Spanish government entered the war at once. This Franco in turn had refused to do; and with the refusal vanished the chance of feeding the hungry Spaniards with grain from the East.

Thus Spain remained dependent upon what could be brought from overseas. Almost a million tons of cereals were still needed to fill out a meager diet for the people; a hundred thousand tons of oil each quarter to enable them to earn their own living; fertilizers, insecticides, tools, and tractors so that the next harvest might be good. Thus several times again in January and February the Americans were asked for credits and the goods Spain lacked.

---

ening reports about pending German marches to Africa. The most alarming of all seemed to have originated with Marshal Pétain.

But still being without direct knowledge of the turn of events, and without pledges, we ignored the hints. What reason was there to trust, what hope of gratitude? Not enough, the answer still seemed to be, after Colonel William Donovan talked with Serrano Suñer the last day of February. Serrano Suñer made no attempt to hide his views. He said that he hoped for and believed in the victory of Germany. When asked what he thought Spain would gain from the German victory, he answered that it would get Gibraltar together with a further recognition of Spain's natural rights in Africa.

Weddell tried to make sure that the Department would not be thrown off its balance by these remarks. He urged that American policy should not be deflected by such words, which might mean little or much. The Secretary of State agreed. But he remained skeptical of assuring Spain's good behavior by calculated generosity. However, the American government took no measures to prevent Spain from meeting its needs where it could. We allowed the cash purchase of all American products that were to spare. We abetted the arrangements made by the British government to move wheat from Canada and Argentine to Spain. But otherwise we permitted these months to run by despite Britain's pleas that we were neglecting a crucial chance. On March 20th the British Embassy made a more formal request than ever before that we share in a new inclusive program of assistance.[4] Another period of debate whether to do so or not began.

But before carrying this account of American action further, let us revert to the record of what had been going on between Spain and the Axis—while we had agonized and stood aside.

---

[4] At about the same time Lord Halifax presented to the Secretary of State another memorandum advocating an extension of our supplies for France. A passage of this memorandum follows: "His Majesty's Government feels that the most immediate danger is the penetration by German experts of French North Africa, which they know is being actively pursued and which, they fear, will pave the way either for the entry of German troops into French North Africa from Tripoli or for the collapse of Spanish resistance to Germany. His Majesty's Government thinks that the latter would certainly occur if Spain felt that Germany had succeeded in taking her in the rear, and there are already signs that Spanish resistance to German pressure is likely to weaken if German infiltration into the Mediterranean area is permitted to continue." Quoted in Langer, op. cit., pages 137–8.

XVIII

THE OTHER WING OF THE MIRROR AGAIN: AFTER HENDAYE

The Fuehrer Pleads for Haste

ALL through the winter of 1940–1 food was short in Spain. The previous harvest had been bad and prospects for the next were not good. Many factories remained idle for lack of raw materials. Trucks and buses broke down for want of parts. Railroad equipment was short, old, and overused. The Spanish people continued to be miserable. As just recounted, Franco could have, by one straight statement to us, obtained relief. But he held his tongue. The men around him hinted, though Franco himself never said so squarely, that this reserve was a refuge—against the powerful German Army along the Spanish frontier. But they did not say that certain units of that Army, in accord with plans to which Franco had given assent, were being trained to seize Gibraltar and the Straits. Of the existence of some engagements there were many signs, but no one in Washington was sure how firm they were or how far they went. The actuality was buried in crevasses from which only now it can be extracted.

At their meeting at Hendaye (October 23rd), Franco and Hitler, it will be recalled, had approved a written agreement about the basis and plan for Spanish entry into the war. This was a tangled mesh. On some points obligations were vaguely defined. Future steps to be taken by one party were left dependent on measures to be taken by the other. Parts contained obscure conditions. Essential supplements were unfinished or unsigned. In short, even a court of truthful and honest men would have found it hard to construe the abortive pact.[1] It is clear, however, that Franco reserved the right to decide *when* he would enter the war.

[1] Still, as Sir Samuel Hoare has pointed out, it greatly strengthened German influence in various phases of Spanish life. Germany was granted a free

The planning and preparation for action went on outside and inside Spain. Hitler hastened with the next measures in his scheme of combination. Even before Article 5 (that dealing with Spanish territorial claims) of the Hendaye Protocol was signed, he had rushed off to lure Pétain into the cell assigned to France. Next was the ritual act of obtaining Italy's formal assent. Mussolini at Florence had already expressed his approval. On November 2nd Ciano wrote in his Diary: "on my way to Sudetenland." There he and Ribbentrop went hunting. How many of the Axis pacts were concluded by spirits refreshed by the sight of dead stag or boar! The hunters at eventide put their names to the secret protocol, drawn up in triplicate. It was, except for some minor changes, the pact worked out at Hendaye.[2] Ciano described it, in the memorandum that he made of this meeting at Schoenhof on November 4th, as a secret protocol for Spain's entry into the Italo-German alliance and the Tripartite Pact of Berlin.

Up to the last hours of this meeting between Ciano and Ribbentrop it had been hoped that Serrano Suñer would meet them at Vienna and add his name to theirs; but Hitler telephoned that it could not be arranged. Thus the three copies were sent by courier to Stohrer at Madrid. He was told to have Serrano Suñer sign them in his presence. On doing so, he was to inform Serrano Suñer that Hitler had told Pétain that France had lost the war but now had a way to ease its lot by working with the two Axis powers during the final conquest of England; that Pétain and Laval had professed themselves "in principle" ready to do so; but that the Spanish government was to know that all the discussions concerning Africa were kept within the terms of the agreement of Hendaye.[3] Whether or not this message pleased Serrano Suñer, he signed (November 11th).

---

hand in the Spanish police, press, and censorship. "Spain was in fact to become an occupied country in the second degree."

[2] Ciano asked and obtained a change in Article 5, but whether in favor of Italy's claims or Spain's, or both, is not clear.

[3] For an account of the Hitler-Pétain-Laval talks at Montoire, see Langer, op. cit., pages 89–96. He concludes that although "Pétain had agreed that the defeat of Britain at an early date was most desirable, and he had accepted a program involving colonial readjustments at Britain's expense . . . all this was in very general terms. All the details were to be worked out later and so the door was left wide open. . . . So Montoire settled nothing" (page 96).

Lacking the text of this accord, it is impossible to be certain as to whether its terms were more incisive than the earlier draft composed at Hendaye. But it is safe to surmise that there were still several large vacuums beneath its phrases. The largest was that intent could be turned into action only upon the completion of measures deemed adequate to assure safe success; and the Spanish government remained the judge. Franco retained the right to delay decision until such time as he felt wholly ready. And both he and Serrano Suñer intended to wait until "the hour of the last cartridge." [4]

But Hitler believed that the accord reached was a reliable basis for action. He seemed almost sure that permission for German forces to move through Spain would be granted whether or not Spanish forces joined in the attack. Only a few days before, Franco had assured Hoare that if German troops crossed the frontier, force would be met by force.[5] Was this said behind Hitler's back? If it was repeated to Berlin was Hitler told that it was a Delphic utterance? Or that it was intended to soothe until the day of action came? Who was deceiving whom? In any case, Hitler was in mid-November confident that he was about to gain a new ally. And certainly he had grown desirous of commencing the action against Gibraltar quickly.

On the same day (November 4th) that Ribbentrop and Ciano signed the protocol, Hitler reviewed the situation created in the eastern Mediterranean by the Italian defeats with the heads of the German Navy and Army.

"The Fuehrer," the record of this meeting reads, "is determined to occupy Gibraltar as soon as possible."

Then the record states an opinion that could have come only from Hitler:

"Franco is obviously prepared to enter the war on Germany's side within a short time; the Army General Staff has already made preparations to send the necessary troops." [6]

[4] As expressed by Serrano Suñer in an interview after the defeat of Germany, "It was my intention to enter the war at the moment of the German victory, at the hour of the last cartridge. . . ." Interview with Charles Favrel, printed in *Paris-Presse*, October 26, 1945.

[5] See page 101.

[6] "Fuehrer Conferences," 1940, Vol. II, page 32.

On November 12th—the day after the tripartite agreement was signed by Serrano Suñer—Hitler issued a directive summarizing the advance measures to be taken by the German High Command for the conduct of the war in the near future.[7] The outline of the program began with the sentence:

"Political steps have been taken to bring about an early entry of Spain into the war."

In this directive the plan of the Iberian military campaign was set forth in much detail. It seems—to the amateur student—that the authors supposed that Spanish forces would play a part in the action, but allowed for the chance that they might not. It was a German plan, not a joint Spanish-German one. But there was an intimate secret liaison at the time between the German and the Spanish staffs, and it may be presumed that the latter knew its main features.

"The object of the German intervention in the Iberian Peninsula (code name 'Felix') will be," the directive read, "to drive the British from the western Mediterranean."

Gibraltar was to be taken, the Straits seized, and the British forces prevented from landing either on the Peninsula or the Atlantic islands. Both strategy and tactics were outlined from the first phase of reconnaissance to the final phase of assault. The reconnaissance was to be carried out by German officers in civilian clothes. The assault on Gibraltar was to be carried out by German units mainly.

"The units," the directive read, "earmarked for Gibraltar must be strong enough to capture the Rock, even without Spanish assistance."

The Straits were to be closed by Spanish forces with German naval, air, and ground assistance; German planes would disperse and pursue the British fleet. The defense of the Canary Islands was apparently to be left to Spanish forces with German support; but the German forces were to seize immediately the Cape Verde group of islands.[8] These military details have now lost interest as

[7] This was Directive No. 18, November 12, 1940, issued by Hitler as Fuehrer and Supreme Commander of the Armed Forces. It is printed in *Nazi Conspiracy and Aggression*, Vol. VI, pages 957-60.

[8] According to the naval minutes, "It is planned to strengthen the defenses

such, but they show that if the plan had been carried out, the German Army would have become masters within Spain as they were in France.

The Fuehrer ordered that the contents of this directive should be closely guarded.

"Special measures," its final paragraph reads, "will be taken to ensure secrecy. . . . This applies particularly to the operation in Spain and to the plans relating to the Atlantic islands."

It was soon brought home to Franco that the plan was tagged for quick application. Serrano Suñer was, as related, invited to Berchtesgaden. According to his own account, before leaving he informed Franco and the military men who were called in council that the summons probably meant a demand to close the Straits; that if he went he might be able to persuade Hitler to postpone the move; that if he did not go, German troops would cross the Pyrenees within forty-eight hours; and so was told to go and

---

of the Canary Islands primarily by Spanish action. Spanish resources will be reinforced by German measures." The Chief of the Operations Division opposed the plan for seizure of the Cape Verde Islands, and Raeder thought it "unnecessary, but with luck possible." Minutes of meetings of senior naval officers with Hitler, November 4th and November 14th. "Fuehrer Conferences," 1940, Vol. II, pages 32 and 40-1.

In passing, it may be noted that there is much scattered evidence to show that the Germans would have in fact assumed direction of military operations in and about the Atlantic islands of both Spain and Portugal. The proposals advanced by Hitler to Serrano Suñer revealed the German wish to retain one or more of them permanently. Hitler was not only thinking of the risk that, if these islands were captured by Britain or the United States, the operations against the Straits might suffer. He was looking forward to the time when the United States might challenge his rule over Europe and Africa.

This train of thought is illustrated in a memorandum prepared on October 29, 1940 by General Staff Major Freiherr von Falkenstein, Luftwaffe Liaison Officer with the Operations Staff of OKW, called "A Brief Résumé on Military Questions Current Here." "The Fuehrer," this memorandum reads, "is at present occupied with the question of the occupation of the Atlantic islands with a view to the prosecution of the war against America at a later date. Deliberations on this subject are being embarked upon here." Printed in *Nazi Conspiracy and Aggression*, Vol. III, page 376.

When questioned by the International Military Tribunal at Nuernberg in regard to this matter, Goering explained that ". . . it was connected with a study of the occupation of Gibraltar, North Africa, and perhaps of the Atlantic islands—first of all, bases for combat against England, secondly, in case—and I underline 'in case'—in case America should enter the war. . . ." Mimeographed transcript of the proceedings, pages 5958 et seq.

win delay.[9] At all events, he went, leaving Weddell and Hoare to hang about with unanswered questions.

On arrival (November 18th) Serrano Suñer was confronted by Hitler and Ribbentrop with direct assertions that the time for action was at hand. The Italian troubles in Greece and the British occupation of Crete, the Germans explained, made it imperative to close the Mediterranean both from the east and from the west.[10] They urged Spain to enter the war as soon as possible. January and February, they said, would be good months. For thereafter German troops would be needed for other purposes. Hence Spanish preparations for closing the western strait should be quickly completed. Apart from the defense of the Canary Islands, Hitler said, there was no military problem to worry about.

Hitler tried to forestall a plea for delay till Spain had enough food and other vital supplies. It was foolish to think, he averred, that Spain could obtain them from the Allies; conditions would not improve with waiting; there was plenty only on Germany's side in the war. The British policy in supplying Spain, it will have been observed, had been shaped to prove the contrary. It prevailed. The Spanish government decided to import awhile longer rather than fight.[11]

With far more vigor than at Hendaye, Serrano Suñer opposed the demand that Spain should enter the war early in the new year. While seeming to swing with Hitler's talk, he unhinged its conclusions. The man who had a few months before admitted no obstacle now saw many. His assurance had been shaken—by Britain's continued resistance. His impulses had been checked—

[9] Interview *Paris-Presse*, already cited, October 27, 1945. No available document indicates that Hitler considered entering Spain without the consent of the Spanish government—unless the United States or Great Britain attacked either Spain or the Canary Islands.

[10] In the November 12th directive already cited, Hitler had also outlined the plan of the campaign in Greece. This began: "The Commander in Chief of the Army will make preparations for the occupation from Bulgaria of the Greek mainland north of the Ægean Sea, should the necessity arise. . . ."

[11] It is of interest to record that during the year between the 1940 and the 1941 harvests, Spain managed to import from overseas about 800,000 metric tons of cereals, mainly from Argentina. For the calendar year 1940 the official Spanish statistics record imports of 674,000 metric tons of wheat, 31,000 tons of flour, 32,000 tons of corn, 55,000 tons of rice, and 6,000 tons of barley, as well as substantial quantities of potatoes, fruits, beans, and other vegetables.

by Franco and the generals. His animosity had been aroused—by German refusal to grant Spanish territorial claims. His self-importance (or pride for Spain) had been hurt—by the German refusal to court. He has made known the way in which he felt himself (and Spain) treated in this talk:

"The decision [to attack Gibraltar and the Straits] had been taken and it was being communicated to me through mere courtesy just as a colonel might in passing salute the farmer whose crop would have to be destroyed by being turned over to the passage of troops." [12]

First and foremost among his objections was the need of more time to secure food from overseas. As if to prove that this was not merely a pretext, he beguiled his listeners with an account of his deceiving ways. The widespread hunger, he said, had made it necessary for him to foster the illusion that Spain would not enter the war; even then he was seeking at least 400,000 tons of Canadian wheat without which Spain's entry into the war would be foolhardy.[13] Therefore, Serrano Suñer continued, he, as Foreign Minister, had had to navigate with great astuteness. His staunch loyalty to the Axis had cost Spain 30,000 tons of wheat, which the American government had been about to send. The American Ambassador, Serrano Suñer said, had impertinently asked Franco publicly to state that Spain's foreign policy would remain unchanged and that Spain would not enter the war. Naturally he had refused. What greater proof that he was in earnest, though not ready for the war?

When Hitler outlined how Spain's needs would be met with German help, *when* Spain was in the war, Serrano Suñer harked back to another grievance. He complained that both he and Franco, ever since Hendaye, had been depressed because in the secret protocol Spanish claims had been dealt with in so vague a manner. If the Spanish people knew how vague, he said, they would be even less inclined to enter the war.

Hitler ignored this complaint as he had at Hendaye. He answered that any other way might cause the loss of North Africa

[12] Interview *Paris-Presse*, already cited, October 27, 1945.

[13] There never was a chance that Spain might have secured so large an amount of *Canadian* wheat. Did Serrano Suñer speak carelessly or choose to mention Canada as the chief source of supply since it was so clearly under British control?

and that he would prefer to have Gibraltar in English hands and have North Africa remain with Pétain. Spain should trust his policy and not insist upon a more definite written agreement. But he implied that the last trick had not perhaps been played; his strategy, he said, would be satisfied if the agreements with France remained valid until the conquest of Gibraltar, after which the danger of revolt in Morocco would be greatly lessened.

No differences were settled, but none were admitted to be insoluble. Hitler again spoke of his promise that Germany would leave the glory to Spain and provide the best equipment and soldiers.[14] Serrano Suñer explained that upon his return to Madrid he would inform the British Ambassador that Germany had agreed to deliver wheat. He would thus incite Britain to speed up deliveries; he would, Hitler might be sure, use the time spent for military preparations in getting as much Canadian, American, and Argentine wheat as possible for Spain.

The results of these turns and twists of Serrano Suñer's on Spain's food situation, I may pause to comment, was this: greater amounts of imports from the British Empire were scared into Spain than would otherwise have been sent; but supplies from the United States were scared away.

In farewell, Ribbentrop said they would await word that Franco had agreed to Hitler's proposal. But if Hitler expected decisive word to arrive by return courier, he was disappointed. Perhaps in part because of the different reading in Berlin and Madrid of recent military occurrences. Hitler had cited the Italian difficulties in Greece as a reason for haste; to Franco they must have seemed a reason for delay.

A week later (November 25th) Franco gave his answer. He maintained the position that Serrano Suñer had taken at Berchtesgaden and asked again for more definite written assurances from Hitler regarding Spanish claims. He wished for further study and discussion of the military problem. But these signs of a lagging will were followed by a more hopeful message. The German

[14] Serrano Suñer later, and without directly saying that Hitler threatened to invade Spain without consent, sought to give the impression that such action was imminent and that he, Serrano Suñer, had staved it off by telling Hitler, ". . . just as did Napoleon, you are going to awaken Spanish national sentiment and run up against a savage resistance. . . ." Interview *Paris-Presse*, October 27, 1945.

Ambassador reported on November 28th and 29th, relying on Serrano Suñer's notes of a talk with Franco, that Franco agreed that Germany should go ahead with the preparations even though he would not now designate an exact date for the start of operations; and that he urged the secrecy of all preparations be most carefully guarded lest Britain take alarm and retaliate or attack. It was about then (November 29th) that Franco told Weddell that no one could foretell the future.

Franco's message seemed compliant enough to cause Hitler to try again for an instant decision. The Spanish operation would have to be begun soon or abandoned. For all German forces would be needed before long for other tasks. The Greek invasion was to be launched before early spring. The attack on Russia was scheduled in Hitler's mind, though further months of preparation for this would be required. There was still time, but only enough time, to close the western Mediterranean without postponing or giving up these other major campaigns. About him were men, first among them Goering and the Supreme Naval Commander Raeder, who were earnestly advising against any plan to turn to the east before the west was won.[15] Goering's disappointment was the sharper for he was so sure that all of west Africa could be taken in a brief and easy expedition.

"The attack on Gibraltar by the air force was so methodically prepared that according to all expectations no failure could be thought of. The British air forces on the small airfield north of the Rock were irrelevant. The attack of my paratroopers on the Rock would have been a success . . . the exclusion of the Mediterranean as a combat area, the key point of Gibraltar, North Africa down to Dakar, Suez, and possibly in the south . . . could have been possible with small forces." [16]

[15] In a file of the High Command of the Navy there is a minute of a discussion with Hitler on November 14, 1940 of the Russian operation. It reads: "Naval Supreme Commander with the Fuehrer: Fuehrer is 'still inclined' to instigate the conflict with Russia. Naval Supreme Commander [Raeder] recommends putting it off until the time after the victory over England. . . ." Printed in *Nazi Conspiracy and Aggression*, Vol. VI, page 977, and again in a minute of a meeting December 27, 1940, "Naval Supreme Commander voices serious objections to Russian campaign before the defeat of England," page 990.

[16] Mimeographed transcript of Nuernberg trial, page 5958.

Dewitt C. Poole has given in *Foreign Affairs* of October 1946 a full account of the laments that Goering made to American interrogators.

This would be true if Spain consented, and quickly. Otherwise Germany would have to defer or weaken the scheduled operations in the Balkans, give the USSR time to grow stronger and the United States more chance to act first and seize the Atlantic islands. Time was the meter of strategy.

XIX

THE OTHER WING OF THE MIRROR AGAIN: THE SEPARATION BETWEEN HITLER AND FRANCO

The Rock is Left Alone

ON December 5th Hitler wrote Mussolini:

"I therefore propose to address a new strong appeal to Franco to set a date for Spanish entry into the war so that the necessary military preparations may be carried forward. The sooner the better for all concerned, as I cannot keep German forces scattered on the periphery." [1]

Admiral Canaris was sent to Madrid to extract the answer.

The Admiral's proposal (made on December 7th) was in the following terms:

"[the] Admiral presents [the] Chief of State [the] Fuehrer's greeting and conveys Germany's wish to undertake [an] attack upon Gibraltar within a short time in connection with which German troops are to march into Spain on January 10. . . . [The] Admiral reports that as soon as [the] march of troops begins, the economic co-operation would at once begin."

The essence of Franco's reply was:

"That it was impossible for Spain, for reasons duly presented, to enter the war on the suggested date." [2]

The main reasons he advanced were: risk that Britain would seize the Canary Islands and Spanish Guinea; incomplete military preparations; lack of food and inadequacy of transport. When Canaris suggested that it might be possible to fix a later date,

[1] Letter, December 5, 1940, printed in *Les Lettres sécrètes échangées par Hitler et Mussolini*, page 100.
[2] State Department Documents No. 11.

Franco answered that since the removal of the difficulties did not depend only on the will of Spain, he could not do so. However, he tried to soften his answer by adding that his attention and his effort would be directed toward hastening and completing Spain's preparations.[3]

Almost at the same time another section of the program that Hitler had carried to Hendaye and Montoire began to crumble. On December 13th Pétain dismissed Laval. Even though Pétain might write, as he did two days after, that this action did not mean an end of the policy of collaboration, it showed how unfirm the ground was.[4]

Hitler concluded that he could wait no longer for the unwilling, faltering collaborators of the west to fall into line. They would come running when he had finished off his last great enemy on the continent; he would not have to woo or bargain with them then. A few days later (December 18th) Hitler issued the fateful order for the start of serious preparations for an attack on Russia (Operation Barbarossa). These, according to the original schedule, were to have been concluded by the May 15th following.[5]

Vague reports began to circulate in Madrid about Franco's refusal to take the decisive step on the road to war along which he had gone so far. In reporting them the American Embassy offered creditable, if not complete, explanations. His Cabinet was deeply divided; some of its members, including the Minister of Marine, threatened to resign if Franco moved in haste. Some generals in the Army went further—they spoke of open revolt. The Navy was afraid of the loss of the Spanish islands; the Army afraid that ill-equipped divisions could not stand up against an Allied landing. Neither wanted to fight under German command. Further, between the leaders of the Falange there were bitter feuds. But above all else, the Spanish people wanted peace and would not be subserviently brought into a world war to help the Germans, whom they did not like.

---

[3] The German record of this conversation is printed as State Department Documents No. 11.

[4] *Le Procès du Maréchal Pétain*, testimony of General Doyen, Chief of the French Mission on the Armistice Commission, page 95.

[5] *Nazi Conspiracy and Aggression*, Vol. VI, page 990.

Even Stohrer had about this time become aware of the lethargy of Spain. His notes to Ribbentrop began to tremble with comments on the terrible economic conditions and the widespread dislike of Serrano Suñer. Even making allowances for the fact that these might excuse failure, they were in substance correct. Stohrer's advice, timidly advanced, began to resemble Sir Samuel Hoare's; Germany should court the Spanish people and government by sending larger amounts of supplies. But Hitler had no thought of doing so unless Spain adopted his program. All parts of his war organization were clamoring for the carefully measured stocks of oil, food, and steel.

How promising the strategic chance seemed, and how keen the disappointment at having to give it up, is vividly shown in the minutes of the meeting between Raeder and Hitler on December 27th. The Naval Staff reported that in view of the events in Greece, Albania, Libya, and East Africa:

"The significance of the German occupation of Gibraltar is increased by the recent developments in the Mediterranean situation. Such occupation would protect Italy; safeguard the western Mediterranean; secure the supply lines from the North African area, important for Spain, France, and Germany; close the British sea route through the Mediterranean to Malta and Alexandria; restrict the freedom of the British Mediterranean fleet; complicate British offensive action in Cyrenaica and Greece; relieve the Italians; and make possible German penetration into the African area via Spanish Morocco."

The passivity of Hitler's response to this strong summary reflects the fact that by then his intense purpose was centered elsewhere.

"The Fuehrer answers that he is in full agreement regarding the significance of the occupation of Gibraltar. At the moment, however, Franco is not ready; his decision is delayed by British promises of food supplies. One day these will prove to be a fraud and Spain will find itself without supplies. The Fuehrer will once more try to influence Franco through the Foreign Minister via the Spanish Ambassador." [6]

The minds and energies of the German government were beginning to be absorbed into other operations: the conquest of

Greece, the domination of the Balkans, and the invasion of the USSR. The troubles in the east had become heavy. No longer could it be thought that a swiftly executed march on the Straits might end the war. But Hitler did not cease to regret the lost opportunity.

On the last day of 1940 he wrote to Mussolini that he was:

"deeply disturbed by the situation, which Franco believes changed. Spain has refused to collaborate with the Axis powers. I fear that Franco is about to make the greatest mistake of his life. I find extraordinarily naïve his idea of getting raw materials and cereals from the democracies as a kind of compensation for staying out of war. They will keep him talking until the last bit of grain has been eaten and will then commence the fight against him. I deplore all this since, on our side, we had completed our preparations to cross the Spanish frontier on January 10th in order to attack Gibraltar at the beginning of February." [7]

Franco, despite his rebuff of the German request, did not cease the preparations of which he had again spoken to Canaris. Or from then on should they be called "exercises"? The steps first planned in September had been carried far along. German specialists in Spain had finished the mapping out of a route for the march. Their study of the tactics for assault had maps of the fortress of Gibraltar as exact as those of the streets in Berlin. German paratroop and assault divisions had completed their practice outside of Spain; a mountain resembling Gibraltar had been found in the French Juras upon which specialized German units had trained at length and with particular enthusiasm and energy. At the same time Spanish assault divisions were being trained in Spain.[8] Supplies had been collected near Bordeaux and Hendaye. Bridges over the Spanish-French frontier and on the road to Gibraltar had been strengthened. Roads leading to Gibraltar had been broadened. New gun installations had been made at points commanding the Straits. The works within Spain Franco continued to extend. But the pace of effort gradually became Spanish.

[7] *Lettres sécrètes échangées entre Hitler et Mussolini,* pages 106–7.

[8] See the story in the *New York Times,* March 16, 1946, based on captured German documents, and the July 1, 1946 issue of the *New Times,* published by the newspaper *Trud* of Moscow containing the testimony of Colonel General E. Jaenecke, Chief Quartermaster of the German troop units organized for the assault on Gibraltar.

The momentum began to wane. Presently Canaris's "hunting" trips to the estate of General Vigón grew fewer and shorter. The design for war began to gather dust.

But not all at once. Hitler tried again directly and indirectly. Franco repeated what he had said in December. Wheat in advance was his standard reply. So he answered when, on January 20th, Stohrer informed him that Hitler was dismayed at the postponement and that he was under orders to demand that Franco make up his mind at once and for all, within the next forty-eight hours.[9] Upon receipt of word that Franco would not do so, Ribbentrop blustered. Stohrer was told to remind Franco that without Mussolini's and Hitler's help Franco would not be Chief of the Spanish State, and to say that if he now refused to enter the war at once, the refusal would be taken to mean doubts of German victory. Germany, the Foreign Minister wound up, must have an answer at once, and for all.

Stohrer, after securing permission slightly to soften the language of his order, did his best. But Franco on the 25th, after repeating his previous replies, cited a new hazard—the weather—observing that the climate was very bad; in January there is too much snow, while in February there is too much rain.

Thereupon Hitler gave up the plan of entering the western Mediterranean before the fighting in the east began.[10] Preparations for Operation Felix had already been slowed up, shunted aside to clear the way for other operations which the Army had

[9] It has since become plain why each day of delay interfered with the German military planning. Two large operations, one to overcome resistance in Greece, the other to drive the British Army out of eastern Africa, were scheduled to start in the first weeks of spring. The vast task of organization for the invasion of the USSR was also under way; for many reasons this could not be delayed beyond early summer. The German timetable for conquest contained no allowance for delay or failure. This was a vital mistake in German planning. The operations had to start on schedule or be abandoned. The program did not permit the indefinite retention in idleness of special German units and equipment while waiting for Spanish decision.

[10] But the plan of campaign was kept in the action file to be used when the eastern wars were over. How soon this was expected to be is illustrated in the letter (sent by the German Naval War Staff to the Commanding Generals of Groups West, North, and South). One line of the section entitled "Objectives for the further Conduct of the War upon the Termination of the Campaign in the East" read: "Plan 'Felix' must be executed still in 1941." Nuernberg Trial Document 57, USSR 336.

in prospect. Now they were definitely displaced.[11] In a conference summoned by him on February 3rd to assess the progress made in the plan for the Russian invasion, the Chief of the Army Staff reported:

"Felix is no longer possible as the main part of the artillery is being entrained." [12]

Hitler's feeling found outlet in a long letter sent to Franco on the 6th of February. This letter was compounded of warning, contradiction, and reproach.[13]

Warning:
". . . If your struggle against the elements of destruction in Spain was successful, it was only because the democratic opponents were forced to be cautious by attitude of Germany and Italy. *You will be forgiven, Caudillo, but never for this victory*."

Contradiction:
". . . *If it later should be asserted that Spain could not enter the war because she received no supplies, that would not be true!*"

Reproach:
". . . It is clear that, on January 10, if we had been able to cross the Spanish border with the first formations, Gibraltar would today be in our hands. That means: two months have been lost, which otherwise would have helped decide world history."

Franco in his reply tried to assuage the German resentment and to cling to the chance of sharing in German victory. He informed Stohrer that he was fully in accord with Hitler's conceptions. He denied that he had intended to suggest that Spain would not enter the war until the autumn or winter; he had merely thought it sensible to call attention to the weather. Sancho Panza had hold of his tongue again:

"You will have no cause to weep, for I will entertain you with the telling of histories until it be day, if you will but alight and take a nap upon these green herbs, as knight errants are wont, that you may be the fresher and better able to attempt the monstrous adventure which you expect."

[11] "Fuehrer Conferences," 1941, Vol. I, page 3.
[12] The record of this meeting is contained in *Nazi Conspiracy and Aggression*, Vol. I, page 801.
[13] State Department Document No. 12.

Hitler had some weeks before asked Mussolini to try to inspire Franco to action—"to bring back home the Spanish Prodigal Son."[14] The two men met—with purpose already dimmed—at Bordighera on February 12th. Mussolini did not appear greatly upset by Franco's conduct. He spoke as a sympathetic man who could hear a comrade's excuses without passing judgment. He presented the case for action in Hitler's name, then listened calmly as Franco blamed the Germans for not accepting the proposals that he had made in the previous June and September, when there was still enough to eat in Spain. At the end of a rambling morning of talk, Mussolini summed up what he had gathered of Franco's attitude. The terminal point of this conversation might be summarized in dialogue form as follows:

Duce:
Spain, then, will enter the war when these two conditions are recognized: first, the sending of sufficient grain, and second, agreement with her colonial aspirations.

Caudillo:
That is just the way it is.

Duce:
Should the Germans suspect that Spain did not wish to enter the war because the German invasion of Great Britain did not come off, or because of the Italian setbacks in Libya, can I assure the Fuehrer to the contrary?

Caudillo:
Absolutely, the faith of the Spanish people in the victory of the Axis is the same as on the first day.

In the course of the talk, Franco managed to bring out a new wrinkle in his thought. The admiring assent given in Franco's letter of September 27th to Hitler's tactical plans for capturing the fortress and the Straits was now withdrawn. Spain, Franco explained, was convinced that she must seize Gibraltar by her own forces and her own methods. He also reverted to his earlier view that this was a job for artillery rather than for bombing planes. The meaning of this talk on tactics was made quite clear. For Franco said that since the capture of Gibraltar was a Spanish

14 Entry, Ciano Diaries, January 21, 1941.

venture, the Spaniards would never allow foreign troops to do what it fell upon Spanish troops to do. Hitler's later comment on this plan was rude:

"Franco's statement that the assault on Gibraltar should be carried out by Spanish troops can be regarded only as an ingenious way of exaggerating the strength and potential offensive of the Spanish Army." [15]

Perhaps it was more than that; perhaps it was the surest way to keep German troops out of Spain, the hardest evasion to challenge as disloyal to a common vow.

Franco did not (at this Bordighera meeting) conceal his hurt that Hitler had chosen to file down Spanish requests to French taste. France, he avowed, would never collaborate; it was the lifelong enemy of Spain as well as of Germany. Then stopping off in Montpellier, on his way back to Madrid, he told Pétain that Hitler had been asking permission to cross Spain to attack Gibraltar and move against the Straits. He asked Pétain to support his refusal. He did not, of course, reveal the rest of his dealings with the leader of Germany.[16] Presumably by this talk Franco was trying to safeguard Spain against the risk that Pétain would permit German forces to enter Algeria or French Morocco, hemming in Spanish Morocco from the rear.

After studying a copy of the record of the talk at Bordighera, Ribbentrop instructed Stohrer to bring up the subject no more. If the Spaniards, he added, ask about supplies, be reserved about the whole question, since they have refused to set a date. A few days later (February 26th) Hitler received Franco's formal reply to the letter he had sent three weeks before. Amidst its vows of loyalty, it conveyed a message of separation:

". . . the facts and their logical development have today left far behind the circumstances which in the month of October had to be taken into consideration . . . and the Protocol then existing must at present be considered outmoded." [17]

[15] Letter Hitler to Mussolini, February 28, 1941, *Lettres sécrètes*, pages 115–16.
[16] *Le Procès du Maréchal Pétain*, testimony of General Serigny, page 174.
[17] Letter Franco to Hitler, February 26, 1941, State Department Documents, No. 13.

Thus while the American government kept its hand in its pocket until it knew what Franco was about, the immediate danger that the war would be carried into the western Mediterranean went by. The British and American Embassies, as already observed, gathered an impression that a crisis had been passed. They were fairly sure that Germany had asked consent to pass through Spain and had been denied. But the full measure of divergence between German and Spanish wishes was well hidden. Even had it not been, the American and British governments could not have felt tranquil about the future.

Franco stayed behind his hedge, while favoring Germany in various ways. A deal for payment on the Spanish Civil War debt was known to be under discussion. The new harvests were due in June. If they were good, Spain would have enough food for a short war. If the German attacks in the east, expected in the early summer, succeeded, Spain might still join Britain's enemies. Spanish military preparations were being carried forward, though at a pace—some watchers said—more suited for the Peninsular War than for the present one.[18] Time, essential time, had been granted, but the future remained in hazard.

---

[18] The reports of the meetings between Hitler and the German Navy during 1941 show that the defense installations in the Canary Islands and certain Spanish ports (El Ferrol and Cádiz, which the German Navy hoped to use) were weak and lacking in many respects. Notes on the situation at various times in 1941, as viewed by the German Navy, may be found in "Fuehrer Conferences," 1941, Vol. I, page 64, Vol. II, pages 26 and 29—particularly the Annex "Defenses of the Spanish Harbors of El Ferrol and Cádiz and of the Canary Islands." In contrast to these weak situations this report (August 26, 1941) stated that "On the south coast of Spain and on the coast of Morocco coast artillery is well placed and work is progressing satisfactorily." There seems to have been a lack everywhere of special equipment such as anti-aircraft guns, mines, searchlights; and the supplies of oil, and probably even of ammunition, would not have lasted long in serious battle.

XX

PATIENCE IN THE FACE OF AFFRONT: THE FIRST HALF OF 1941

The Spring of Rumor

EACH passing day of the Washington spring of 1941 was drenched by a rain of rumors. The news was saturated with foreboding that Germany would gain control of the western entry to the Mediterranean and Africa. Either Pétain would yield consent to enter the French colonies or Franco would agree to a march against Gibraltar and the Straits. One would lead to the other. These were the thoughts that the German government wished us to think. Lazar, Press Attaché of the German Embassy, used every channel provided by the compliant Spanish government to spread these fearsome stories.[1] The purposes were several: to disguise the plan to attack Russia; to deter us from giving friendly aid to Spain; and to keep Spain mindful of German power.

Now we know that by the spring of 1941, Germany had moved its attacking force elsewhere; that its whole war program would have been spoiled by a campaign in the Peninsula until it won in the east. But this was not known at the time. American and British opinion remained on edge. The extreme state of nervous gloom is illustrated by the April 30th issue of the New York tabloid *PM*. Across the whole front page ran these short but immense lines:

> "THE MEDITERRANEAN IS LOST
> SUEZ AND GIBRALTAR DOOMED"

These headlines were followed by the following statement over the initials of the editor:

[1] See Thomas J. Hamilton: *Appeasement's Child*, page 242.

"We are so certain of these terrible facts that for us it is as if they had already happened." .

German armies swarmed over Greece and the Balkans. Their successful air-borne conquest of Crete hurt hardly less; for it showed that a dominant air power could skip over water. The British in order to support the Greeks had weakened their forces in North Africa and were soon falling back before the Afrika Korps. Germany, it seemed probable, would soon have near-by air bases on both sides of the Mediterranean to attack the British fleet off Egypt. These events seemed to warrant the editor's forecast.

The American and British governments were worried, but they did not accept the sentence of doom. Weddell continued to affirm that Spanish policy remained in the balance and that the condition of the Spanish people would compel Franco to keep Spain out of war. The British government did not permit itself to doubt; it maintained the belief that Spain would remain quiet unless Suez fell, and the grim determination that it should not fall. The German line in Spain was met with more open advertisement of Britain's will and ability to help the Spanish people regain a normal life. Bread in the basket, oil in the jar, wine in the bottle, shirt on the back, men in the fields, children at play, trucks on the road, priests in their parish, nights in bed; could the brightened prospect of these repel the thoughts of war? Britain thought so, and acted without waiting for us to come round to the same view.

Thus the British government relaxed its blockade restraints. It culled the Empire for those products which Spain most wanted, such as wheat, tin, rubber, and cotton. And finally, in April, it announced the large new sterling credit of which it had spoken to the American government the previous autumn.

The British during March and April scoured every crevice of influence to find new means. As already told, it urged the American government, first on March 20th and almost daily thereafter, to announce that we also would provide foods and raw materials for Spain, would increase our purchases, and grant a credit. But the prevalent view in the United States was different from the British; Americans in general were averse to helping

Franco and did not believe that either generosity or the resistance of the Spanish people would influence his course.

The State Department veered between these two streams of feeling and opinion. It did not like to go contrary to the popular view—which most of its officials shared. But British experience in such matters was impressive. A half-hearted search was begun for some type of offer that would supplement Britain's appeal to the Spanish people. But nothing would have come of it had not a new reason emerged. It became expedient to devise an appealing way to remain in touch with the Spanish government. For Serrano Suñer was trying his utmost to create a vacuum.

With Animosity Added

He tried to turn a light taunt of Weddell's into a break with the American government. The American Ambassador had adapted himself well to our hesitant course. He had conveyed American sympathy for the welfare of the Spanish people and with practiced calm had shown faith that they would respond. He had tried hard to read a decent meaning into Franco's purposes and excused his reticence.

Weddell called upon Serrano Suñer on April 19th to make a grave affirmation—as instructed by the Secretary of State. The message was short but meaningful; the American government wanted the Spanish government to appreciate that the United States was determined to see the war crisis through to a successful end, no matter what the cost or how hard the struggle. Weddell spoke as told. The Minister made no reply. Weddell then turned to current business.

He protested against the increasingly hostile tone of the Spanish press, denoting, perhaps, some change in Spanish policy. This Serrano Suñer denied, but Weddell did not let him off. He said that he was sorry that the Minister had chosen, in a recent speech, to take credit for what appeared in the press.[2] For, Weddell

---

[2] Serrano Suñer, in opening a German press exhibition at Madrid, had

explained, he had drawn comfort from a comment of the Minister's predecessor in office, that the Spanish press represented neither the Spanish government nor public opinion. Serrano Suñer still made no reply. Weddell went on; he remarked that when he read the newspapers these days, he sometimes had the impression that their articles were translated from some foreign language, perhaps from German. The tone of this remark was easy, as of a man who was curious about a vagary of nature, but Serrano Suñer winced. The truth hurt—for it smashed the image of self-esteem. He had to believe that he was leading Spain in a great common cause. Any suggestion that he was sacrificing Spain's independence was, as he answered, disagreeable.

The talk ended in a cold separation. For six months thereafter Serrano Suñer barred the way to Franco. At first this may have been only a way of hurting the Ambassador; he hated the cool ease of the Virginian. But gradually it was used as a way of keeping the American and Spanish governments apart. This was the time of Serrano Suñer's greatest influence with Franco, and Franco took no step to heal the breach. It suited his purpose, as he watched the unclear course of battle in Russia and Africa, to keep the prying American government at a distance. For he knew that before granting aid, we intended to insist upon having from him a firm promise to stay out of the war and reduce aid to the Axis. This promise he was not yet ready to give. Suez might yet fall, and Axis power become free to sweep the whole length of the African shore of the Mediterranean. The Germans in Madrid were boasting that Rommel would have the Canal by May 1st.

It was no time, the British insisted, for us to permit ourselves to be put off by the unpleasant behavior of a scheming Minister. Churchill was expounding his policy in the House of Commons (April 22nd):

"This policy has been most carefully considered . . . we do not wish to do anything which could give any excuse for a breach at the present time between us and the Spanish government; and I certainly consider that the starving condition of the people of Spain fully justifies assistance being given by Great Britain and by the United States, if she

with great satisfaction taken credit for the way the controlled press served Germany.

chooses so to act, irrespective whether any expressions of gratitude are forthcoming or not." [3]

Despite Serrano Suñer's repulse, Weddell urged Washington to fall in with British policy and display its willingness to help the Spanish people. It was not enough, he said when reporting his talk of April 19th, merely to discourse to Franco about our ultimate determination. If we wanted to sway Spanish policy, some alluring offer should be made, even though we might not go through with it. Both the British and Weddell, at the time, were afraid of battle movements which, we now know, neither Spain nor Germany was in a position to make. The rain of rumors wet the windowpanes through which they looked; and not only they, also the opponents of aid to Spain; *vide* the front page of *PM*.

Secretary Hull was persuaded, but not flurried. On April 29th he gave Weddell leave *when* he saw Franco to state that the American government was ready to consider at once the means whereby it might be possible for Spain to secure goods in surplus supply in the United States, such as wheat, corn, and cotton. The looseness of the language was intentional. The United States, it was pointed out, might not be able to provide much or any of certain other products in scarce supply and needed for defense. Weddell was told to bear in mind, when making this restrained offer, the conditions that we had previously attached to our aid to Spain. By then, it may be observed, the variety of conditions that had been typed into and out of the dozens of cables were difficult for anyone even to identify. But the essential one remained: we asked Franco to state in some form or other

[3] This speech apparently was made as a desperate attempt to prevent an event that Churchill, at the moment, thought imminent. According to Langer (op. cit., page 145), he warned President Roosevelt that he thought the situation of Spain to be hopeless and feared Gibraltar would be lost or at least demobilized. If he used the word "hopeless" it must have been to impress the President with Britain's plight and to influence us to act faster. For he never actually gave up hope of keeping Spain out of the war as long as Britain held Suez. Certainly at no time did Hoare; on May 1, 1941, after reviewing the events that made the picture black, he reported that all his best sources of information united in supporting the view that there was no change in Spanish policy and that Franco did not want the Germans in Spain. Hoare, op. cit., pages 110–11.

that Spain would remain out of the war and would not aid the Axis. This we wanted said "in the space of a creed."

Our offer was a test rather than a business bid. It was intended to enable Weddell to stay in the game rather than to play the hand. The Ambassador tried to have it made more tempting. He wanted to lure rather than drive Spain to declare itself; and to do so by making our offers worth more, by promising goods in short supply, vitally needed by Spain. The list of such products was getting longer as the Spanish industrial plant ran down—scrap iron, lubricants, carbon black, chemicals, electrodes for steel furnaces, ferromanganese, tin plate for canning, machine tools, rubber, were all urgently wanted. We had repeatedly denied export licenses for anything more than the smallest quantities of them. To permit Spain to obtain them now might be a real lure to the courted Caudillo.

The State Department yielded slightly. It agreed to shorten and simplify the conditions attached to American help. But it refused to promise goods in short supply. They were being rationed out sparsely to all countries except those actually fighting Germany. Furthermore, even the continued flow to Spain of goods of which we had an adequate supply was still under animated attack. The Secretary of State had to ask the Senate and the House to table a vigorously sponsored resolution to investigate the trade in oil.[4]

The officials of the Department need not have stayed overtime to rewrite their proposal. For Weddell could not see Franco. He was repeatedly put off by notes that Serrano Suñer phrased with decorous rudeness. They were construed both by Weddell and by the Department as a sign that the Spanish government had come to think it would not have to pay attention to our views much longer. The loss of Crete was being taken in Spanish military circles to forecast the capture of Suez. This gloomy reading of the situation seemed confirmed by the fact that Franco was also refusing to see Hoare, canceling three appointments in close order. And reports from other sources were of the same blue tenor. For example, Admiral Leahy, after talking with Pétain, at the beginning of May, cabled:

[4] S. Con. Res. 10, known as the Gillette-Coffee Resolution. *Congressional Record*, May 5, 1941. Vol. 87, Part 4, page 3550.

"The Marshal expects an early advance of German troops through Spain with the purpose of either taking Gibraltar or occupying some place on the coast from which the Straits can be controlled by gun-fire and from which troops can be sent to Spanish Morocco." [5]

Was Pétain misled, misleading, or merely wrong?

It was not easy to know what to do next. If the American government merely waited, Serrano Suñer would be pleased. If it did the wrong thing, an unwanted break might result. After consultation Weddell sent, on June 11th, a note intended to try the edge of Serrano Suñer's influence. It asked him to inform the Chief of State that the Ambassador's purpose in seeking an interview was to discuss the possibility of increasing trade between Spain and the United States. By so long denying him the chance, despite his repeated requests, the Spanish government seemed willfully to be disregarding the rights of an Ambassador. If this conduct marked a change in the views of the Spanish government, the American government wished the Chief of State to know that it would have to reconsider its own policies.

This note drew a touchy and studied rejoinder. Serrano Suñer posed as a defender of Spain's affronted honor. It was his duty, he said, to prevent anyone from speaking before the Chief of State in such inadmissible terms as the Ambassador had used in recent visits to the Ministry of Foreign Affairs. This, Serrano Suñer said, was the only reason for what had occurred and he wished the American government to know it. Weddell's recall would probably have served Serrano Suñer's purpose—though perhaps not his final advantage. The Secretary of State therefore decided to continue to be patient—in the face of affront.

Weddell was told to deliver a formal note stating that he had been ordered to make of record the fact that each step he, the Ambassador, had taken to see Franco had been with the full knowledge and approval of the American government. This stiff little notice was to make clear to Serrano Suñer that he was in for a stubborn fight. But not much was hoped for from this slight snap of the will. Franco, it was known, was well acquainted with the situation. Informed agents explained his remoteness by a wish to avoid our probing. It was also, they implied, a way of giving

[5] Quoted from Langer, op. cit., page 144.

satisfaction to Germany without serving it in other ways. He still was eager to stand well with that powerful German force which might, at the end of the summer's campaign, be master of all.

The Summer of Recrimination

Now came the event that made Spanish conduct of smaller account. Germany invaded Russia (June 22nd). The Spanish government was excited, but half-dismayed. Fear and hatred of Communism increased its longing for German victory. But hope that its chance for empire might be close at hand vanished. Spain could do nothing but await the outcome of the fighting in the east and recruit a miserable division or two to send to the front.

The new surge of hostility against Britain and the United States was permitted to register itself. On July 4th all the invited Spanish officials stayed away from Weddell's reception. And on July 17th, the day of Franco's annual speech to the Falange, he gave free rein to his resentment at having to take heed of British and American power—especially the power to grant or deny what he wanted. "The war," he orated, "was badly planned and the Allies have lost it." The United States had no just reason to intervene, and if it did so, would be guilty of "criminal madness."

"I would speak to you with this crudity," he went on, referring to our attempts to pledge him to neutrality, "because the time has come to take steps against these snares, pretexts, and maneuvers. . . ." For whenever

"it seemed that the prospects of help and collaboration were appearing for Spain, there always appeared behind the generosity of a credible operation the effort of political intervention, uncongenial to our sovereignty and our dignity as free people."

Finally he accused the American government of having prevented shipments of wheat that Spain had already bought; this was the same as telling the Spanish people that we had tried to starve them into submission.

This was indeed, to borrow a phrase of Justice Holmes, "churning the void to make cheese." But why? Did he wish to mark time or make a break? Or, as Carceller shortly thereafter implied, were the words intended to gratify Hitler while Spain withheld effective co-operation? Or, as rumor went, had he spoken so to please an extremist audience that had been tending lately to look to Serrano Suñer as its true leader? A piece of political oratory, nasty and troublesome, but nothing more?

The American and British governments could not tell. Anthony Eden, British Foreign Secretary, in an address before the House of Commons on July 24th, mingled correction with gentle warning. After viewing the facts, he concluded:

"If economic arrangements are to succeed there must be good will on both sides, and General Franco's speech shows little evidence of such good will. His statement makes it appear that he does not desire further economic assistance for his country. If that is so, His Majesty's Government will be unable to proceed with their plans, and their future policy will depend on the actions and attitude of the Spanish government."

The American government decided to keep silent, to continue with its aid to Britain, and with slow reflex to apply its controls over exports, ships, and funds more stringently.

In the light of later knowledge, it seems clear that all the bother about the course of trade with Spain during this first half of 1941 made little difference one way or another. What really counted were the tanks, planes, and soldiers that were hurried during this period out to the Suez region. When the British held the line there, it was held in Spain.

XXI

THE DISMAL AUTUMN (1941)

Spain was Still Grubbing to Meet History

PRUDENCE, not pride, had governed American policy through the first half of the year 1941. Spain had been permitted freely to supply itself with all products not in short supply, including all ordinary grades of oil. The only limits to this economic transfusion had been the lack of dollars and the British blockade. Spanish and foreign tankers under charter for Spain had moved across the ocean with fair regularity for wartime.

But by summer the dislike for trade with Franco's Spain began to find new ways of expressing itself. The list of American products subject to export control had been extended to include most of those desired by Spain. Even before Franco made his offensive speech of July 17th, delays began to ensue in the clearance of oil cargoes for that country. This happened without any explicit order. There was an unarranged click of attitude between various sections of the American government whose consent was required. The rude treatment of Weddell caused the political officers of the State Department to be less alert than usual to clear away obstructions.

After Franco's speech the restraints were applied with more system. A newcomer in the Department, Dean Acheson, began to guide the strategy of gradual pressure. On August 1st it was announced that exports of oil to all points except the British Empire and the Western Hemisphere would be limited to "usual pre-war quantities." This formula could easily be twisted on the statistical wheel. Then on August 3rd Welles fell in with the idea advanced by Secretary Ickes that in view of the growing scarcity of tankers, none that were American-owned or controlled should carry oil to Spain or to the Canary Islands. Whatever Ickes's intention in advancing the idea, the State Department's purpose in accepting it was to cause the Spanish government to behave more decently, not to force a collapse. The restraints were relaxed whenever a risk appeared that Spain might completely run out of oil. But the amount received during the summer was small; and the gauge of Spanish stocks fell low.[1]

About this time the first signals of a possible turn of mind came into sight. They were hoisted in an unexpected spot, by the Ministry directed by Carceller, the former close working associate of Serrano Suñer. First the Under Secretary of Industry and Commerce and then the Secretary himself showed sudden interest in that vague trade proposal which Weddell had vainly been trying to present to Franco. Carceller, it will be recalled, had formerly been head of the oil monopoly in the Canary Islands. The failure of tankers to arrive on schedule would not have escaped him. On July 31st he put himself out to persuade us that we should ignore Franco's spray of animosity and refusal to see Weddell. The American government, he counselled, should examine actions, not words—implying that Franco's speech had been designed to rejoice the German heart without satisfying the German wish. Why should we not, in fact, join in the deception? For example, he asked, why should we not send Spain 500 tons of coffee and allow the Spanish government with a great show of secrecy to smuggle it into Germany? The scheme would be sure to work, he suggested, because there was not an intelligent man in the German Embassy; he could, he boasted, fool them all.

Coming so quickly after Franco's speech, these advances caused surprise, though they did not greatly please. The relations between the Minister of Commerce and Industry and the Minister of Foreign Affairs had evidently become crossed. Rogues had clearly fallen out. But Carceller's purpose seemed dark and his authority dubious. It was, in reality, simple and practical; to get as much as he could from both sides for Spain. A few weeks later he advised the Germans to pay no heed to what Franco might

[1] During July and August and September 1941 the United States sent only 185,000 barrels of gasoline (less than one half of normal), and 156,000 barrels of fuel oil (about two thirds of normal). Unpublished records of the U. S. Department of Commerce.

say to Weddell, that the words would be merely suction pumps.

The State Department, after some delay, decided to explore the meaning of Carceller's talk about trade. But it did not promise to send the 500 tons of coffee, the better to help Carceller fool the Germans. There was no practical way of putting poison in it.

The discussions that ensued were inhibited and confused. Neither government was really of a mind to give anything to the other. The Spanish government was pledged to send most of its available surpluses to Germany. The American government was mistrustful and afraid of critics. We soon began to find the Spanish ideas of a bargain annoying, since, as the State Department informed Weddell on September 18th, we were not willing to supply scarce and essential goods merely to retain Spanish goodwill. The products that Spain was asking were in urgent demand elsewhere; what favors or advantages would Spain grant in return?

September, and Rommel was still not in Cairo, nor Hitler in Moscow. The oil of Europe was being spilled into the Mediterranean, or hauled over the long Russian plains. Civilians and Military both, leaning over empty gas tanks, had begun to mock at Serrano Suñer's clamor. For throughout this period of empty talk with Carceller (August to October 1941) our contact with both Serrano Suñer and Franco remained broken. Serrano Suñer sulked in haughty spite. The American government permitted the situation to develop, the Spanish oil reserves to fall. The German armies were moving deeper into the USSR—maybe to victory, maybe to death. The dispute with Japan over its expansion in the Pacific was showing itself to be an irresolvable conflict. The hardening American spirit grew less inclined to try to buy peace for a short night longer.

In September, Cárdenas, the Spanish Ambassador in Washington, took upon himself the task of conciliation. Secretary Hull, after plainly showing his feelings, blessed the peacemaker's errand. Cárdenas earnestly busied himself to find a way to end the quarrel. Carceller was doing the same, and had prepared the German mind for a make-up meeting. They prevailed. On the 28th Weddell informed the State Department that Cárdenas, who was in Madrid, said Franco intended to invite him to call. In the same cable Weddell reported that Cárdenas had also said the Spanish need for gasoline was desperate.

Weddell met with Serrano Suñer on September 30th. Only brief allusions were made to the origin of their angry alienation. The main accent of the talk was on the improvement of economic relations, a subject in which Serrano Suñer had never before shown an interest. He had belonged to that school of political alchemy which preached that a furious will to greatness will always find the necessary material means; a school whose leaders always end with charges of betrayal. Now he said that Spain felt it was being strangled and could not understand why oil shipments failed to arrive. Weddell defended the American record firmly without provoking a fresh dispute.

A few days later (October 6th) Weddell was admitted to Franco's presence. Despite Serrano Suñer's sniping, the talk was affable. It centered upon Franco's statement that Spain was finding it very difficult to obtain wheat, cotton, oil, and foreign exchange. Weddell rebutted any notion that it was our fault. At the end it was agreed that the trade talks should go forward.

Amiable talk this was, but it did not have any result. The formulas did not mix. The State Department found the Spanish offers without interest. They would have contributed very little to our defense and taken very little from the Axis. Further, many of the departments represented on the Economic Defense Board were by then decidedly opposed to increasing the flow of oil to Spain. There was animated and well-based suspicion that some of it was being used to fuel German submarines and merchant ships.

Oil became again the primary Spanish worry. The reserves were, as Serrano Suñer now pleaded, dangerously low. Weddell, who fretted during these weeks of confused bargaining, now began to repeat his warnings of the danger of internal disorder and German occupation.

The Spanish tanker fleet was barely adequate to haul the needed supplies when in full and effective use; and the time consumed in making the round trip between Spain and the United States was drawing out toward Nirvana. Drags and delays occurred in the stream of consent necessary to the quick and smooth trans-port of oil. Now the Navy objected to some tanker movement or action; now the Treasury took a very long time to examine a cargo or its financial cover; now the Coast Guard delayed a sailing order to quiz the crew; now the records of the Export Control Administration became confused; now the State Department suspended its approval because of reports of diversion to Axis use. Each delay meant loss of sailing time. Then, too, the Spanish authorities wasted tonnage. Orders regarding the kind of oil to be obtained were changed while tankers were en route. Tankers showed up at loading points where they were not expected, and did not show up where they were. Little wonder that Spanish tankers during the last half of 1941 often swung idly for long days inside American harbors.

During the autumn the chore of deciding what should or should not be sent to Spain was shifted again. It glided out of the hands of the diplomats to the officials concerned with economic and defense matters. This transfer in management was followed by a change in the character of the program that was put together bit by bit toward the end of 1941. It ceased to be only an extension of the British policy of providing goods lest an angry or threatened Spanish government would bring the country into war, and to make the Spanish people more resistant to any attempt to do so. The American government began to bargain for reciprocal benefits.

After long weeks a memorandum based on this idea was stitched together—with haste because another crisis was near. Lack of oil was bringing the whole Spanish economy toward a halt. About a week before Pearl Harbor, Cárdenas was given a statement of our terms as provider of essential goods to Spain. Given without warmth, given because the American government did not think it could afford disorder in Spain.

The reports of current Spanish activities still contained many displeasing facts. Fortifications at many coastal points bearing on Gibraltar and the Straits (Cádiz, Tarifa, and Algeciras) were being made stronger, with German help; a new bridge had been built at Hendaye with the aid of German troops: two reputedly strong and well-equipped Spanish army units (one at Andalusia and the other at Huelva) were being trained in assault tactics; staff contact with the German army was still intimate; the production of war weapons in Spanish factories was growing under German guidance; lookout stations on the islands and coast of Spanish Morocco were transmitting intelligence to Germany; the German airline Lufthansa acquired a large interest in the network of airlines operating from Spain to Portugal and the Spanish colonies. Some of these measures were designed to help Germany in the war. Others could be construed as features of defense in case of attack, or as preparations to snatch first if the moment came when Britain and Russia were down. Their utility would be settled by the fighting in the frozen fields of Russia, the seas and skies of the Atlantic, and the deserts of Africa.

Spain, under Franco, was at the end of 1941 still grubbing to take advantage of history. But grubbing by itself. By small steps, with glance concentrated on safe pay dirt, Spain had been edging farther away from Germany's side. With the help of the captured documents, it is possible to mark briefly some of the points of withdrawal.

XXII

SPAIN AND THE AXIS DURING 1941

Fortune and the Wiles of Men

FORTUNE and the wiles of men had failed to bring Spain into the war when the step would have been most damaging. During the spring of rumors (1941), which kept the British and American governments so on edge, Germany and Spain in fact were tending toward separation. But that was not permitted to show. The diplomats of the Axis kept up the appearance of close association.

The exchange of favors went on. During the early months of 1941 the trade accord between Spain and Germany was broadened. The Spanish government bid constantly for German military equipment, especially airplanes and artillery. It secured some, but less than bargained for and later than promised. In return it shipped substantial amounts of raw materials like mercury, wolfram, and hides. But the bargainers were becoming annoyed at each other's stinginess.

Of more value to Germany than these raw materials were the other forms of Spanish obligingness. The Spanish government lent itself freely to German purpose in the fields of secret intelligence, press, and propaganda. It entered into an agreement with the German government on March 12, 1941:

"To organize an office to represent the Spanish and German news and press-political interests in South America."

In June of 1941, shortly before the invasion of the USSR and in ignorance of it, Mussolini again urged Spain to cast in its lot wholly with the Axis.[1] The Spanish government again refused. One of Serrano Suñer's reasons for not doing so is of special in-

---

[1] Ciano Diaries, entry June 3, 1941.

terest. Such action, he observed, would hasten American entry into the war, since Roosevelt would regard it as a threat to the Western Hemisphere. Spain was still afraid of losing its Atlantic islands.

Yet, as recounted, Serrano Suñer was permitted to keep the United States at arm's length and to prevent the British program of economic aid from impressing itself well on the minds of the Spanish people. The (nominally) Spanish press and radio varied their abuse against the enemies of Germany by predictions that their doom was at hand. The Foreign Minister assured Stohrer that he was using any and all means to provoke Britain and the United States. Serrano Suñer and Franco were, it has since become known, at this time scheming against each other for the loyalty of the Falange. Perhaps Franco's reproachful and insulting speech of July 17th—the speech that anchored Spanish tankers in American ports—should be read as his way of keeping that following. The whole Spanish people paid the cost of this courtship of the mob.

In August, as related, Carceller, the Minister of Commerce and Industry, emerged as an opponent of Serrano Suñer's tantrums, if not of his plans. He wanted American products and began to devote his talents to draw them into Spain. For us, bland confidences that Spain would stay at peace and curtail aid to the Axis, whispers that Spain's services to Germany were intended to deceive. For the Germans, soothing assurances that his main purpose in dealing with us was to enable Spain to help Germany more.

Early in September, Carceller went off to the Leipzig Fair and found himself in Berlin. As a result of the pro-German attitude of Spain, Carceller explained to the German officials, it was becoming more difficult to bring in essential overseas imports. He therefore intended to try to patch up economic relations with the United States. This should not bother Germany, he said, since it would be the means whereby Spain would strengthen itself for war. Moreover, Spain could secretly pass on to Germany part of what it got—he mentioned tin, not coffee. Germany, he said, should assent to such acts of conciliation as might be necessary to get the goods. The first of such steps would be to tone down the press and radio attacks on Britain and the United States. Then

Franco might receive Weddell, if only for a quarter of an hour. He would not, Carceller went on to explain, have to give Weddell any definite promise; he could manage merely by stating that the Spanish government intended to continue with its present policy; the Americans would take the remark to mean that Spain would continue to be neutral, while its real meaning would be obedience to German wishes. The man was enjoying himself. He left Berlin without receiving either assent or rebuke.

The Spanish government, as recounted, then proceeded with the effort to come to terms with us. Germany watched with chagrin, but without formal protests. No great concern was shown over the possible Spanish trade concessions to the democracies.

But over an occurrence of another type it showed itself really hurt. Two German ships, the *Corrientes* and the *Charlotte Schliemann*, had, by agreement between the German and Spanish navies, remained at anchor in the outer harbor at Las Palmas. They were supply ships for U-boats. The purpose of their presence at that spot had long been suspected, but actual proof came to hand only in September. Then the British government demanded their removal. The Spanish Minister of Marine, without prior notice to the German government, ordered them to withdraw into the inner harbor. In Berlin this was regarded as a great blow to U-boat warfare in the Atlantic.

The German Foreign Office informed Stohrer on October 9th that the transfer to the inner harbor was directly harmful to the effectiveness of the German submarines in the battle of the Atlantic. The German Navy, therefore, requested the Foreign Office to make every diplomatic effort to cancel the measures of the Spanish government. The German government reproached Spain for its infidelity, the same message recalling that Franco, after a thorough examination, had promised that Spain would make possible such aid for German submarines. Germany, it continued, had been most considerate of Spain in using this privilege, and took it for granted that Spain would not go back on its word.

The reproach did not avail. The Spanish government said it did not dare permit the ships to move back to the outer harbor lest the British torpedo them. The German government had to be satisfied with the statement of the Spanish Minister of Marine on

October 14th that he was willing to continue to protect other supply measures in the Spanish mainland harbors.[2]

The incident illuminates a later event. It makes clear why the Spanish government was so disturbed by one feature of the trade arrangements that the American government proposed in November. That was a request for permission to supervise the use and distribution of oil within Spain and the Spanish colonies. As long as it could, the Spanish government refused—until its oil stocks were near exhaustion. That story carries the narrative back to Washington.

[2] The agreement for such supply measures in mainland harbors was re-ported to the Foreign Office by Stohrer on December 5, 1940, as follows: "In reply to proposal made by [German] Embassy as instructed [the] Foreign Minister has now informed [me] that the Spanish government has agreed to the placing in readiness of German tankers in out-of-the-way bays of the Spanish coast for the supplying of German destroyers with fuel. [The] Foreign Minister vigorously requested that we observe the greatest caution in carrying out the measure." State Department Document No. 10.

XXIII

THE SHARP POINTS OF A BARGAIN
(WINTER OF 1941–2)

No Longer for Political Effect Alone

THE disturbing November 1941 crisis in Washington as to whether, and on what terms, to continue to send oil to Spain developed something like this: in October several Spanish tankers were sent over without forewarning; doubtfully, but in accord with the rule of "usual pre-war" quantities, they were given cargoes. The radical press began another slashing campaign against the whole traffic. Statistics given out by the Treasury seemed to tell of large recent shipments of aviation-grade gasoline and lubricants to Spain. This would have been contrary to both public orders and public statements. The figures were taken as proof of some devious plan to work with Franco against the popular will. After some days the Treasury publicly explained that its records were wrong, that no oil of these types had been sent. But the stories caused the already strong protests against what was conceived to be State Department policy to become stronger.

The pressure gauge by which it had guided our trade relations with Spain broke down. There were too many pressures. Too many groups, inside and outside the government, thought the State Department was making false readings. Surrounded by a negative disposition, it had to come forward with an affirmative program, one that rested on something more than the fear of consequences. The British government believed that the strategic and political usefulness of supplying Spain was enough, but American public opinion did not.

The State Department took heed. Though the diplomats were worried, it decided that oil should be sent only if Spain made some useful return. Also that it was time, and more than time, to make really sure that we were not helping Germany. These were the thoughts that shaped the new terms that the State Department in November put before the Spanish government. But the primary motives in proceeding with any program at all remained strategic and political; the economic-warfare gains sought were, as they had to be until the Allied position was stronger, incidental.

To place an unclothed proposal in the hands of Serrano Suñer might doom it without trial. Therefore the State Department decided to transmit it through Cárdenas, the Spanish Ambassador in Washington, rather than through Weddell. On November 29th he was given an aide-mémoire containing our terms for the continued conduct of wartime trade. The text had been much fought over between those who wished it to be firm and plain and those who wished it to be loose. In both language and structure it was patched. But it is the business of diplomats (and lawyers) to read between the patches.

In this case, they found that:

1. The American government offered to supply Spain with enough, and just enough, oil "to meet Spain's requirements for transportation and other essentials."

2. This oil was not to be used "in any manner useful to Italy or Germany, directly or indirectly."

3. Its distribution and use within Spain and the Spanish colonies was to be subject to our supervision—to prevent diversion to the Axis. American agents were to be given free access to all Spanish facilities for receiving, shipping, storing and refining oil.

4. The American government also offered to permit Spain to obtain such other American products as could be freely bought in the American market.

5. In regard to goods in short supply, we promised to see what we could do to provide such amounts as were necessary for a low wartime level of economic activity. These were not to be used in ways that would benefit Germany or Italy or countries under their rule.

6. In return, Spain was asked to obligate itself to assist us to secure various Spanish products—wolfram, cork, mercury, zinc, lead, fluorspar, olive oil, and various roots and drugs.

7. The Spanish government was to try to transport these products in Spanish ships.

The Department advised Weddell of this proposal. In doing so, the Department explained that our primary purpose in putting it forward was strategic; we thought it well to permit Spain to secure minimum amounts of what it needed to get along, so that it would not be dependent on Germany and bitter against us; but our need for the Spanish products that we asked was not vital; we did not wish to enlarge the trade for its own sake; and we had no thought of nursing Spain's friendship by close attendance upon its wants. Later on, the State Department was, at times, going to find it hard to make this attitude clear to Weddell's successor, Hayes. One more comment on this American proposal: the attempt to draw a line around our supply offer where it might overflow to Axis benefit was somewhat unreal. Anything that enabled Spain to maintain production made it more possible for Spain to trade with Germany, except in such avenues as were blocked. More and more energy and money had presently to be spent in building blocks.

The longer Cárdenas studied our offer, the more depressed he seemed to become. No doubt he foresaw that his government could not accept it without mending its ways and amending its vows to Germany. This would be, he knew, far from agreeable and perhaps even unsafe. Over one feature in particular he shook his head: the request for the privilege of watching over the use of the oil we sent. This, it was appreciated, might be felt to be humiliating; and it was certain to make Germany fume. But how else to make sure that the oil might not kill our own men; how else reconcile the American people to the risk? The Spanish government had forfeited trust, as well as the right to have its feelings considered.

Or so it seemed after the receipt of Weddell's report on his talk with Serrano Suñer on December 1st. The Foreign Minister was again under the spell of recent contact with his Axis associates.[1]

---

[1] He had been in Berlin meeting with representatives of the signatories of the Anti-Comintern Pact. The meeting had not been completely harmonious. Ciano recorded in his Diaries on November 24, 1941: "The atmosphere of the anti-Comintern meeting was truly singular. The state of mind of the delegates differed very much. Serrano Suñer was aggressive and sharp but quite pro-Axis."

Serrano Suñer on November 25th delivered a speech in Berlin which promised that millions of Spaniards would fight to save Germany from

He accused the United States of creating Spain badly. With an airy and detached manner he rubbed in his view that the Axis was invincible and showed how pleasant he thought it would be to be among the future rulers of the world. Weddell met point by point with cold dislike. He dismissed the thought of German victory. But he also warned that if Serrano Suñer was right and Germany should win, Spain would lose its independence.

Cárdenas in Washington spoke in a gentler tone. After a few unhappy days he accepted the idea that we should maintain watch over the use of our oil. But he urged changes in our language. These changes would make it easier to swallow the dose. New phrases were found which made it appear that our request was a practical aid to the supply program; a means of minimizing delays by reason of inadequate information. For this purpose the American government was to appoint agents who, in consultation with the Spanish and the British, would carry out the necessary observation.

Having so rounded the point, Cárdenas presently passed it on to Madrid. An anguished argument, we know now, ensued within the Spanish government. No answer was made for many weeks. In the interval cargoes were sought for Spanish tankers waiting at Port Arthur, Texas, and on their way to Venezuela. The Spanish tanker fleet was growing.

In the midst of these talks about oil, the Japanese attacked Pearl Harbor. The Spanish government reaffirmed its position of nonbelligerency. But the Spanish press glowed with praise of Japanese patience and sparkled with accounts of Japanese naval and air victories in the Pacific. As before, the Germans and their friends cheated themselves. The American government read summaries of these stories with cold anger. Besides, Secretary Hull was on the

Russia. In the course of his speech he called the Russians "cannibals." It is possible to guess the origin of these remarks from an entry in Ciano's Diaries on November 25, 1941. He notes that Goering "was impressive when he spoke of the Russians, who are eating each other and have also eaten a German sentry in a prison camp. He recounted the incidents with the most absolute indifference. . . . Goering told me that hunger among the Russian prisoners had reached such an extreme that in order to start them toward the interior it is no longer necessary to send them under armed guard; it is enough to put at the head of the column of prisoners a camp kitchen, which emits the fragrant odor of food; thousands and thousands of prisoners trail along like a herd of famished animals."

alert in regard to a possible German march through Spain and Portugal. What a blunder if German armies on their arrival on the Spanish coast were met by Spanish tankers full of the oil of Texas!

Thus for some weeks after Pearl Harbor the American government simply sat tight. For the time being, it ceased to concern itself lest Spain might suffer and resent the deprivation.

The Spanish tankers in American ports were kept there for the time being; the British government was asked to deny navicerts; the Dutch, Venezuelan, and Mexican governments were asked to consult us before providing cargoes in the Caribbean, and so were the American oil companies. The Navy disliked the presence of three Spanish tankers anchored just off the harbor of Port Arthur. These ships had been using their radios for the probable purpose of reporting other ship movements in and out of the port. The Navy therefore asked that all three be denied clearance, and they were.

But as the December days passed, fears of a German attack faded and reports of trouble within Spain again began to grow loud. Spain's oil reserves were rapidly being used up. The heads of the oil monopolies pleaded that soon all transport and fishing would come to an end. They asked for interim shipments while they were getting together the information sought and the Spanish government was making up its mind. Both Weddell and the British government begged us to accede.

On December 29th a representative of the British Embassy called upon Ray Atherton, chief of the Western European Division to plead for a more yielding attitude. Atherton implied that the stubborn vine ran across Executive Avenue. He suggested that if the British wanted to make sure that their views were understood, Churchill's presence in Washington provided an excellent chance. The Prime Minister is believed to have grasped it. On the same day the British Ambassador called upon the Secretary of State. He explained once again that the British still felt it wise to do everything reasonable to encourage Spanish opposition to the possible entry of the German Army into Spain on its way to French Morocco.

Whosesoever the decision, the Under Secretary shortly thereafter approved cargoes for three Spanish tankers that were waiting in

Venezuela. Again it had been decided that the time for a flat showdown had not come, that the risk was still too great.

We reverted to the parcel-by-parcel method of trading with Spain. The inclination to compromise was favored by well-founded reports from Weddell that the Spanish government was sending less to Germany and was seeking German consent to use Spanish ships to carry goods to the United States. The State Department did not then know that this stubborn Spanish front toward Germany was part of a tactic to force the delivery of arms; Germany was being scared into equipping the Spanish Army on the score that it might be necessary to resist an Allied landing.

No sooner had these tankers received cargoes than a fourth came. From somewhere (and the best guess was the British Embassy in Madrid) the belief was being sowed that the American government would not insist upon all the demands contained in its November memorandum. The Spanish government was complaining sadly over what we asked. To Germany it promised that it would concede the least possible, though it had to have oil.

The diplomatic officers of the State Department, reporting to the Under Secretary, had again assumed charge of the situation. Theirs was the duty, they thought, to see that a blunder was not made. The Secretary of State, when sounded, did not seem to want to ease the ban on oil until we had our way. But his view was not pressed; it was an exhalation that did not condense itself into a firm order.

In January a new report arrived that German ships were being fueled in Spanish ports and waters. The British Naval Attaché in Spain, on going aboard a captured German submarine, found that the crew was carrying Spanish matches. Members of the crew admitted that the ship had obtained supplies in Vigo harbor. But the incident was not pursued to its depths. Hoare's view was accepted, that even if the fact was so, it was an isolated case made possible by the corruption of local officials. But now it is known not to have been.

Six weeks had passed since Cárdenas was first given our proposals. Then doubts arose as to whether he had ever passed on its full text. Therefore on January 8, 1942 Weddell was told to do so. He was reminded that we did not believe that economic favors would win over the Spanish government, and that we would therefore require a tangible and substantial benefit in return. We would match, and presently overmatch, Germany in the tactics of pressure. Weddell began to work along these lines while urging greater liberality. The British government did the same.

The pass reached in January 1942 could be easily identified on the strategic map. Two paths were open. One was to maintain a minimum program of supply for Spain without insisting upon much return advantage in our own war effort. Thereby we might lessen the chance that distress and disorder would in one way or another cause the Spanish government to line up more closely with Germany. The British favored this path. The other was to insist upon an adequate return and to leave Spain to suffer if it was not given. There still seemed to be—in the spring of 1942— several dangers in going all the way down this path. The Spanish government might so resent the terms of the bargain that it would risk its chances on the German side. Or attempts to meet our demands might so strain relations with Germany that an ultimatum would result, to which Spain would yield.

The American government went as far down the second path as it dared. But every now and then some noise or sign caused it to halt, look about, and take shelter in compromise. Hoare, anxious over the effect of the British retreat in Africa, seemed more disturbed by our stubbornness than did the Spanish government. Later knowledge shows that his worry, and those of the American government at this time, were excessive. They counted too little upon the Spanish resolution to be independent and to stay out of the war.

XXIV

THE SHARP POINTS OF A BARGAIN (Continued)

Like a Game of Bagatelle

THE three-cornered game went on into the spring of 1942. Now only a few of the major points and phrases remain of interest. The shortage of oil was proved when, in February, the Spanish refinery at Teneriffe was forced to close down. The Spanish government tried to keep its tankers in motion. Cargoes were provided from time to time, enough to keep the bargaining alive, enough to keep the Spanish economy going. Similarly, from time to time we approved the export of other goods that the Spanish wanted—like fertilizer and tin plate.

The most troublesome point was our wish to exercise watch and ward over the Spanish oil situation. The Spanish government did not want us to have the right to poke into every corner of its oil-supply situation and follow every ton to its final use. Furthermore, it seemed genuinely afraid that if it agreed to permit our agents to carry on such activities (and what else might they not do?) Germany would demand the same permission.

True, Germany was allowed privileges of a more intrusive kind —not only in the trade field but in the direction of the Spanish press and radio. But the Spanish government wanted to reduce rather than extend them. At first it ignored our request; next it suggested a poor substitute; but finally, early in February (1942), it agreed to the proposal in principle. But with the plea, spoken in every office, for the greatest of discretion.

The Spanish government, we now know, went through a difficult ordeal. It was not easy to persuade Ribbentrop and the German Naval Command that Spain had no choice. By the end of February the necessity was accepted. Germany could not, and it knew it, supply the oil that Spain wanted. The utmost that a disheartened Stohrer could get from Berlin was a promise that Berlin would send a skeleton economic mission in order to give a psychological satisfaction.

Germany was at this time suffering from a critical shortage of fuel oil, which affected even its military operations. Thus in December 1941 the quota for the German Navy had been reduced to 50,000 tons per month, about one half its requirements, causing drastic cuts in all naval uses except submarine training. Urgent Italian requests for supplies for operations in the Mediterranean had to be partly refused. This shortage itself put out of the question any extensive German operation in the western Mediterranean in this first period after Pearl Harbor.[1]

Thus Spain had to accept our demand for a supervisory watch. But other hard corners had to be rounded before our program could be made effective. How were we to buy and fetch the Spanish products we demanded? Within this problem there were three kinds of difficulties, not entirely of Spain's making.

First, the American government was asking for certain products the whole surplus of which had hitherto been reserved for Germany. Of some of these, for example zinc and cork, the Spanish government was ready to share the supply. About others, such as wolfram and mercury, it was reluctant. Whatever was sent to us, it seemed at the time, would be taken away from the Axis. The American request required change in Spain's contribution to the opposed sides. But the Spanish dodges were not wholly due to the wish to arrange this smoothly. It saw a chance to gain from the rival bidders for these products and wished to make the most of it.

Second, the American government was not in a position to acquire some of the products sought. These were not to be had by ordinary business methods. Their prices were much higher in Spain than outside the blockade. Further, they could only be obtained if the buyer was willing to enter into long-term contracts; private buyers would not take the risk of doing so. Because of these and other elements in the situation, wartime trade with Spain in scarce materials could be conducted only by a govern-

[1] Memorandum on "The Fuel and Diesel Oil Situation of the Navy as of 6 December 1941," Annex 4 to Minutes of Meeting between Hitler and Raeder, December 12, 1941. "Fuehrer Conferences," 1941, Vol. II, pages 90-1.

ment organization. As will be related, earlier efforts to create such an agency had come to nothing. But now that the need was showing itself so clear, another effort was begun. In the meanwhile, however, we were asking the Spanish government to do what we alone could do.

Third, there was the question of whether and how we could move the Spanish products that we sought to the United States. We were not willing to send American ships to Spain. The Spanish government did not dare to ship war materials in Spanish vessels without prior German consent. Germany had brought that lesson home by one or two torpedoes. Even a partial solution of this difficulty took time. The Spanish government during this period tried hard to obtain German consent to the use of Spanish ships on the ground that it was essential to the maintenance of Spanish economy. But Germany would not agree to give safe passage to such products as wolfram, zinc, and mercury.

These were the compounded problems that caused the negotiations with Spain to string out so long. Only the pertinacity of Weddell and his staff, and Hoare's grave laments, kept them going. By March (1942) brittle bits of a trade agreement were approved. But it required many more months to plane and fit them together. In the meanwhile the movement of goods between Spain and the United States resembled a game of bagatelle. Someone pushed the plunger from time to time and the marbles bounced off the pegs until they settled into a hole.

The Spanish leaders did not always make it easy to carry on even such a game. American anxieties focused on the question of whether Russia would prove itself able to withstand the German assaults. The Spanish leaders freely expressed their hatred of Russia and wish for German victory. Thus Franco told the officers of the Spanish Army on February 14th:

". . . if there were a moment of danger, if the road to Berlin were open, it would not be a division of Spanish volunteers who would go there but a million Spaniards who would offer themselves."

This declaration coincided with Rommel's rapid advance in Africa and the fall of Singapore. And Serrano Suñer as usual outdid Franco. The American public could not know that in between speeches he was now telling Beaulac, Chargé of the American Embassy, that Spain's foreign policy was directed toward staying out of the war. When reporting these voluntary assurances, Beaulac reminded the State Department that almost exactly a year before Serrano Suñer had said to Colonel Donovan that Spain would remain aloof until its honor, interests, or dignity were in question.

The Revolt at Port Arthur

The oil chart at this time was shaken up by a revolt at Port Arthur, Texas. German submarines had been cruelly busy off the Atlantic coast and in the Caribbean. During February they sank some American tankers while the Spanish tankers went safely on their way. They also attacked the islands of Aruba and Curaçao, where the great refineries were located. In these attacks they had sunk other Allied tankers and shelled the tank farms. Many in the crews of the sunken ships came from the towns along the coast of Texas.

By order of the Navy, all loadings at Port Arthur for Spain had been suspended after Pearl Harbor. But at the special request of the State Department two cargoes had been provided at this point in February. Another Spanish tanker, the *Campechano*, was loading in the harbor on February 25th.[2] The news of these shipments was restricted, but word spread among all classes in the vicinity. Sailors from the tanker were loud and hard in their remarks about the company. They were aroused by the memory of having seen, while on their dangerous voyages, Spanish tankers sailing through the Gulf of Mexico, lit up like a Christmas tree. They were convinced that these Spanish ships were serving as spy or signal ships for the submarines. The whole town of Port Arthur joined in their angry words.

The Texas Company became afraid to complete the loading even though it was officially authorized. It decided to break its contract with Campsa rather than accept the bad name and the

[2] This particular shipment was, in fact, destined for Portugal.

risk of sabotage to its loading gear. It arranged to have the *Campechano* proceed empty to New Orleans (where, to follow the incident one step further, the Treasury for other reasons long held the ship in port).

This revolt ended the visits of Spanish tankers to American ports. Thereafter, they went for their oil to Venezuela and the Dutch West Indies. This made no difference in regard to the actual movement of oil to Spain, for we continued to control all shipments. This change in point of supply would have been made anyway. American war needs were growing so great that the Texas fields no longer had oil for other uses.

XXV

STEPS TOWARD AN EFFECTIVE PROGRAM

Many Minds with as Many Purposes

THE agreement of March 1942 with the Spanish government was, as remarked, a thing of loose bits and pieces. It included a promise to send enough oil to meet Spain's most urgent needs. When the American government said that it would send only 63,000 tons during the current quarter, the Spanish government was appalled.[1] But it accepted the figure as better than nothing. The oil-inspection system quietly found its place.

But at the American end confusion reigned. Besides the State Department, the Board of Economic Warfare, the Navy, the Treasury, the Reconstruction Finance Corporation, the Office of Strategic Services, the Petroleum Administrator for War, and the War Production Board were all concerned in one way or another with the Spanish program. Closely joined judgment and action within and between all these branches of the government were needed. But it did not exist. No one was in charge of the whole.

Inside the State Department it was hard to tell who was doing what. The Secretary did not concern himself with details and the Under Secretary gave orders only now and again. Spanish diplomats, men from oil companies, officials of the British Embassy, swung in and out of a dozen different doors. Spokesmen from other branches of the government, such as the BEW, scattered their views wherever they thought they would be best regarded. The Petroleum Adviser, Thornburg, and his staff, seemed to be passing out hints and half promises on their own. The diplomatic officers of the Department, under Atherton, were in worried col-

---

[1] This total was not to include any crude oil, since Washington was not satisfied regarding stocks at Teneriffe, the distribution of the products of the refinery there, or the situation in North Africa.

loquy with their Spanish and British colleagues. Intelligence reports from the Navy seemed to be short-circuited at the wrong points. Jones and Clayton, of the RFC, who controlled the funds that might be used to buy Spanish products, still waited to be told what to do; then they did what they thought best. In short, the scene, in its way, resembled the beaches of Morocco on the afternoon of the landing.

Nor was the outward prospect much less confused. The State Department did not know precisely what Spain had offered us. The Spanish Embassy in Washington was of little help, for its exchanges with its own government were mixed up. The only thing that was clear was that the Spanish government was stating in frantic language that our failure to provide oil was imperiling its existence. Half its tanker fleet was either in or on its way to American harbors. The British government from high to low was beseeching us to hurry. Churchill was expounding the reasons for doing so to the President in round phrases.

But besides the confusion there were other deterrent causes. Franco and Serrano Suñer were still placing wreaths on the doorsteps of the dictators, and it was suspected that they were still slipping notes through the slots. Spain was completing a new trade and loan agreement with Argentina; the Argentine Ambassador to Spain puffed it up into a plan for the joint conduct of banks, shipping companies, and airlines. This Axis-tainted deal worried the Treasury. For it seemed designed to improve the channel for re-exports to Germany, the carriage of contraband goods, and the smuggling of looted valuables from Europe. American public opinion was as displeased as ever. Despite Presidential advice, several of the departments represented on the BEW would have preferred to let Spain riot or rot.

If the Spanish program was ever to be more than a game of bagatelle, it was apparent that some new measure of order was necessary. The Under Secretary of State asked me to organize and act as chairman of an interdepartmental committee to manage economic relations with the Iberian Peninsula. This group (which was named the Iberian Peninsula Operating Committee) was formed by appointment from several branches of the State Department, the BEW, and the United States Commercial Corporation (of which more later). A liaison officer from the British government was present at all of the meetings. Each of the two governments could thus know what the other was doing. Gradually this group, which became known as IPOC, became the main Washington bearing in what developed into a very large supply-purchase program for Spain and Portugal. Its system later became the rough working model for other groups set up to deal with other countries, particularly Turkey and North Africa. The Committee held some hundreds of meetings during its lifetime.

But the account has jumped in advance of the story. It was essential that the Committee have a confirmed basis for its assignment. Acting Secretary Welles approved the idea of submitting to the President a full statement of what was planned. If approved, all the straggling branches of the government could be brought into line. Then perhaps individual initiative would be a bit subdued.

While this statement was being drafted (March 5–14) many things were done. Plans for the creation of a government organization to do the buying in Spain (and elsewhere) were, after a rough tussle, settled. A State Department officer, Labouisse, who had been immersed in this work, was sent to Spain to start off its work. The American Embassy in Madrid was instructed to begin, along with the British, to arrange for the purchase of wolfram and other strategic materials. The Office of Strategic Services was asked to recruit a group of men to act as oil observers in Spain, to which task it turned with gusto. All these and other steps were hurried along in the thought that the basic statement of policy would be placed on the President's desk as soon as written. It was completed by March 14th.

But before it was sent to the White House the whole bustle of preparation was brought to a chilled halt. For Atherton and Thornburg, who had hitherto been the most constant advocates of oil for Spain, now combined to produce a strange chit. They took a look at the sky and discovered rings around the moon.

Spain, they noted, was chartering tankers to Portugal and these were in American waters. There was no other Spanish ship in our ports, and clearances in our direction had been suspended. The Spanish diplomatic mission in Havana was sending identical messages to the other Spanish missions in Latin America telling them so. The trade agreement with Argentina was being hurried. The

Spanish Chief of Staff and the Chief of the Spanish Air Force were in Berlin. There was unusual cable activity in the Spanish Embassy in Washington. Such were the evil portents.

Acting Secretary Welles ordered a halt until we could find out what was afoot. Along with my colleagues on IPOC, I was puzzled by this swift burst of alarm. I could not resist the thought that its authors were trying to show either how right they had been in the past or how wrong it was to transfer authority to the new Committee. However, the alarm soon ended. All of the signs had innocent meaning.

When this became clear, the Acting Secretary submitted the program to the President (March 20th). Approval was given at once. A summary was thereupon, "upon direction of the President and with his approval," sent to all other branches of the government concerned. The IPOC was formally entrusted with the management of the daily details. The way was open, in conjunction with the British government, to strive for a ruling place in the economic fortunes of Spain.

Up to then we had had only one good weapon, the power to provide, or to refuse to provide, American products. From this time on we were to have another: great sums with which to buy Spanish products of use to the Axis. But the voucher for these sums was stained with the blue-black ink of office warfare in Washington. This flowed freely in the battle over the creation and control over the new organization that was to conduct our economic program in the Iberian Peninsula and elsewhere. This was named the United States Commercial Corporation.

XXVI

THE HARD BIRTH OF THE USCC: WALLACE AND JONES FALL OUT

Were We About to Buy the Sky?

THE birth of the United States Commercial Corporation was long and hard. To minds soaked in the salt of sound private finance, it never became legitimate. Differences over its necessity and policies caused a break between Vice President Wallace and the Federal Loan Administrator, Jesse Jones. The tale is worth the telling—at the risk of interrupting the main narrative. To do so, it is necessary to turn back from the spring of 1942 to the end of 1940.

The task to be done was to deprive the Axis of vital war materials heedless of cost. Operations to this end came to be known as "preclusive." The British had begun them early in the war. On November 19, 1940 a memorandum prepared in the Office of the Economic Adviser of the State Department had recommended to Secretary Hull that the American government should do the same. The American program for the purchase of strategic and critical materials was hobbled. We were buying only such products, and in such grades and quantities, as were thought necessary for our own defense program. The estimates were on the scanty side and the buying slow. We were permitting the Axis to secure war materials which could be put out of its reach —particularly in Latin America. Large amounts of such products as copper, tin, mercury, chrome, and mica were being sold to Japan, whence part was passed on to Germany. The United States, it was urged, ought to be buying up the whole supply.

Patient attempts were made to persuade Jones to do the job. He seemed to respond and said that he would gladly consider specific suggestions for action. Leon Henderson, busying himself with economic preparations for war, was known to have proposed to the President that a new organization be created which, among other duties, would assume charge of the raw-material buying program. Other officials of the State Department, especially Thomas Finletter, Chief of the Defense Material Branch, held similar talks with Federal Loan Administrator Jones and with his deputy, Will Clayton. They too found what they thought to be receptive listeners. But the weeks passed and nothing much was done. Our buying stayed within the safe, low limits of our own defense needs.

And so Secretary Hull had been persuaded by his staff on January 29, 1941 to try again himself. In a long letter addressed to Jones, he summarized the reasons for action and listed the neglected situations. This letter brought a useful response. Jones undertook to deal with the situations mentioned. But he showed himself unconverted. Our purpose, he wrote, should not be to buy merely to keep someone else from getting the same materials, but rather to have on hand an ample supply of what we might want.

Following upon this exchange of letters the various agencies run by the Federal Loan Administration had begun to be bolder, to consider longer-term contracts, and to be less apt to hang back in order to get the best price.[1] But still there was a lag in buying both for defense and for preclusive ends. It should have been carried on with the wish to get everything that could be had. Instead, it was still restrained by the wish not to buy what might not be needed, and not to take avoidable loss.

During the winter months various officials of the State Department managed to draw the Federal Loan Agency into this or that activity. But the effort was like carrying firewood through a gate that latched itself after each armful. Weariness is reflected in a memorandum prepared for the Under Secretary of State on May 7, 1941:

[1] Mr. Jesse Jones was both Federal Loan Administrator and Chairman of the Board of Directors of the Reconstruction Finance Corporation (RFC). That organization had created three new subsidiaries to buy critical and strategic materials, the Defense Supply Corporation, the Metals Reserve Company, and the Rubber Reserve Company. Mr. Jones and the Deputy Loan Administrator, Will Clayton, supervised the activities of all these organizations closely and personally.

"It cannot be said that the program for the acquisition of available supplies of strategic and critical materials produced in the Latin American countries is making satisfactory headway."

Some deals of great value—either for supply or for preclusive purpose—were arranged in the summer of 1941. We agreed to buy all the copper produced in Latin America, all of the Bolivian tin and wolfram ore, to secure control of most of the zinc production of Argentina and the manganese production of Brazil. But many parts of the purchasing program (as recommended by the Interdepartmental Committee on Strategic and Critical Materials) were still "in a rather frustrated state" [2] at the end of the summer. While Jones and Clayton gave much time and patience to it, their temper was not aggressive. Their habit was just to keep pace with the obvious national danger rather than to get in front of it.

By renewed persuasion, in which Welles took a leading part, the effort was carried forward. During the autumn the attempt to acquire an inclusive command over the resources of the hemisphere was made effective. We arranged with the governments of all important Latin-American sources of supply, except Argentina, to buy *all* their production of critical and strategic war materials. [3] These agreements were a real achievement. They greatly cut the flow of war materials to Japan. They marked the transition from a buying program kept within the limits of identified defense needs to one that overflowed into the unknown in order to keep supplies away from the enemy. As a matter of record it may be observed that almost all the materials bought from Latin America under these contracts were later needed in the war.

[2] Memorandum by Feis, Chairman of this Committee, to the Secretary of State.

[3] In order to do buying that went beyond evident defense needs, the Federal Loan Administrator felt it necessary to secure extensive amendments to the Reconstruction Finance Corporation Act. When once he was reconciled to the necessity of extending his operations beyond customary bounds, he set about obtaining this added authority with vigor. He had much influence "on the Hill" and Congress responded quickly to his request for additional power. The amended Act (Public No. 108, June 10, 1941) clarified the extended power of the RFC broadly enough to permit it to buy anything that it felt advisable anywhere, of any grade, at any price.

Still, in this phase we did not stray far from ordinary bases of trade in wartime. We devised ways to limit government purchases to such quantities as private American buyers did not purchase. We did not found organizations within foreign countries to seek out supplies. We remained careful about the prices that we paid. Some of them seemed high and were much higher than prices before the war. But they were within familiar commercial range and proved to be much lower than the prices which have prevailed since. In other words, these Latin-American arrangements did not lead to risks that would make a banker quiver.[4]

But the strange jobs that lay ahead in Spain and Portugal, in Turkey and elsewhere, were of another kind. There, within the dual blockade area, the rival sides were bidding wildly for vital materials; they were also plotting to get control of the sources of production. There, governments controlled exports, and used that control to bargain for supplies wanted from the nations at war. Buyers had to provide goods as well as cash. Trucks carrying these materials might be waylaid or ships sunk. To enter these situations another attitude was called for, another kind of organization, and tactics that used money as a tool rather than an asset. Ralph Ackerman, the Commercial Attaché of the American Embassy in Madrid, had, in several able dispatches, made amply clear that this was true of Spain.

The dragging differences in Washington as to how far to move into this field came into the open—became stuff for the press—in November 1941. The British government asked us on November 4th to share in a wolfram-ore buying program. This had been begun in an effort to injure German war production by depriving it of a vital metal. But it was becoming too burdensome for Britain to carry alone. Would the United States, Britain now asked, join? Would it share the expense and stake out a claim for part of the Portuguese production? To do so, we would have not only to spend a substantial sum but also to provide American

[4] For example, the prices specified in some of the important agreements were as follows: 5.4 cents per pound for Mexican lead, 8.25 cents per pound for Mexican zinc, 12 cents per pound for Mexican and Chilean copper, 48 to 50 cents per pound for Bolivian tin, 21 dollars per unit of Bolivian wolfram ore. All of these are much lower than current (October 1947) prices—e.g., lead at 15 cents per pound, copper 21.5 cents per pound, tin at 80 cents per pound.

products in scarce supply. What we might do in Portugal, it was foreseen, we should also be called upon to do in Spain.

It was entirely in order to doubt whether an expensive fling in Portuguese wolfram was justified even as a war measure. Neither its value nor its feasibility could be proved.[5] In this field statistics were doubtful and the course of the future supply unpredictable. The only convincing basis for the view that we might achieve a significant military result was the behavior of the German government. It was making the utmost diplomatic effort to obtain and export Portuguese wolfram ore. It was bidding for mines and their ore in disregard of cost. In June 1941 the unit of wolfram in which the trade was ordinarily conducted was selling for $19.50 within Portugal. By September 1941 the price was up to $123 per unit, and toward the end of October the Germans had bought some lots at between $300 and $370 per unit. The price for the same product in the United States was at the time about $21. The British officials concerned with economic warfare were convinced that the German buying policy proved, first, that the ore served a vital purpose in German military production and, second, that the Portuguese (and Spanish) sources of supply were vital to Germany.[6]

But these evidences of intense German interest did not dispose of the causes of doubt. Could not, if absolute need be, Germany substitute other metals for most of its uses? Could we and the British together, in the light of the diplomatic and military situation, engross so much of the Portuguese supply as really to hurt Germany—no matter how much we spent? How much might we ultimately have to buy?

No one found it easy to gulp down these doubts. But the officials concerned in the State Department and the BEW agreed that it was worth while to pay to test them. If billions could be

[5] Wolfram, or tungsten as it is more commonly known in the United States, provides an alloy invaluable for hardening steel, and in many other processes and products. It was one of the most vital of materials for military purposes, and distinctly limited in supply. Command of the wolfram supply of the Iberian Peninsula was to become later the main object of Allied economic-warfare policy. A full account of this struggle, its meaning, and its outcome will be found in later chapters.

[6] At that time Spanish production was about one tenth of Portuguese production. Shortly thereafter it began to increase extremely rapidly.

spent to wreck war plants from the air, millions might be ventured to deprive them of such vital material. But they could not convince the Federal Loan Administrator, Jesse Jones. Vice President Wallace as chairman of the Economic Defense Board took over the pleading of the case. A few days before Pearl Harbor he called upon Jones in an attempt to induce him to go all out for the greatest part of Portuguese wolfram. Jones said the idea was silly; he would not squander money on it. The question was one almost certain to divide these two men angrily. The one so impetuous in working for a desirable end that he would not pause to count cost or practicability, or even to address himself persuasively to a man who did; the other so measuring and concerned with questions of expense and return. Even Secretary Hull, who had supported every previous initiative in the buying field, seemed to share the opinion that this one was foolish. Wolfram at the price of moon-dust!

Thus the matter stood for many weeks longer (November 1941 to February 1942). The officers of the State Department badgered their bosses. They went further, time and again pointing out to Jones and Clayton the need of a suitable organization for jobs of this sort—one equipped to conduct economic warfare, to spend freely, to act quickly and secretly, and to bargain with American goods as well as money. The British government had an organization of this kind, the United Kingdom Commercial Corporation (UKCC).

In February Finletter and I were joined in our efforts to accomplish this by Assistant Secretary Acheson, who thereby spoiled his reputation for stability in the building on Vermont Avenue that housed the Federal Loan Agency. Notice was given that if that organization continued to balk at the assignment, others would be found to take it up. Harry Hopkins had promised to ask the President to provide the necessary funds out of an emergency appropriation. These would be managed by a new subsidiary of the newly created Board of Economic Warfare. That agency, of which Henry Wallace was Chairman, was eager to do the job.

Faced with this choice, Jones and Clayton agreed to accept the assignment. Henceforth they supported the preclusive program, no matter what their doubts. The USCC was brought into existence. The wolfram buying program, for better or for worse, was launched. It had caused one of the deepest splits in the wartime government.[7] Later it was almost to divide the Allies.

On February 10th the State Department informed the British Embassy that:

". . . it has been determined that the loan agency will establish . . . a corporation which will be prepared from time to time to conduct preclusive operations."

It also stated that the American government would enter into a joint program to acquire certain Spanish materials of importance that could not be had by commercial methods or at commercial prices.

Before many months had passed, the USCC had a competent group in Spain hunting for whatever the Axis wanted. It was signing drafts for tasks licit and illicit. These were directed by Walton Butterworth, a Foreign Service officer who knew how to find three ways around an obstacle. "Indestructible" his col-

[7] The BEW before long won control of the new organization away from the Federal Loan Administrator.

The actual transfer of control over foreign buying was made by Executive Order No. 9128, issued on April 15, 1942. The meaning of this order was stretched to its fullest in the rules and regulations issued on April 17th by the Executive Director, Milo Perkins, of the BEW. These authorized him to issue orders to any agency (including the State Department) in regard to foreign buying, production, and the financing of the same.

These rules and regulations caused several months of anguished struggle between the RFC and the BEW. But the latter gradually secured effective control over expenditures, which had been Jones's particular province of power.

The State Department had exercised control of another sort, both negative and positive, over buying policies. In order to effectuate the large buying programs already in existence, the State Department had to use all our diplomatic and military resources. It felt it necessary that all economic warfare activities, including buying operations, should be adjusted to its pattern of purpose. This narrative illustrates clearly how they may involve the question of war or peace. But Milo Perkins was loath to recognize these facts.

For a while the authority of the Secretary of State seemed threatened, but it was confirmed by the issuance on May 21 of a Presidential statement "to clarify certain relations and functions of the Department of State and the Board of Economic Warfare in the administration of the President's Executive Order No. 9128. . . ." This specified that the Board should "continue to recognize the primary responsibility and position, under the President, of the Secretary of State in the formulation and conduct of our foreign policy and our relations with foreign nations."

leagues had nicknamed him, after he had emerged from a Pan American clipper beneath the waters of the Tagus—resting on his briefcase. He worked under the gaze of the Ambassador and in good accord with the Embassy staff. Weddell had left Madrid, retired at his own request after the crucial battle over Spain's role in the war had been won. His successor, Carleton J. H. Hayes, at once took an active interest in the whole economic program.

XXVII

TRADE WITH RESERVATIONS
(THE MIDDLE OF 1942)

Again, How Much Oil?

THE new program had been conceived with inner cramps. One cause is illustrated by an anecdote of Labouisse's upon his return from Madrid.

He was sent there to work out the schedules of products to be traded. High on the list of those desired by Spain was rubber. On the anniversary of the capture of Madrid by Franco there was a great parade down the wide avenue Castellano. Crowds filled both sidewalks under the watchful eye of the police. Labouisse and a British colleague, forgetful of the occasion, were on their way to see Spanish officials. To get to their meeting-place they had to cross the line of the parade. At several points they tried to excuse their way through the massed spectators but failed. The third time they got through only to run into the policeman on point duty. He carried a long night stick, a flexible "billy." While Labouisse tried to explain why they had to cross the street, the night stick hit him on the knee. He turned to his British companion and said:

"The Spanish government is asking us for rubber, but if this is the use to which it is put . . . !"

That was the constant query—would the products we sent be used against us?

The main assignment of the USCC was to secure as large a part as possible of those Spanish products useful in war production—to ourselves or the enemy. The act of purchase was merely the first step. Yet even this was far from simple. The approval

of the Spanish government had usually to be obtained before
buying contracts could be signed. Then there was the matter
of obtaining enough pesetas to pay. At first this was routine, but
as the Spanish balances of gold and dollars grew, it ceased to be
so. The government had to be persuaded to accept larger amounts
of reserve funds when it wanted larger amounts of American
goods. But these hindrances were less constant than two others.
They were, first, to obtain permits to export what had been
bought and, second, to arrange transport out of Spain. Each required diligence and constant bartering with the Spanish government—favor by favor.

Still, as the months of 1942 passed, the joint British-American
effort grew in scope and promise. The beam of our buying power
was shifted to each and every point at which we thought the Axis
vulnerable—from mercury to zinc, fluorspar, and strontium, to
skins and woolen goods, then on to wolfram. The arguments
regarding give and take were long and full of reproaches. What
wolfram was to us (and iron ore to the British), oil, fertilizers,
rubber, coal, and various items of industrial equipment were to
the Spaniards. They sought to get as much of these as possible.

The determination of how much oil we should send to Spain
always caused the most trouble, despite the new controls. When
in April new gusts of rumor struck, the whole patched structure of accord trembled. Were German submarines drawing on
convenient Spanish supplies? They were, at the time, haunting
the American coast line and sinking American merchant ships
even under naval escort. Naval officers, back from convoy duty
in which they had watched American seamen die in burning oil,
vented their agony of mind. The State Department officials who
were sanctioning the flow of oil to Spain grew fearful lest they
were making a mistake for which they would not be forgiven.
Our policy rested on a choice of risks that were, in the final
analysis, military. For this reason on April 28th the whole program was submitted to a senior Army and Navy group under
the chairmanship of General Eisenhower, then Chief of War
Plans. The military men were far less perturbed than the
civilians. They wanted the program carried on even though now
and again a little of the oil might leak into German tanks.

How much oil were we to send? We had promised enough for essential civilian needs. The IPOC looked to Walter F. Smith, the head of the Spanish oil-control organization, to estimate suitable quantities. But it balked at his first brisk suggestion that many tankers be given cargoes at once, because of the low level of Spanish reserves. It wanted to bring home the fact that leakages would not be tolerated. It also waited for more adequate information about Spanish needs or stocks. Neither then (April 1942) nor later was this easy to obtain. The IPOC never was really satisfied with the reports on the oil situation received from Madrid. Smith seemed prone, especially at the beginning, merely to accept the records that Campsa furnished. In several proved instances the figures provided by Campsa (and passed on by Smith) turned out to be wrong, incomplete, or misleading in form. He was there to probe, not to copy. The IPOC at the time had the unhappy impression that Smith either was careless or did not understand the limits of the program. His seeming zeal to sell oil impaired his usefulness as an adviser for a program that had other aims.

Thus shipments were delayed in April. This worried the British government greatly. It did not like the prospect that the Spanish government would soon be compelled to reimpose rationing regulations which would end all private motoring and reduce economic activities. Hoare lamented that this would bring about a renewal of press attacks and destroy the joint pre-emptive program. Without being as disturbed over these possibilities as the British, we agreed at the end of the month to license four tankers. In informing the American Embassy of this action on May 2nd, the State Department explained that while it did not wish Spain to conduct a propaganda campaign:

"we certainly do not feel called upon to prevent the Spanish government from curtailing the civilian use of gasoline in Spain, especially at a time when we are about to carry our own domestic restrictions further."

It was hard to maintain this attitude in the face of the plea that if we were more generous we could win Spain over to co-operate with us in many ways. Our new Ambassador, Hayes, was strongly of this mind.

The American Embassy in Madrid on May 26th next submitted its ideas regarding the supply program for the whole year 1942. The chief features were: (1) That peninsula Spain be supplied with 637,000 tons. (2) This total was to include 10,000 tons of aviation-grade gasoline; 4,000, it was explained, was for the Iberia Airline; 2,400 for use in industrial aviation, permitting the manufacture of aviation motors; 3,600 for the use of the military.

The IPOC rejected these recommendations for several reasons:

First, the total was too high. During 1941 Spain had consumed 577,000 tons. This amount had been enough to permit great economic improvement. There seemed no good reasons to authorize an 11 per cent increase over the 1941 rate of use, in order to enable Spain to relax its restrictions.

Second, the total was in excess of the then existing capacity of the Spanish tanker fleet. This was estimated to be about 492,000 tons. To offer more would encourage an expansion in the fleet.

Third, there was no reason at all for supplying any aviation gasoline. None of the three uses named were to American advantage. Germany held an important share in the control of the Iberia Line.[1] German diplomats, military men, and secret agents used it all the time. Judgment was against aiding Spanish industry to make airplane engines or parts. They were in close working touch with the German Air Force.[2] Judgment was also

[1] The question of whether or not to provide aviation gasoline for the Iberia Line was the subject of protracted discussion between the State Department and Ambassador Hayes, which is recounted in Supplementary Note III.

[2] In connection with the Spanish request for aviation gasoline, the following information is pertinent. On January 12, 1942 General Gallarza, Chief of the General Staff of the Spanish Air Force, explained to Baron von Bülow, the German Air Attaché in Madrid, the aims of his prospective visit to Berlin. Among other things, he was going to ask help in arming the Spanish Air Force in ways that could be useful to Germany and to Spain in equal manner. He explained that with German technical assistance certain Spanish factories (Elizalde, Hispano-Suiza, and others) could begin to produce airplanes and airplane motors at once. This would be valuable to Germany in two ways: first, the Spanish aircraft industry could deliver a certain number of airplane motors to Germany, and second, if the German Air Force units came to Spain, they could obtain spare parts and repairs.

Franco made virtually the same point in a talk with Stohrer on July 14th. He observed how advantageous it would be for Germany if he were able to put at Germany's disposal Spanish-made war materials and especially planes,

against making it easier for the Spanish Army to conduct training maneuvers. Early in July 1942, it may be added as a postscript to these remarks, it was learned that the Spanish government had undisclosed stocks of aviation gasoline. The Embassy excused this as mere negligence and the State Department passed it by with a mild rebuke.

Besides such specific reasons for saying no to Madrid's proposals, it seemed a time to keep Spanish supplies small. The program just barely survived another access of alarm in May. Darlan, with Pétain's public blessing, was known to be discussing with Hitler an agreement to permit the Axis to use the ports and railroads of Tunis and Dakar. The prospects so alarmed the President that he ordered the Chief of Naval Operations to be ready in three days with an expedition of 25,000 men which could, if necessary, seize the Azores.[3] During June the British met disaster in Libya. The State Department could not detect any signs of a change in the policy of the Spanish government. But in view of these movements of diplomacy and of battle, the smaller the oil supply at hand in the Iberian Peninsula, the better. Again it may be observed in the light of later knowledge that all these fears were overdrawn; Spain and Germany were beset by recriminations. Franco was really going up the hill toward independence.

But mistrust, and the always present dislike of aiding Franco more than need be, imbued the reply that the Department sent on July 2nd. This stated that we thought that the flow of oil to Spain during 1942 should not exceed 50 per cent of the average amounts consumed during the years 1929–35. This was the maximum current rate of supply to the American republics. The average Spanish use during these early years had been 760,000 tons; we proposed to send half, or 380,000 tons, instead of the 672,000 tons that the Embassy had proposed. No oil of aviation grade would be sent. Smith was also told that the Spanish government must not be informed of the basis or quantities of this program, inasmuch as we did not regard it as a definite commitment.

---

quite aside from the fact that Spain would have become a greater military factor.

[3] Langer, op. cit., pages 153–5.

The Embassy found this program (of July 2nd) to be harsh, shortsighted, and not in accord with what had been promised Spain. It asserted, and correctly, that the quantity in mind was less than the barest Spanish needs. As for keeping the figure to ourselves, that was likely to be impractical.

The customary circuit of anxiety whenever we were being strict or demanding began to vibrate. On July 14th the British Embassy in Washington began to relay warnings. It passed on reports from Hoare that Carceller was angry over the American delays in sending oil; that he had submitted his resignation to Franco in view of his past opposition to German demands; and he also said that Spaniards would rather walk than be constantly humiliated and kept in a state of suspense as to whether or not they were going to get gasoline. We were, Hoare said, helping the enemy in a situation that was dangerous and delicate. Hayes sent similar messages. The usual adjectives of the period seemed always to come out of a clinic where a prolonged childbirth was taking place.

Alarm over possible German entry into Tunis or Morocco had waned. The conduct of the Spanish government—as far as the State Department knew of it—seemed to justify Carceller's reproaches. Therefore, on July 30th the limit was raised to 492,000 tons. This was about the capacity of the Spanish tanker fleet and about 60 per cent of past Spanish consumption. Smith was again plainly reminded that the American government did not wish to get into an obligated position regarding any specific rate of future supplies. Our wish to retain freedom of action no doubt seemed unfair to the Spanish government, being a hindrance to advance planning. But it had always reserved the same right in every sphere; no one ever got an option on Spanish resources or influence.

The record showed that we and the British had not been making Spanish life intolerable. Franco, in his usual July 17th speech, dwelt on the many signs of returning economic health: the progress in farming, forestry, industry, and mining; the increased supplies of essentials; the normalization of transport and finance; the new bridges and ships being built. Trade and production in the colonies were also beginning to thrive. These were evidence, he said, of the economic victory that had been gained, and he added:

"Do the people know what it means to achieve this in the face of a menacing international situation without recognition of belligerency, having to win the war without unfriendly countries knowing that we are winning it?"

Spain was on its way to becoming a prosperous neutral.

Also, though Franco did not mention this, our oil was making it possible for Spain not only to maintain a large army but to service it actively. The force in Morocco alone was about 100,000 men. Its food, supplies, and equipment were carried by trucks. Training used oil. In short, out of even the scant supplies some could be spared to better the condition and morale of the Army. We did not quarrel with that fact. Possibly it helped to create a measure of goodwill among the Spanish army commanders which, perhaps, was of use when our troops landed in Morocco.

The newly confirmed schedule of oil supply (492,000 tons per year) entered into effect with an autumn flurry. Spanish tankers still suffered long delays in American ports. Weeks sometimes went by before the hose was laid across their sides. Spanish officials were bitter. They said that even while they had been taking risks to meet our wishes, their people were being punished. Was this the deceit of which they had been warned in Berlin?

Ambassador Hayes became aroused. His cables sent in the middle of August urgently asked for a remedy. Apparently with the thought that those causing the delays might also disregard ordinary messages, he sent a personal one to the President. The thunder in this was loud, perhaps too loud, for there were very many other clouds in the wartime sky. He asserted that the American government was failing to carry out its pledged word to supply Spain with oil for its essential needs. The failure of arrivals was using up the already too small stocks. He said he was compelled to conclude that there was either a sad lack of co-ordination within the American government, or systematic sabotage. The results threatened, in his opinion, to destroy Spain's pitiably weak economy and our own buying program. It would result in the surrender of Spanish economy, with its reservoir of manpower, into Axis hands. A truly alarmist message.

The men who had put together the Spanish program fingered it with chagrin. True, the flow of oil to Spain so far during 1942 had been very small. But this was mainly because we had to good purpose shut off all supply early in the year. A quick survey showed diverse causes for the most recent delays. In some cases they had been due to the slowness of the British government in granting safe-conduct. In others, and these consumed the most time, they had been caused by the Treasury, which had taken from ten days to three weeks to give financial clearance. In still others they had resulted from Spanish mistakes or failure to co-operate with the United States Naval Command.

The call for reform was justified. This was admitted in the reply sent to Hayes on August 29th. A promise was given that the delays would be reduced. But it was also pointed out that the Spanish government would have to improve the management of its tanker fleet. All shipments during wartime were caught in the crowded pressure around the dam of formalities. The State Department could not do all the nagging for Campsa and Cepsa.

The time of voyage thereafter shortened. The flurry showed that in Hayes the program had a sedulous care-taker. As quick proof of the sweets of amiability, he was able to cite a notable betterment in the way in which the Spanish press dealt with the news from American sources, particularly war communiqués. Oil for the winepresses of the provinces, for the news-presses of Madrid. What could we not, Hayes came to think, get for plenty of it?

XXVIII

WITH OPERATION "TORCH" IN MIND

The Great New Incentive

ON JULY 25, 1942 the Combined Chiefs of Staff decided upon
Operation "Torch"—a combined American-British landing in
French Morocco, Algeria, and possibly Tunisia.

As Sir Samuel Hoare observed:

"The Allies by entering the Mediterranean and making their chief
naval and air base in the Straits were taking very grave risks, unless
Spanish inaction could be assured." [1]

The American and British planners did not take that for granted.
They conceived Spain and Germany to be in closer working
accord than they were, and more able to send a real attacking
force against the Straits. The fear of exposing the invasion forces
to defeat caused by loss of Gibraltar and the Straits determined
one of the main features of the invasion. Original plans were to
make all landings inside the Mediterranean. But it was judged
prudent to have a railroad and supply line that could not be cut
by the Spaniards. This was a main reason for deciding upon the
expedition to Casablanca. [2] The risks of landing in bad Atlantic
weather and strong surf were taken, rather than risk the chance
that the Germans might come through Spain, or that the Spaniards might strike out from Morocco. As further protection, the
Allies organized a task force in England, ready to step into

[1] Hoare, op. cit., page 151.
[2] Harry C. Butcher: *My Three Years with Eisenhower*, entries August
15, 16, 22, and 24, and September 2, 1942. The fortress of Gibraltar was regarded as most vulnerable. Lt.-Gen. Sir F. Mason MacFarlane, Governor
and Commander in Chief, is reported by Butcher as saying (on August 16th)
that if Spain became a belligerent, "both the naval base and the naval station
would go out of commission at once."

Spanish Morocco if necessary.[3] This task force was known as Operation Backbone. The anxieties that inspired both these elements in our military plans seem, in the light of present knowledge, unfounded. But they cannot be called foolish. If our troops had met disaster on the beaches, who knows whether Spain might not have been carried, or forced, by Germany into the battle?

The trade program came into new esteem as another kind of insurance. The benefits of trade, it was thought, would induce a friendly and quiet frame of mind among the Spanish people. That became, for the time being, the prime incentive. Preclusive activities were pushed, but quarrels and crises were avoided. We asked nothing that might alienate Spain. At the same time, as already related, care was taken to see that Spanish oil stocks did not grow. Who knew what impulses might rise to the top?

The pursuit of these policies was made smoother when, in September, Serrano Suñer was dismissed from office. No longer would Hayes have to stride past armed Falangist guards on the stairways to the Foreign Office, or witness the Minister's quick dash into the armored car drawn up at the side entrance. No longer would we have to reckon with his bent ways and secret dealings, or put up with his studied offenses.

Serrano Suñer's shrill attempts to keep himself before the Spanish people, to shine as a leader in all but name, had tried the Caudillo's patience too far. His tongue had ridiculed too often. His personal conduct had bruised the intimacy within the Franco household. And, above all else, the Americans were in North Africa. When the chance came to drop him, Franco took it. Dissension between the Army and the Falange, and between Serrano Suñer and other more extreme leaders of the Falange, made the change expedient, woven into an extensive rearrangement of the upper ranks of Spanish officialdom. Even the Germans did not regret his going. The change—according to what our Embassy could learn—was not meant to mark a change in Spanish foreign policy, but it did.

It turned out to be greatly in the Allied favor. General Jordana, the new Foreign Minister, was an elderly, orderly, and

[3] Story of the North African operation by General Mark W. Clark, *New York Times*, May 24, 1947.

thoughtful military man. His loyalty to Franco had survived an earlier blow. He had been Foreign Minister before, in 1939. Then, by his own account, he had been dismissed to appease Italy after Spain's refusal to join the Axis in the summer of 1939.[4] He was reputed to be eager for good relations with the Allies.

Hayes's first talk with Jordana on September 8th confirmed the hope that the change was for the good. The Foreign Minister referred appreciatively to the supplies that the Nationalists had received from the United States during the Civil War. He responded—as Serrano Suñer had never done—to Hayes's expression of a wish to extend trade with the United States.

That he meant it was proved a few days later in the game of give and get. He instructed the Spanish negotiators with Germany to trade with closed fists; while with us they began to open their fingers. Thus there was equity in his protests against the delays in oil shipments. He, if not the whole Spanish government, had become entitled, under the rules of bargaining, to a more regular inflow. This was recognized, as already told. Except for a few unreconciled minds, the officials concerned with the oil-supply program did not want to starve Spain for oil. But they did not want to send a gallon more than they had to for the sake of winning the war. And they were determined to maintain strict control of the size of Spanish imports and reserves. Dependence was regarded as more reliable protection than the word of any Spanish official, no matter how friendly. But oil began to move on an appointed schedule and continued to do so for the rest of the year 1942.

Toward the end of October both Hoare and Hayes began the formal preparations for Operation Torch. On the 19th Hoare, in a talk with Franco, dwelt upon the way in which Spain was being enabled to satisfy its main needs from overseas. In view,

---

[4] This would appear to be borne out by the entry that Ciano made in his Diaries for September 4, 1942: "A governmental crisis in Spain. It had grown to be inevitable. I was convinced of this in Leghorn when I heard how Serrano was talking about Franco. He talked of him as one speaks of a moronic servant. And he said this without caution, in the presence of everybody. It is too early to say what the consequences of this development will be. The only indication might be the choice of Jordana, and this is not favorable. Jordana has always been a man not whole-heartedly with the Axis and a sympathizer with France and Great Britain."

he said, of the mutual wish to have this continue, Spain should be on guard against incidents that might be caused by Axis activities in or near the Straits. Then he reassured Franco that Britain had no intention of intervening in Spain's internal affairs then or *after* the war. He also flatly affirmed that Britain would not occupy or invade either the Spanish mainland or Spanish colonies. Franco answered that Spanish policy was "unchanged." Once Serrano Suñer had explained to Ribbentrop how this form of words could be used to mislead.[5] But on this occasion Franco gave them clear meaning; he had kept Spain out of the war up to then and expected to keep it out until the end.

The American government waited until Operation Torch was close at hand before giving similar assurances. On November 2nd Hayes sent a message to Franco, personally authorized by the President of the United States and Commander in Chief of the American Army and Navy. Its two main points were:

"It is the purpose of the government of the United States of America to do everything possible to prevent Spain from being brought into the war, and Spain's desire to remain out of the war is fully recognized by the United States. The government of the United States has no intention of infringing upon the sovereignty of Spain or of any Spanish colonial possessions or islands or protectorates. The United States will take no action of any sort which would in any way violate Spanish territory.

"Moreover, the government of the United States of America, perceiving with much gratification the improvement of relations between the two countries which has been taking place in recent months, strongly deprecates any activities by purely private organizations or individuals within the United States which would seem intended to prejudice the growth of good feeling between the Spanish people and the people of the United States."[6]

Franco seems to have placed faith in these British and American statements. More faith than the American authorities put in what he said. The American Embassy in Madrid reported that it could detect no signs of any change in Spanish policy and no special preparations for military action. But it had become habit —a habit thrust upon us—to mistrust even Franco's infrequent

[5] At the meeting at Berchtesgaden.
[6] The full text is published in *Wartime Mission in Spain*, by Carleton J. H. Hayes, pages 87–8.

direct remarks. Thus the fear lingered that he might permit, or even connive in, a military action to defeat the North African operation. The headquarters of the Supreme Commander were much worried over this risk in the weeks before the landing; this anxiety was connected with the dread that the Germans knew much about our plans.[7] There were diverse last-hour reports that a German expedition was being prepared to anticipate our landings. Thus Robert Murphy, who was in touch with various sections of French officialdom, cabled about the middle of October that:

"The Germans appear determined to settle the western Mediterranean issue during the coming weeks and will have the use of the Spanish mainland and of Spanish Morocco for this purpose. Gibraltar is under constant surveillance. In French opinion, definite action is not a question of weeks but of days." [8]

There was not, as far as can be learned, any danger of such a German-Spanish operation then or soon after our landings. Even if at last the Spanish government should have consented to allow German troops to move into Spain, Germany was not ready to attempt battle in the western Mediterranean. The fighting forces, equipment, oil, and food could not be spared without risk to other important operations.[9] The only service—but this might have been of critical use—that the Spanish government performed for Germany in the days before the landing was to transmit full news of what was afoot around Gibraltar and the Straits. This infor-

[7] How hard General Eisenhower found it to shake off the fear that Spain (or Germany with Spanish consent) would strike at the time and place (Gibraltar) where the whole Allied expedition was most vulnerable is shown by a chit he passed out to Captain Butcher a few hours after the first landings and before the arrival of news. Entitled "Worries of a Commander" item number 1 read: "Spain is so ominously quiet that Governor of Gibraltar reports himself uneasy. No word from any agent or Ambassador."

[8] Quoted in article of General Mark W. Clark, *New York Times*, May 19, 1947.

[9] Shortly after the landings the Navy submitted a report to Hitler on the situation. "It would likewise be," the report read, "of the utmost strategic importance to us to take over the entire Iberian Peninsula. . . . However, since we do not want to divert either the military or economic forces necessary for such action, unless it is imperative, we must strive to maintain the neutrality of the Iberian Peninsula." Annex 3, Report by Naval Command to Hitler, December 22, 1942. "Fuehrer Conferences," 1942, page 145.

mation went mainly through military intelligence channels. But on November 5th the German Ambassador cabled to Berlin a personal report that the Spaniards were disturbed about Allied military preparations in and about Gibraltar. He said that both Franco and Jordana were asking for immediate arms deliveries. They believed that the massing of planes and ships clearly pointed toward an invasion of French Morocco.

After the landing Hayes reported that Jordana had been most helpful in preventing any adverse reaction. According to this account, Jordana had put through an agreement with the Ministers of the Army, Navy, and Air to give full publicity to the British and American guarantees, and to publish straight stories of our military movements. This group, Hayes said, had prevailed over others who wished to arouse Spanish feeling against the invaders. The Spanish press and radio behaved creditably.

After the actual landings (begun on November 8th) Spain made no hostile move. The American commanders in Africa kept an alert watch upon the forces in Spanish Morocco, but were given no trouble.[10] In numbers they were sizable, and well enough equipped to send tribesmen into the hills or quell revolt. But they lacked the means of facing Patton's divisions. The Spanish people on the whole seemed to be glad of our successes. Some appeared to hope, others to fear, that they might ultimately lead to a revolution in Spain. The first signs appeared that Franco was thinking about a change in the status of Spain.

Throughout the months before, with rubber tread, he had been turning away from Germany, toward the Allies and the goods they could supply. Records since come to hand make it possible to trace the footsteps of withdrawal, which had left him free when the American soldiers landed at Casablanca.

[10] Butcher, op. cit., entry November 15, 1942, made at Gibraltar, reads: "At lunch we learned through diplomatic channels that Hitler had demanded of Franco free passage for his forces through Spain." Hayes, op. cit., page 92, writes that Germany made two such requests and was refused twice. No record of any such requests or refusals appears in the captured German or Italian documents available to me, and none of the German leaders, when interrogated, spoke of them.

If the landing attempt had been a failure and the expeditionary force had been badly defeated, it is probable that Germany would have hastily organized an attacking air and land force and entered French Morocco, and (with or without permission) Spain and Spanish Morocco as well.

XXIX

SPAIN AND THE AXIS: A GLANCE BACK
OVER 1942

The Stages of Spanish Retreat

THE retreat was well under way at the time of Pearl Harbor. The lag in oil shipments during the autumn of 1941 made a deep impression upon the Spanish government. Franco appears to have been struck by a sudden fear that his regime might be destroyed by a complete Allied blockade. On December 19, 1941 he called in Hoare to deny it. The fear was strong enough to counter his strong dislike of what the United States asked in its November memorandum. The memorandum, it will be recalled, in which the American government stated it would only supply Spain in return for equivalent benefits and firm guarantees against diversion to the Axis.

To satisfy, even in part, our demands for materials, Spain would be forced to withhold from Germany.[1] If it admitted American oil observers, secret aid to Germany would be imperiled. But the need for oil, as already emphasized, was imperative. The Spanish people would not do without it in order to drive a nail in Roosevelt's coffin.

Thus while the Spanish government was still trying to whittle down our lists, it let Germany know that it would have to rearrange its distribution of war materials. When Ribbentrop fumed (in January 1942), Franco gave in to a German demand to continue wolfram shipments even though Germany could not send equivalent values of German goods. However, Stohrer, when reporting this concession to Berlin, gave warning that such favor could not last. He said that Spanish officials were caustic at being

[1] Though with wolfram this did not turn out to be the case until 1943, because of the increase in production. See Chapter xxxiv.

186

asked to send large amounts of raw materials to Germany while getting so little in return. Germany had failed to send machinery and equipment of various kinds promised the year before. The large credit balance in Spain's favor was growing in the books of the Spanish-German clearing arrangement. The magnet of German victory was losing strength; respect for German efficiency was fading as it failed to supply Spain; fear of the German forces in the Pyrenees began to succeed friendly admiration as the war went into its third winter without decision.

The American insistence upon obtaining wolfram, cork, and mercury, and even more upon setting up an oil-inspection system (backed up by constraint of current oil shipments), drove Serrano Suñer into an anguished dilemma. On January 24th he read the whole of the American proposal to the German Ambassador as a prelude to telling why Spain would have to yield. Of course, he added, Spain would delay some deliveries and cause others to miscarry, and of course Spain would never consent to having American agents investigate and control. He said the same thing again ten days later. But other branches of the Spanish government had by then virtually agreed to do so.

Ribbentrop rose to the crisis with his usual graces. On February 4th (1942) he wired Stohrer that the German government would certainly not allow Spain to carry on compromising negotiations with the Allies because it was frightened by the presence of Allied armies in North Africa. But Stohrer found no way to make the commandment "shall not" effective. Carceller, and Serrano Suñer as well, kept asking who would supply Spain with oil, coal, and rubber if the Allies did not. Short of the use of force, there was no way to prevent Spain from entering into deals to obtain these and other products—even at German expense. The German government did not dare or care to use force. Disgruntled, it watched the progress toward a settlement with its enemies. As balm it got another promise that wolfram exports to the Allies would be kept as low as could be, and permission to export the stocks of wolfram and lead that it had stored up in Spain. The agreement with the Allies began to operate. The agents of Sofindus (the trading organization of the German government in Spain) began to pass those of the USCC on the stairways to the offices where strategic materials were sold. Oil observers began to spot out the Spanish hirelings of the German secret service.

During May-June-July of 1942 the German government could feel elation over events in the eastern Mediterranean but not in the west. As the German armies again came close to Suez, the American government, as recounted, worried lest Spain swerve, for German victory in the east opened up a vista of vast new sources of supply. But the Spanish government chose the supply in hand. Time enough, its idea seemed to be, to apply for the oil in the Middle East when the Germans had the wells.

At any rate, the Spanish negotiators with Germany showed themselves less, rather than more, giving than before. They stood out for the rule of equal deliveries, no increase in credit. Serrano Suñer wearied of the haggling. He went off on a long visit to Rome, drawn by a wish to share in the excitement of the Libyan victory. At the end of his visit (June 25, 1942) Ciano wrote in his Diaries:

"Serrano has left, after an eleven-day visit. A too lengthy trip is never useful; it creates boredom."

On July 14th, under instruction, Stohrer reviewed the relations between Germany and Spain in a long talk with Franco. He protested the Spanish demand for payment in goods and its reluctance to issue export permits for the products that Germany needed. To contribute to the victory over Bolshevism, Stohrer asserted, was the self-understood duty of an allied nation like Spain. Though Franco avowed that he was still entirely faithful to Germany, Stohrer found his remarks to contain many deviations. Franco made much of our power to deprive Spain of oil if we did not get what we wanted. Then he promised export licenses for goods that Germany had already bought, particularly 175 tons of wolfram. As for further deliveries, he suggested that their amount be determined in future negotiations.

This was a partial victory, to which Germany did not find it easy to cling fast. For the German government would not offer anything in return—not even "booty-weapons." The apparent extreme shortage in Germany of equipment, machinery, tools, coal, and fertilizers that Spain wanted made our offer look most attractive.

Hitler wasted little regret upon the discharge of Serrano Suñer in September. He passed on a strange version of the event to Ribbentrop: it had been brought about through Serrano Suñer's machinations for the monarchy; this was shown by his recent trip to Italy, which did Serrano Suñer immense harm, and by the Vatican's plan to form a bloc of Catholic countries. Serrano Suñer had worked harder for these ends, Hitler summed up, than for those of Franco.

The German Embassy in Madrid tried hard to believe that the change was of little account. One member at least was sure that he had firm ground for this belief. Lazar, the Chief of the Press Division of the German Embassy, cabled to Berlin on September 5th that the Chief of the Press Bureau of the Foreign Office, Minister Doussinague, assured him that he had received instructions from the Foreign Minister, General Jordana, to change nothing in the foreign-policy principles for the Spanish press; all heretofore transmitted instructions, including the treatment of new material and the composition of captions, were to remain the same.

But in the economic field the effect of the change became evident at once. Talks with Germany were suspended. When they were resumed at the end of September, Jordana showed himself uncooperative. His only favor was to agree to keep secret the fact that Germany admitted the sinking of the Spanish merchant vessel *Monte Gorbea*. Had this torpedoing been meant as a warning against the carriage of contraband goods to the Allies? It was so construed.

In October Carceller, who had recently been left on the side lines, tried to gain control over negotiations with Germany by entering into a "gentlemen's agreement" behind Jordana's back. But the gentlemen fell out.

The crisis of the American landings in Morocco did not bring the Spanish and German governments any closer together. As already observed, Germany made no serious attempt to draw Spain into an attack upon the Allies; it merely increased its effort to make sure that the Peninsula would continue to remain neutral. Ribbentrop found Franco's reply to the President's letter of assurance more obliging than necessary. Franco made clear that he was thinking first and last of Spain. The one thought of the Spanish government seemed to be to keep out of the war, which had now reached the borders of Spanish Morocco. Or if that was not Franco's only thought, it certainly was the salient one. Whether a wish to serve Germany activated in part the transfer of troops from Spain to Morocco is a matter for surmise. But the instinct of defense is enough to account for it, since no one could be sure that the fighting might not overrun French frontiers. Did he know about the American forces in England (Operation Backbone) that were standing by in case of trouble?

Whatever his inner thoughts, Franco focused his messages to Hitler upon his wish for arms from Germany. A hint was given that if Germany did not send them, Spain might ask the Allies. Franco's expositions to Stohrer of the critical need for arms might have been puzzling to another auditor, for it bobbed around the question of who he expected to attack Spain. His thoughts were hidden within the fluffy flounces of his talk.

Hitler did not want to give up any arms. But on November 24th he decided to offer some as a gesture. The talks on economic matters were resumed as the American troops pushed on toward Tunis. The Spanish government braced itself against coming American demands. It correctly surmised that we would presently make it harder to continue even the reduced forms of special favor shown Germany.

How different was the image of the present from the one Franco had conceived when he told Hoare that Britain should give up so futile a struggle! Hitler did not stand before the cenotaph in Whitehall. He did not parade through the Red Square. But there—look—Roosevelt and Churchill sat under tents in Casablanca. They were among the Moors.

XXX

THE CHAPTER OF HARMONY OF EARLY 1943

By Favor or by Firmness?

BETWEEN Spain and the Allies there opened a brief chapter of harmony. After our landing in North Africa the Spanish government had promised orally and in writing to remain out of the war. Jordana assured Hayes secretly that Spain would resist any attempt from any quarter to bring it into the war or to cross its frontiers. These promises were kept, and Secretary Hull decided that they would remain unbroken as long as we did not suffer serious military reverses. The fear of nourishing Spain for war, by sending supplies, thereafter passed, though not without a few last gasps. In February the trade program was reviewed by the Joint Chiefs of Staff (JCS) and their British colleagues. Both gave their endorsement. The greater our forces committed to the Mediterranean, the more essential they thought Spanish neutrality.

The program had been started as a way of relieving Spain of any need to join the Axis and to make peace tolerable. During 1942 another aim had been added—to reduce the flow of war materials to Germany. After the successes in Africa it became possible to pursue this goal with less fear of consequences if Franco resisted and hated. But neither Washington nor London was ready to take a serious risk of provoking him to desperate action. The military men wanted a tranquil Spain. If our demands put Franco's regime in great danger, he might—it was thought—seek safety in an alliance with the Axis. Or if in our wish to have our way we brought misery to Spain, misery might bring revolt, and revolt might bring the Germans.

Though still hobbled by such thoughts, the will to deprive the enemy of Spanish goods became stronger, and the wish to rub

out all the other war advantages enjoyed by Germany in Spain.
The Spanish government was still far from impartial. Its press
and propaganda system was serving the enemy as faithfully as
ever. Doors were still being held open, on the sly, to German
secret service and military intelligence. The American government began to look forward to the day when we could demand
that Spain end these aids to the enemy. By favor or by firmness?
That was to be the most argued question for the rest of the war.
For a time the American government tried the first, then resorted
to the second.

While the landings were in prospect, the State Department
had authorized Hayes to promise more friendly regard for Spain's
wants. The President's words, transmitted when our Armada
was on the water, were cordial. The Spanish government was
entitled to think we at least half meant to be—and for a time
we were. The American government began, early in 1943, to
assist Spain to secure products in scarce supply.

Spain sought above all else from (or through) the United
States oil, cotton, copper sulphate, ammonium sulphate and other
fertilizers, repair parts for tractors and agricultural implements,
electrodes for steel furnaces, and from the sterling area, coal,
rubber, cellulose, and fertilizers.[1] As the Allies began to provide
more of such goods, the USCC and the UKCC in concert began
to ask in return a larger and larger part of Spain's production of
materials useful in war. The combined American-British outlay
for strategic Spanish products began to run at a rate of about
70 million dollars per year. The United States began to have
to hunt for enough pesetas. Spain and Germany had entered into
secret accords which: one, reaffirmed Spanish promises to serve
as a source of supply to Germany; two, provided Germany with
the means of paying for wolfram.[2] Spain was practicing a policy
of profitable harmony on two pianos, in two different sound-
proofed rooms.

There was still no single coherent agreement between the

[1] The improvement of trade relations is shown by the rise of the value
of American exports to Spain from 14.3 million dollars in 1941 to 22.8
millions in 1942 to 28.2 millions in 1943. The figures for the later years
contain no oil products, which were sent from the Caribbean. The largest
single item of export was raw cotton.
[2] See Chapter xxxii.

Spanish, American, and British governments. All attempts to arrive at one frayed out. There was only a conglomerate group of avowals, accords in principle, brief bargains. This made it necessary to argue and fret over every transaction; the sun never set on the trading that went on in Madrid, London, and Washington. But it had one advantage; copies of any formal accord would certainly have come into German possession; this way the Spanish ministries could evade German claims and reproaches.

The Americans and British in London and Washington at this • time worked together congenially. Joint committees in both cities went over every question of consequence. The exchange of information was unguarded. The outlays for preclusive buying were shared equally and resources were pooled. The individuals who shared in this work were united in a single group to their mutual enjoyment.[3]

Competitive war buying, at high prices, changed the whole economic prospect within Spain. Hayes has described the change well:

"Higher prices for Spanish products, increased production stimulated by higher prices, created a mild boom in the country particularly in wolfram producing areas. This, with the accompanying increase of helpful imports from the Allies as well as from the Germans, immeasurably strengthened the Spanish economy. Gradually food stuffs and textiles became less scarce. Rationing was reduced. Transportation was improved. Simultaneously the Spanish army was enlarged, properly uniformed and better equipped." [4]

Spain had chosen to bid for the comforts of peace rather than the risky rewards of war. They were being garnered. The British government took a kindly view of that fact. Many members of the American government observed it with wry displeasure. The

[3] The same was true of the Joint Economic Warfare Committees that conducted operations in Portugal and Turkey. It extended also over the whole field of acquisition of raw materials for defense production. Of all the Combined Boards, the Combined Raw Materials Board worked most smoothly.

The same measure of cordial co-operation between the American and British representatives did not, unfortunately, exist in Madrid. While the local staffs of the USCC and the UKCC co-operated, the regular staffs of the two Embassies often did not. Hayes and Hoare were not attracted to each other.

[4] Hayes, op. cit., page 86.

thousands who were still rotting away in jail or exile were a constant reminder that the regime rested on cruel force. But outside of trying to give no favors without return, nothing was done to interfere with the movement of Spanish affairs.

The joint preclusive program was guided in Washington by two simple, in fact over-simple, ideas. They were: first, if the Germans wished to buy a product, it was needed by them; and second, therefore, they should be prevented, if possible, from getting it. The chief method of doing so was to buy as much of the supply as possible. But available funds were limited. Various measures were taken to stretch them. Most important of these was the use of a surcharge on the sale of certain American products, particularly oil, sent to Spain. This was amply justified, since the prices paid for Spanish products, particularly wolfram, were enormous. We tried to impose a 200 per cent surcharge on oil. But we reduced it by half in return for a promise of pesetas in exchange for dollars and gold. In 1940, it will be recalled, Spain had not had enough foreign exchange to pay for essentials such as wheat. How greatly its situation was changed by the spring of 1943! By then the Spanish government was loath to accumulate larger dollar balances.[5] It had to be induced to do so.

Just as well that the American government did not have all the pesetas in the world. Fear of running short was a healthy rein on ardent spirits who might otherwise have bought up the Spanish shrubbery. They were compelled to choose between the products they were trying to corner. It kneaded their bargaining will and caused them to search for economical ways to succeed.

There was always uncertainty as to what was being achieved. Insight into Spanish obligations was blurred; knowledge of Axis needs of Spanish products was incomplete; information as to how much the Axis was receiving was unreliable. The preclusive campaign was like a naval battle conducted beyond the horizon.

[5] For pre-emptive operations the United States and Great Britain on joint account alone spent about 75 million dollars in Spain from January 1, 1942 to July 1, 1943. Both the UKCC and the USCC independently spent besides substantial sums for products desired to meet genuine needs—the so-called "supply purchases." In addition, privately arranged trade, especially with the United States, went on.

The exact range was rarely known, and the gunners were dependent upon aerial observation to tell whether they were hitting or sinking anything.

The American Embassy in Madrid and the USCC went ahead with enthusiasm. Officials in Washington could draft schedules, but they were the ones who did the hard work. It was they who had to extract out of the Spanish maze approval for their buying, contracts, and licenses to export. It was natural that they should be eager to have much to offer. That was one of the reasons why the Embassy and the State Department found themselves apart in the late spring of 1943 on the question of how much oil to send to Spain.

XXXI

THE QUARREL BETWEEN HAYES AND THE STATE DEPARTMENT

The Sweet or the Dry

THE quarrel between Hayes and the State Department disfigured the spring of 1943. In the account of his mission written by the Ambassador it is treated with deft lightness.[1] But his messages at the time surged with the sense that the life of Spain, and perhaps even the outcome of the war, were at stake.

The causes of the dispute concerned both wish and method. The State Department wished to send as little to Spain as might be needed to avoid internal trouble, and to win the battle against Germany for strategic supplies. It wanted to drive a hard bargain and was not wholly averse to coercion. The BEW favored a policy of sending even less and did not seem to worry over what might happen in Spain. Hayes wanted to gain our ends by generous and trustful aid; to win over, and perhaps reform, a grateful Spain by making it prosperous.

The two attitudes clashed over the question of how to interpret the principles that were supposed to govern the flow of oil to Spain. These were, one, that the supply should be enough for Spain's essential civilian economic needs in wartime. It was presumed by the authors of the program that Spanish ration controls would be maintained, thereby keeping the current rate of consumption low. Two, that the rate of flow would be so adjusted that stocks in Spain would never exceed two months' consumption (three months' for lubricants). This would be enough to protect Spain against an unexpected failure of supply, but it would not be enough to enable Spain either to fuel a war or dispense with shipments for a long time.

[1] Hayes, op. cit., pages 143-8.

The procedure for applying these principles was this: Smith prepared and submitted supply schedules for an advance period; the IPOC, after studying these and other pertinent facts, settled upon a program; this was cleared with other officials concerned with Spanish affairs, and with their superiors; in the event of a significant change, the Joint Chiefs of Staff were consulted. The program, thus fixed, was sent to the Embassy at Madrid as a basic guide.

The Navy did not wish Spanish tankers to be moving in and out of the Caribbean at all times. Therefore it set two brief periods in each month during which they might call for cargo at selected loading ports. These were Puerta de la Cruz in Venezuela for crude oil, and Aruba for refined products. Lubricants were bought in the United States and shipped out of American ports in ordinary cargo vessels. The Spanish oil monopolies, Campsa and Cepsa, notified the Embassy of the names of the tankers it wished to dispatch to meet each loading date. The Embassy was then supposed to approve such voyages as fitted into the total supply program and to discourage any that did not. The Embassy's consent was construed by the Spanish government to mean the promise of a cargo upon arrival.

The American government, it will be recalled, had authorized shipments to peninsula Spain during the second half of 1942 at an annual rate of 492,000 tons. Actual imports during this period had been, however, much less. Supply had been short and Spanish stocks had been much depleted. Still, toward the end of 1942, when the inflow of oil at this level became regular, the Spanish government found it possible to raise the rations for private cars, trucks, buses, and factories.

In December 1942 Smith came to Washington to discuss the program for the first part of 1943. At this time the prevailing thought was to avoid any trouble that might upset our African operations; the Spanish government had recently improved its behavior; and the period of harmony, just reviewed, was starting. It was then agreed to permit Spain to secure, during the first half of that year, oil at the annual rate of flow of 541,000 tons. This Smith estimated to be the maximum carrying capacity of the Spanish tanker fleet.

All interested departments of the government, including the

military and the Petroleum Administration for War, concurred. But some officials of the State Department, myself included, did not fully appreciate its import. It was their fault, their carelessness in reading the committee minutes. When later they concluded that the quantity was too large, no question of obligation seemed to be involved. For the Embassy had been told time and time again that the quota figure was for our use only, and the Spanish government was not to know of it. Never had we promised to supply any specific quantity of oil—only to supply enough for Spain's essential civilian needs.

In January 1943 the members of the IPOC noticed that the trips of the Spanish tankers were much more frequent. The fleet had grown. There was a spurt of worry. The outcome of the fighting in Tunis was still uncertain. The military and Hayes thought it critically important to do nothing at this time to affect Spanish goodwill or lessen the influence of our friends within the government. No one else wanted to give Spain just cause for inviting or aiding the Germans. But there seemed, by then, little or no danger that Spain would do so, because it got less rather than more oil. The country was beginning to taste almost placid comfort after long, deep suffering. Another danger seemed more real: that the German Army, opposed or not, would come through Spain and find reserves waiting.

The situation was reviewed in a meeting called by Under Secretary Welles on February 11th. All present agreed that the tide was running too fast; that less oil should be sent to Spain from then to April, to lower the level of Spanish stocks. But Hayes was pleased by the tide. What matter if it overflowed a bit? The Spanish people would be grateful to the source. Thus the Ambassador spoke to them in Barcelona on February 26th, saying in part:

"I am happy to say that during the last four months of 1942 and to date in 1943 the flow of gasoline and other petroleum products from America to Spain has equalled the full capacity of the Spanish tanker fleet. Already by January 1 of this year stocks had sufficiently accumulated here to enable the Spanish authorities to increase gasoline rations, put more trucks on highways and recently to start street busses running again in Madrid. At the present time, the amount of petroleum products available in Spain is appreciably higher than the quantity available for non-military use [2] to any European country and is considerably larger than the present per capita distribution to people along the Atlantic seaboard of the United States."

And at another point:

"The United States stands ready to continue and extend any help it can to Spain which itself is doing so much with such obvious success to develop a peace economy that can and will carry this country safely into a future period of world peace."

It was puzzling to know where such a statement left us. It was out of accord with the feelings of both the American government and the American people. They were not pleased that Spain was doing so well while they were in the fires of war. They were not grateful for Franco's artful caution, or eager to see his regime carried safely into the future. The Ambassador's remarks seemed to many to have gone beyond both his title and his task. Only a few days previously Franco had declaimed before the National Council of the Falange:

"The liberal world is succumbing, victim of the cancer of its own errors, and with it commercial imperialism and financial capitalism, with ther millions of unemployed, are falling apart."

The dislike of Hayes's speech was well founded. The feeling of the liberal press, though strewn with needless insult, was natural. Hayes, in his account of his mission, has recorded the belief that the speech did a vast amount of good at a critical time.[3] There seems little reason for thinking that the speech made much difference one way or the other; and none for the view that the hour was critical.[4] But, howsoever that may be, it is hard to appreciate why the criticism should have seemed to him "humorous" and "pitiful." [5]

Apart from sentiment, there were working reasons for being disturbed. Hayes's attitude seemed to skimp two features of the economic warfare problem. First, the more nearly normal

[2] In the version of the speech available to me the phrase appearing is available for "military" use. But this is obviously wrong, and I am assuming that the Ambassador said "non-military."

[3] Hayes, op. cit., page 97.

[4] See Chapter xxxii reviewing Spanish-German relations during this period.

[5] Hayes, op. cit., page 97.

Spanish production and transport became, the larger the surpluses of minerals, farm and fishery products, and textiles that might have to be bought. Second, the more secure Franco was about his economic situation, notably about his oil supply, the more able would he be to hold out against demands to cease trade with the Axis. Officials were thinking forward to that decisive step. They therefore were not as disturbed as the Ambassador when Spain's economic affairs were deranged.

Miscount and Make-up

Hayes's speech of February 26th still echoed when the IPOC decided, on March 23rd, to limit the flow of oil to Spain during the first quarter of 1943 to 100,000 tons. This compared with 135,000 tons provided for in the schedules approved the previous December. This troublesome decision was based on a careful reckoning that Spanish imports and stocks were both on the verge of becoming excessive. The energy to make it was drawn from discomfort because the lot of Franco's Spain was being made easy. The junior officials who met in IPOC were in their own way wrestling with the question that has haunted the Allied nations ever since. How far, in order to gain the easiest victory, should the American government go with measures that might rob the victory of ultimate and lasting meaning? But they did not admit the fact, even in their own company; the measure was discussed as a temporary and expedient move, not as a significant turn in policy.

The reduced figure was selected in the light of reports that Spanish consumption during the previous few months had been about 30,000 tons per month and that imports in excess of that amount had gone into reserves. It was higher than actual Spanish consumption during the whole of 1942 of about 330,000 tons. Further, it was almost identical with the rate of actual imports during the last quarter of 1942 and in the first quarters of 1943. In other words, it gave no ground for the idea that we were oppressing Spain or ruining Franco.

The decision was noted with approval by all thè officers of the State Department concerned. It was passed upon by the Secretary of State. But the first attempt to make it effective failed. Study of the approvals of tanker sailings previously granted by the Embassy showed that unless some canceling move was made at once, shipments would not only exceed 100,000 tons—the new guide figure—but would exceed the 135,000 tons that had been in mind before. On April 18th, therefore, the Embassy was asked to refuse clearance to several tankers about to set out for the next loading period (May 4–5). The Embassy queried the correctness of these figures and took no action about the tankers.

On April 24th Secretary Hull presented the problem to the Joint Chiefs of Staff, since there might be a political or military risk in refusing to supply all the oil that the Spanish tanker fleet could carry. By letter he reviewed the history of the subject and explained the reasons for the change now proposed. The British government, the Joint Chiefs were informed, had reserved its position.

But the Embassy's failure to halt tanker departures (for the May 4–5 period) made it necessary to act again before the reply of the Joint Chiefs was received. Secure in its judgment, the State Department on April 27th informed Hayes of its wish to limit the flow during April-May-June to 100,000 tons and of the reasons why. It pointed out that the list of sailings being proposed by the Spaniards was enough to fetch half again that amount— 150,000 tons. The Ambassador was told, therefore, to thin down the list to the dimensions of the new program.

This order seemed to Hayes to threaten all that he was trying to do. His impression of it, as later stated, was that:

". . . suddenly and without prior consent of the Chiefs of Staff or of the British, the program was arbitrarily to be cut from 541,000 tons a year to 400,000 tons, with obvious grave injury to Spanish economy and, above all, to the Allied position in Spain. Our chief weapon was being turned into a sawed-off shotgun." [6]

In regard to which it may be observed that, first, the reduction was not arbitrary; second, the question had been placed before the JCS, and Hayes had been so informed; if they objected, he

[6] Hayes, op. cit., page 144.

must have known that the decision would be reversed. But they did not object. On April 29th they replied that there was no military reason why the proposed change should not be made.

It had been foreseen that Hayes would not welcome the cut, coming after his talk of bounty. Therefore, on the 29th the State Department had sent him another precautionary message. This pointed out that it would be advisable for the Embassy to defer approval of tanker sailings for the next loading period (May 19–20). The text of this message was initialed by many officers used to scrutinizing language. None raised a question as to its intent.

The Ambassador's answer to these messages of the 27th and 29th reflected his feeling that he was faced with foolish unreason. He cabled on the 30th that in the exercise of the discretion which he found in the Department's messages—those which had been intended to end discretion—he had permitted the Spanish tankers named for the next loading period (May 19–20) to sail. He added that he was ready to justify this action to the President in the light of the President's approval of the oil program and its bearing upon the whole of our Spanish policy. The tankers were soon on their way. The State Department was thereby faced with a choice of refusing cargoes on their arrival or accepting the accomplished deed. The wish to keep shipments within the 100,000-ton limit during the second quarter was thwarted.

The Ambassador's answer of April 30th was addressed to Secretary Hull personally. He read with soft reproach the messages that recorded the clash in which he had been drawn by the zeal of his staff. One quarrel more! Hayes had been the President's selection; he had been sped to Spain to win, with words untaped. Thus Secretary Hull might well have allowed the situation to drift. But the group of subordinates who had nursed the Spanish program were not content to have it do so. They felt that they, not Hayes, were the true custodians of our Spanish policy and programs. With a sigh, the Secretary signed the indignant response that they had drafted.[7] This reviewed the record and spelled out the conclusion; the Ambassador's action not only made nonsense out of the 100,000-ton policy, but would induce a movement of oil in excess even of

[7] This group consisted of Acheson, Feis, Finletter, Labouisse, and Merchant. The last named was then serving as chairman of the IPOC.

the earlier scheduled rate of 135,000 tons per quarter (annual rate of 541,000 tons). This was certain to occur unless some of the Spanish tankers were promptly recalled. Without a refusal somewhere in this transit, the flow during the second quarter would, it was figured, reach 170,000 tons.

For the Spanish government had not been slow to take advantage of the position. Several new tankers had been brought into service. The annual carrying capacity of the Spanish tanker fleet, according to Smith's latest report, had now grown to be between 700,000 and 770,000 tons according to the speed of movement. The Spanish government proposed to use it all.

Hayes's instant (May 1st) reply did not go into the comparative statistics of the oil movement. It dwelt primarily upon the political and military importance of retaining the friendship of the Spanish government. He pointed out the various benefits that he had lately won—such as the Spanish passivity at the time of the North African landing, and the release of French refugees so that they might go to North Africa. For what fanciful reasons, he asked, should these and greater future favors be imperiled by keeping Spain short of oil?

This was but the first of a series of protesting messages. The next implied that the situation had not been adequately explained to Admiral Leahy or the JCS. The next called the State Department's action unfair, unforunate, and inopportune. The next conveyed the news that all of the five tankers nominated for the May 18–19 loading period had already sailed, and that any request for their recall would injure our relations with Spain and impair Jordana's position. The State Department, after consulting Admiral Leahy, again accepted the accomplished fact. It did so in the face of the angry grumbling of the BEW. But at the same time Hayes was told that no oil would be given to still another, a previously unmentioned sixth, tanker that had been sent on its way. Further, he was flatly ordered not to authorize any trips for the next (early June) loading period.

The situation was further confused about this time because of lack of certainty as to the size of Spanish stocks. At the behest of the BEW another try had been made to find out whether the figures received from Smith were all-inclusive. Previous inquiries of the Embassy in Madrid had failed to produce a direct answer.

Now Washington was informed that the reports sent covered only Campsa's stocks. For statistical purposes, Smith explained, when products were passed on by importers to resellers or consumers, they were considered as consumed. The amounts in question were not great. But it was a shock to uncover the point. It was an open door to evasion of stock limits. Campsa at the very time, and with Smith's knowledge, was avoiding our charge of excess stocks of lubricants by some such speeded-up process of transfer. This incident again shook faith in the direction of our system of oil control.

The Embassy apparently construed the mildness of the Department's reproofs up to this point as immunity. The next significant message received from Hayes on May 11th showed that he was going to insist on his own version of the American program. Admitting that the already approved shipments for the second quarter would exceed 135,000 tons, he urged that he be permitted to grant approval for at least one tanker sailing for the next loading period (June 4–5). This request was defended on the score that the excess flow during the second quarter would only make up for earlier deficiencies. There seemed to be no visible limit to the quantity of oil needed to avoid a crisis in Spain. The bogeyman at the window was becoming a fixture; the State Department was being told at the same time that he was really a friendly creature.

The Secretary of State found himself with an incipient staff rebellion on his hands. The Ambassador was instructed on May 14th to postpone the sailing of the disputed tanker (for the June sailing) and to adhere scrupulously to instructions on the point. He was also told that our program of oil supply for Spain was being more vigorously attacked than any other subject in the field of foreign policy. Hayes has since stated that the Secretary of State thus revealed the real reasons for reducing the oil program. It was the need of catering to public opinion in the United States, which Hayes plainly believed to be misinformed.[8]

The Secretary's cable of May 14th did not end the squabble. So on May 22nd the Department sent its first stern telegram. This directed the Ambassador not to authorize any further tanker sailings under any circumstances without the Department's ex-

[8] Hayes, op. cit., page 146.

press approval in advance, and not to make any promises, direct or indirect. Furthermore, Hayes was informed that the JCS had reviewed the program. They had concluded that there was no military reason to supply Spain with more than 100,000 tons of oil in the second quarter; but in view of the clearances already granted by the Embassy, they were willing to agree to a maximum amount of 135,000 tons.

This message of May 22nd for the first time seemed to cause Hayes to realize that the opposition grew out of something more than the ignorant prejudice of a few officials or fear of public opinion. His reply of May 26th suggested that, in view of the divergence of views, Smith be recalled to Washington for discussion. Earlier he had proposed that he himself should return.

Smith's arrival was preceded by a conciliatory personal letter from the Ambassador to the Secretary of State dispatched June 7th. This assured that the Ambassador had no thought of disregarding orders; that he had taken them only to be hints to be dealt with in the light of his own judgment; and he had been certain that the results of acting upon them would be bad and were not clearly grasped. The Ambassador took heed of the repeated queries as to whether the Spanish government had been told of the schedule of supplies. He stated that while, as far as he knew, it had never been informed, it naturally expected that the current rate of supply would not be reduced.

The Ambassador's information on this point turned out to be wrong. On June 9th the Petroleum Attaché of the Spanish Embassy in Washington told an official of the State Department that Smith had given to the Spanish government a copy of the program of supply (the scheduled totals and individual tanker sailings) as approved in December. In a matter-of-fact way he produced a copy out of his pocket, remarking that he had often discussed it with a subordinate member of the Office of the Petroleum Adviser in the State Department. The members of IPOC, upon learning that the Spanish government had been informed of the schedules, became less puzzled about the reluctance of the Embassy to interfere with the tanker sailings named.

While waiting for Smith's arrival, IPOC had to repress various further tanker nominations supported by the Embassy. Madrid was given a full and firm exposition of the reasons for maintaining low limits for both shipments and stocks. When on June 22nd Hayes sent word that he was in complete accord with this statement, the end of the troublesome argument came into sight.

In his account of this episode the Ambassador has described Smith's visit to Washington as a "love feast." [9] Hardly so. But by the end of June the Department and the BEW were willing to revert to the 541,000-ton annual basis—on the condition that there could be no carry-over from quarter to quarter and that the stock limits would be strictly enforced. To that extent Hayes had his way. Both he and Smith accepted this limit contentedly. They had learned that it was really meant to be an effective maximum, no matter how great the capacity of the Spanish tanker fleet. The JCS approved. When Cárdenas, learning what was in the wind, complained, Welles turned the protest aside. Spain was managing well.

Tankers again began to move between Spain and the Caribbean without furore. But only for some months. Then a more critical question presented itself: whether or not to stop all oil shipments to Spain in order to compel the Spanish government to cease shipments of wolfram to Germany. The impulse to do so was aroused by reports of new deals between Spain and Germany which would enable the latter to continue the contest with the Allies forever. Of these deals, and their significance, much more is known now than then. Spanish responses to our demands during the last period of the war can only be understood by turning back to the disclosures in the German documents—turning back to the arrangements made between Spain and Germany after our landing in Africa in November 1942.

[9] Hayes, op. cit., page 148.

XXXII

FRANCO ARRANGES HIS SURVIVAL (1943)

Germany Contributes Arms

How many times Americans had thought they were about to hear the German word of command among the Arabs! But in the winter of 1942–3–it was hard to believe–American soldiers tented in the fields where the enemy had been expected, American generals conferred in villas from which the Axis commissioners had made a hasty exit. American voices traveled through the soft African nights, across the waters from Morocco to Spain.

The diagram of fear became reversed. Germany began to be afraid that the Allied soldiers might cross the Straits of Gibraltar. Even if they did not, they might compel or induce Spain to end all economic and military favors. The Spanish government was quick to search for whatever advantage could be drawn from these anxieties. It had accompanied its advance reports to Berlin about the Allied expedition gathering at Gibraltar with urgent requests for arms. After the landing, Hitler began to take serious notice of them. Ambling talks were rushed to a swift conclusion. Hitler had up to then paid little attention to General Muñoz Grande, the Commander of the miserable Spanish Blue Division on the eastern front. After the feet of the Allied soldiers were firmly on African soil, Hitler had received him warmly. He stated that Germany would provide the Spanish Army, Navy, and Air force not only with arms, but with arms of high quality–if the Spanish government would pledge itself to use these arms in the event of any Allied attempt at infiltration or attack.

A general assurance of this kind being given, an agreement was signed–on December 17, 1942. This provided that Germany would deliver not only arms, but coal, fertilizer, chemicals, and iron and steel products. Spain in return promised to facilitate the acquisition by Germany of substantial amounts of raw materials and foodstuffs. The scheduled trade exchange was greater in both volume and value than ever before, and did in fact become so for a time.[1] The Americans had broken the lock on the German warehouse.

The Spanish Foreign Minister, Jordana, stressed the importance of guarding the secrecy of this accord. The reason, it may be supposed, was that he did not wish to spoil the impression made on the Allies. They had not long before been assured that Spanish trade with Germany was falling off. This was, it will be recalled, a period of harmony in the trade relations between Spain and the Allies; the United States was relaxing its controls and supplying Spain more willingly.

In their haste to conclude the accord of December 17th, the German and Spanish governments had left important features vague—even the Spanish pledge to resist the Allies. Hitler wished to have this confirmed in clear and conclusive terms. Ribbentrop asked for a written promise to resist any Allied entry on Spanish territory at all costs and on all counts.

Franco had little taste for such an unguarded promise. He tried to convince the Germans that it was self-evident that German arms in Spanish hands would serve a good purpose; that a strong Spain would find it easy to ward off an enemy attack and thus make Europe more secure. He also made much, in his talk with the new German Ambassador, Moltke, of his exertions to disrupt unity among the Allies.[2] But the German government was not content with aphorisms. It dallied over essential details of the arrangements to deliver arms. The German military experts who were in Spain on this business absented themselves on longish tours of inspection.

---

[1] German exports to Spain in the first half of 1943 were 98,500 tons (value about 30 million dollars) as compared with 47,400 tons (value about 16 million dollars) in the first half of 1942. Spanish exports to Germany rose from 239,500 tons (value about 24 million dollars) in the first half of 1942 to 283,500 tons (value about 54 million dollars) in the first half of 1943. These figures do not include arms deliveries, and are only rough approximations.

[2] Stohrer, a recognized failure, had been replaced by Moltke as German Ambassador in Spain. The latter died a few months after being assigned to this post and was succeeded by Dieckhoff, former German Ambassador to the United States.

The Spanish government learned that it would get the arms only if it gave a written pledge. Jordana did so in a secret protocol signed February 12th.[3] The Spanish government declared that in the light of the

"intentions of the German government to deliver to the Spanish army in the shortest time possible arms, war equipment and war material of modern quality and in sufficient quantity"

it was determined to resist any entry of Anglo-American forces upon the Iberian Peninsula or in any part of Spanish territory outside of the Peninsula "with all the means at its disposal."
The final paragraph read:

"Both parties obligate themselves to keep this declaration . . . absolutely secret."

They did; the soundproofing was effective for quite a time.

Thereupon the German and Spanish military men began to compare their lists of arms to be delivered. It soon appeared that the two governments were at odds on two vital points.

First, the German government wished to make sure that the arms would be used, and well used, if the Allies ever did attack Spanish territory. For this purpose German training and technical help in the use of the arms were offered. These forms of aid the Spanish government readily accepted. But Hitler's ideas went further; talks between the German and Spanish General Staffs were in February urgently suggested, especially in regard to the possibility of joint action in the event of an Allied attack on Portugal. But the Spanish government evaded, fearing, and fearing correctly, the wrath of the Allies. Franco lagged in giving the required orders, seeming not to know how many weeks were going by. Then in the middle of June, after the arms deliveries had begun, he told the German government that he did not think such conferences were needed since he saw no immediate threat to Spain. He was deeply impressed by the Allied capture of Pantelleria and Lampedusa. The German Ambassador found him depressed by his perception of Allied strength and of Spanish weakness. Arms or no arms, he would not thereafter stand up and be

[3] The text of this protocol bears the date of February 10th but it appears not to have been actually signed until the 12th. The text is printed as State Department Document No. 14.

counted. The German Ambassador's docile report on the talk (June 16th) in which these impressions were received ended by observing that during the whole of the conference—at which Jordana and many bemedaled generals were present—he had the feeling that he was the only one who spoke the military language.

The second point of difference concerned Spanish payment for the arms. Hitler expected to price the weapons high. He hoped to secure enough to pay for large amounts of the products that Spain had promised to provide. Franco expected to price them low, to get them as a fee for the defense of Fortress Europa. The span of difference had become clear during the second half of March.

The Spanish had asked that the arms be sent at once; the Germans had said they would be sent when the related economic agreements were concluded. The German Foreign Office and the German Ministry of Economics had fallen out with each other. The Foreign Office wished to keep the arms until Spain gave in. The Ministry of Economics was afraid of losing Spanish supplies, especially wolfram; for during this interval the Spanish government held back export licenses. It is a fair surmise that in this bargaining over terms the Spanish government was supported by the fact that supplies were coming from overseas in greater volume and variety than before. It could feel sure of a return from Allied sources for whatever was withheld from Germany.

Early in May a partial compromise was put together. This settled for the time being the order of delivery, but it left aside the exact details of compensation. The first three special trains carrying the advance arms shipments crossed the frontier at the end of May. Spanish raw materials began to move in the opposite direction. In June (1943) the Spanish government turned over 125 tons of wolfram to Germany at a very low price. The American government protested. It was informed that this wolfram shipment discharged old contract obligations assumed by the Spanish Ministry of Aviation. Germany had only recently delivered the specified aviation equipment to Spain. This was the truth, but not the whole truth.

These advance exchanges of goods between Spain and Germany soothed only for the moment. The German government valued the arms that it was to deliver at 250 million reichsmarks

matters were being argued, Carceller tossed in a
November 12th he told the German Ambassador
very much like to obtain 100,000 tons of grain from
matter where it was grown, it must be sent from
clearly identified as a German shipment. For his
rranging the transaction was to prove to the Allies
ontinued to demand too much, Spain could get along
ir products. He offered to furnish Germany with
nd olive oil in return. Hitler ordered 20,000 tons of
sent and promised to see about the rest. The wheat
vel in railroad cars, not in trucks. They would be
long way round and their movements would be widely

wheat tour was an incident. Carceller tried to incite
by reading to the German Ambassador on November
emorandum received from Hayes asking a complete
embargo to all destinations.[5] But the knowledge did not
negotiators together. The talk about the Civil War
gged futilely into the lost future.

oves and countermoves in the economic warfare within
ere nearing their climax. The deal just traced, when it
known, caused anger in Washington. German fighting
ad been restored and the American government did not
aving to expend huge further sums in order to deny Ger-
wolfram and other strategic materials. It was beginning to
rong enough to insist upon another solution.

is was the memorandum that marked the start of the Allied attempt to
Germany of all supplies of wolfram, narrated fully in the following
rs.

at 1939 prices. It asked in payment a current sum that would buy
as large a quantity of Spanish products as could have been bought
by this money in 1939. The price increase of the Spanish products sought was reckoned to be fourfold.

But how the German notions shrank as the talks went on! As
Ministerial Direktor Clodius reported to his chief, Ribbentrop, on
June 22nd, the Spaniards stressed the political character of the
deal and refused to admit that it was fair to set prices for the German war material which took into account the rise in Spanish
export prices. Even Franco seemed to be of this mind, and said
that the prices asked were making a very unfavorable impression
on the Spanish government and the Spanish generals.

The dispute reached a crisis at the end of July. The best Spanish offers were greatly below the German hopes. For the revised
list of arms Germany asked 741 million reichsmarks; Spain would
pay only 216 million. It accused Germany of overstating the original cost. The Spanish sum was less than Germany needed. Wolfram prices were sky-high and the Germans lamented that it would
bring only enough to pay for 1,000 tons of that greatly needed ore.

Germany had gold. But it did not want to part with it, and the
Spanish government was not eager to accept it. For the United Nations had announced that the gold held by Germany was "looted
property" and they would not recognize the legality of its transfer. Some sneak transfers had been made, but the Allies were now
more touchy and more likely to win.

To break or not to break? The German government groped
for new springs to move men who were showing a strong will
of their own. It tugged again at Franco's fear that German defeat
might be followed by his own downfall. Once more Franco admitted that this was probable and avowed an ardent wish for German victory. But he stuck to his offering price. The new German
Ambassador, Dieckhoff, on August 5th, urged surrender. He
pointed to the signs that the Spanish government was leaving the
Axis orbit and said that it was essential to have a new magnet.
Hitler and the Foreign Office gave in. The Spanish and German
governments signed a Supplementary Economic Agreement on
August 18th. This accord, which the Spanish government chose
to regard as a firm obligation, was to become later the main line
of assault we had to overcome.

The agreement provided for the payment of 216 million reichsmarks. The Spanish government confirmed the promise, contained in the earlier accord of December 1942, to permit Germany to secure whatever quantities of various listed Spanish goods, including wolfram, it could pay for. This promise the German government sternly brought to the fore when the Allies sought a wolfram embargo.

The Allies learned of the making of the accord with chagrin. Germany had stayed out of the wolfram market during the summer of 1943; spring buying had taken care of its needs, and funds were short. Now it would be able to resume buying. The repletion of the German accounts meant a renewal of the preclusive battle which the Americans and British thought they were about to win. They puffed and they huffed, and began to frame a new and tougher strategy.

But Franco could and did face Allied displeasure with calmness. For he could feel strengthened in four ways by this August agreement; with the Army, for the arms obtained; against rebels; against a possible Allied attack; and against the cessation of the rivalry between the Axis and ourselves, which was enriching Spain. These boons were his, while he was still free to deal with the future. By this August arrangement he managed to guarantee his survival before the Allies had won their victory. He grasped future security out of Axis misfortunes.

True, the promised weapons did not arrive on schedule. But before the end of 1943 Spain had secured a thousand or more railroad cars containing not only arms but other German goods as well.

Spain Resumes the Name of "Neutral," but Clings to Old Habits

The Allied demands made in the autumn of 1943 were beginning to tell. They touched on the remaining inside advantages enjoyed by Germany in Spain: the coastal spy services, which aided the attacks on Allied convoys; the secret German organiza-

tions within Spain that hel
the presence of the Blue Di
Spain was beginning to wave
ises to Germany. As early as
had informed the American g
of Spain was turned toward c

By autumn Franco ceased to
careful not to provoke German
ventured farther along the route
tober 1st he used the phrase "wa
escape the German Foreign Office.
that Spain's dependence made it e
American powers a pretext for co
console. Nor did Jordana's avowa
would never become the enemy of
then cast out and in flight, Franco sp
for whom he had the deepest admirati
He refused to recognize his rump gov
the Spanish government announced th
ligerency" to "neutrality."

Ingratitude. But not absolute. At le
would be paid. The Spanish governmen
mainder of its Civil War debt if the Ger
accept reasonable terms.[4] The total had b
lion reichsmarks as far back as February 19
110 million of this total. On November 10,
Ministers resolved to pay off another hund
This was to enable Germany to pay expor
and textiles already bought. Discussions regard
some 162 million reichsmarks—were begun. T
ment hoped to have the debt reduced by offse
of the Blue Division and by deducting the adve
ing balance.

[4] By doing so it tried to soften resentment at its refusal
to increase its debt under the German-Spanish clearing. At
had been allowed to rise to 220 million reichsmarks. But S
it to 70 million. Carceller, a practical man, did not permit s
his pencil. But he was ready to help Germany to find anoth
tinuing its buying rivalry with the Allies, one that could
proper Spanish obligation.

While these
new item. On
that he would
Germany. N
Germany an
purpose in a
that if they
without the
some lead a
grain to be
was to tra
routed the
advertised.

But this
generosity
27th a n
wolfram
bring th
debt dra

The
Spain w
became
funds
relish h
many
feel st

[5] Th
depriv
chapt

XXXIII

THE RETREATING GOAL

The Achievement Ceases to Satisfy

THE accords between Spain and Germany (of February and August 1943) upset Allied hopes of depriving the enemy of vital supplies. Several times—as during the winter of 1942—it had seemed as though Germany was near the end of its bidding and buying power. The Allies were obtaining an increasing part of the Spanish production of useful war materials, such as wolfram, fluorspar, strontium, and woolen textiles. But each time the Germans reappeared, with pesetas and friends in the right places. Thus, in April-May 1943, after the first trainloads of arms were shipped, they were able to buy and pay for a larger amount of wolfram than in any like period.

Were we also to bid with arms? In the summer of 1943 it was suggested that we might at least display our stock. When in June, as just recounted, the talks with Germany became tangled up, the Spanish government made it known that an American offer to discuss possible arms deliveries would be appreciated. On June 6th the Under Secretary of Commerce and Industry pointed out how we might thereby deprive Germany of influence and funds. On the next day the same proposal was put before the American Consul at Tangier by General Castillo. He advanced the same arguments. But when asked why Spain wanted the arms, he said that they were desired to put down possible internal disturbances or to cope with troubles that, arising elsewhere in Europe after the war, might spread to Spain.

Hayes tried to persuade Washington to agree to discuss the matter "in principle." In so doing he had no thought, he has written, of recommending any actual sale of equipment, and he made clear that no commitment to do so was involved.[1] Presumably, then, his purpose was merely to make a show of goodwill and to assist Spain to give the least possible to Germany. James Dunn, the Political Adviser, suggested that our military representatives might be permitted to go into the matter—thereby, it may be supposed, sterilizing it against political infection. But the other members of the Department, grouped about Dean Acheson, were fearful where such discussions might lead. Secretary Hull upheld them. Thus, having confirmed the fact that the JCS did not think it advisable to furnish military equipment to Spain, on July 20th he instructed Hayes to let the matter drop.

How then, the restless query spread, were we ever to bring our economic warfare program to a decisive end, an end equivalent to the money and energy that had been spent? Would it turn out to have been merely an expensive mode of rewarding Spain's abstention from the war, of detaching her gradually from the Axis side? This is how the British had tended to regard it. But we had hoped for more. More than even slight injury to the German economy—a way to weaken it vitally.

Could we not do so still, by using our power to help or harm Spain? When it became clear that Germany was going to be able to sustain wolfram purchases on a greater scale than ever, the thought was spoken aloud. Out of committee rooms it traveled to London. The British government took quick heed, fearing that we might by impulsive action endanger important military aims. On September 7th it set about by indirect discourse to make us acquainted with its views. Copies of a recent exchange of messages between the British Foreign Office and Hoare were left with the State Department.

The first item, a Foreign Office message, dated August 13, 1943, was an interesting estimate of the situation. Its main points were: that while the Spanish government made no secret of its wish for Axis victory, its present conduct was not seriously prejudicing the course of the war; that no change in the Spanish government could come about without serious internal disorder; and that no alternative in prospect would be better. This analysis led to the conclusion that the British government did not think the current Allied policy should be changed. But, on the other hand, Great

[1] Hayes, op. cit., page 150.

Britain could not forever tolerate wanton attacks on British rights and interests such as Axis sabotage in the Straits. It was therefore instructing Hoare to do his best to make Franco and Jordana realize that the British government was dissatisfied on various scores and urgently wished for remedies.

Hoare acted with vitality. His report, of August 21st, as passed on to the State Department, showed that he had reviewed Allied grievances with the heads of the Spanish state in a thorough and forthright way. As a result, he thought that the remaining deviations in favor of the Axis would be corrected. But he found Franco's complacency unshaken. Hoare's surprise at finding this so shows a dull understanding of the extent to which British policy had aided Franco to deal with danger and distress. Why should he not have felt complacent, whether he looked back over the past or forward into the future?

Spain's situation was constantly improving. Current British proposals would help more. For example, the British government was at this time urging that the quota of oil to Spain for the final quarter of 1943 be increased from 135,000 to 209,000 tons, even though Spanish stocks were adequate. Thus Spain would be able to end all restrictions on the use of oil. The Spanish people would thereby have a simple lesson in the usefulness of the Allied connection; and the Spanish government would be more willing to meet Allied wishes.

This strategic purpose was reaffirmed in a memorandum that the British Embassy gave the State Department on September 22nd. Again it was argued that any reversal in policy might result in disorder in Spain, with which the Allied governments were not yet ready to cope. A more severe economic policy, it was stated, was unwise, for it would imperil not only the preclusive program but also British supply of Spanish products needed for war. Moreover, it was likely to fail because of Spanish obstinacy. Thus, the memorandum concluded, it was thought that the present economic policy would achieve more than one which tried to force Spain to give in by depriving it of the means of living and working.

But the official American feeling was turning in the opposite direction. The demands that the British put to the forefront—closely connected with naval and shipping activities around the

Straits and in the Mediterranean—seemed of less account to the civilian agencies in Washington than to their counterparts in London. Their minds were squinted differently. Several of the departments on the BEW had become impatient with what they regarded as a "soft" policy of permitting the European neutrals (Spain, Portugal, Sweden, and Switzerland) to supply Germany with important war materials. This, they argued, reduced the sense of the vast bombing campaign, so costly of life, directed against German industry. The American government—in contrast to the British—was confident that a stern policy, perhaps after a rough tussle, would win.

The BEW began to review the whole list of its prime objectives. Notorious among them, and a greater drain on the purse than any other of them, was the effort to shut off the flow of wolfram from the Iberian Peninsula to Germany. The impulse to force the issue in regard to that ore broke loose in October. If it led into a bad quarrel with Franco's government, what of it?

To make clear why the American government concluded that it could attain its end only by making Spain realize its vital dependence upon us, the whole wolfram situation must be reviewed.

XXXIV

WOLFRAM: THE MORE WE BOUGHT, THE MORE THERE WAS TO BUY

The Statistical Rainbow

Sir SAMUEL HOARE has written that he felt that the word "wolfram" would be engraved on his tombstone. On one face only, it is to be hoped; and on the other: "no wolfram."

Wolfram is the ore from which the alloy tungsten is derived. Tungsten has many important war uses: for hardening cutting tools, armor plate, and gun barrels; for the core of armor-piercing projectiles; for lamp filaments; for valves; for hydrogenation catalysts; for the making of widia and Stellite. For some of these uses there was no good substitute. Thus to deny it to the enemy was an obvious aim. Pilots and air crews had cities to smash; motorized artillery had bunkers and fortresses; infantry had stone walls and hedges with the enemy hidden behind them. The jinn of the desk had only the targets they could detect with statistical mirrors. Wolfram was one of the most alluring.

The idea of hurting Germany by absorbing the tungsten supplies of the Iberian Peninsula had been first advanced by the British at the end of 1941. It rested on a scaffold of estimates, many parts of which turned out to be awry in one way or another. These were:

1. That during 1942 Germany would need at least 5,800 tons of wolfram ore.[1] This was taken as the indispensable minimum. Germany had consumed 8,500 tons in 1941. During the same year the United Kingdom had used 9,500 and the United States 18,000 tons.

2. That Germany at the beginning of 1942 had stocks of about 2,500 tons. Thus it would have to import about 3,300 tons during

[1] Of 65 per cent W.O. 3 grade.

219

1942 to meet minimum current needs. If no more than that was obtained, stocks would be gone by the end of the year.

3. That Germany could get but little outside of the Iberian Peninsula, not more than 1,000 tons a year. Chinese ore was being shut off and most of the surface blockade runners from the Far East were being caught.

4. Thus, it was figured that Germany would have to secure from the Iberian Peninsula during 1942 at least 2,300 tons and in after years at least 4,800 tons. This might be reduced by the use of scrap (600–800 tons).

5. The then current Portuguese annual production was thought to be about 5,500 tons and the current Spanish production about 350 tons.[2]

6. The chances of getting the main share of the Portuguese production of 5,500 tons were deemed good. The Portuguese government required all ore to be delivered to an official agency at a fixed price; it then allocated the supply among the buyers. The British owned (or had exclusive contracts with) mines producing about 2,400 tons, which they could count on receiving. A French group controlled the source of 500–800 tons; but there was fear that they might be forced by Vichy to sell out to Germany. The Germans directly controlled but little.

Of the rest of Portuguese production (2,600–2,900 tons)—the so-called "free" ore—Britain and Germany were each getting about half. But Britain was hopeful that a greater share could be had.

7. The sum of these reckonings was that Germany could be hurt if three things could be brought to pass: One, if the Allies could keep the French-controlled production in Portugal (500–800 tons) out of German hands. Two, if they could secure more than half of the "free" Portuguese ore. Three, if they could acquire most or all of the Spanish ore. Then the toughening would be taken out of German steel.

But Britain's buying power was being used up. The price of Portuguese ore had sped toward the fantastic (from about $1,300 a ton in January 1941 to $20,000 a ton in October 1941). Funds

[2] This estimate of Spanish production was even then out of date; in the course of the year 1941 it had doubled and by the end of the year was more nearly at the rate of 800 tons.

were running out. Would the United States share the effort and expense?

It has already been told how officials (Wallace and Jones) quarreled over the idea, and how, in February 1942, the American government took it up. In June 1942 the USCC made its first large appropriation of 22 million dollars to buy wolfram in the Iberian Peninsula.

Spain Emerges as a Great Supplier

But the American government became quickly aware that even its golden lariat might not be long enough. It was not going to be easy to snare even the greater part of the wolfram ore of the Iberian Peninsula. For Germany took protective steps. The Allied program was upset almost at once by a secret agreement signed on May 14, 1942. The Portuguese government promised to make available to Germany between 2,000 and 2,400 tons per year. Salazar refused to void or breach this deal; thus the Allies failed in all attempts to reduce the flow of wolfram from Portugal to Germany until the middle of 1944.

The active battle was transferred to Spain. There also the Allied program had to take account of bargains made with Germany. But these were less definite than the Portuguese and less firmly upheld. Producers were permitted to enter into sales contracts with buyers of their choice.[3] But the Spanish government intervened in two ways. It taxed the ore heavily; at first about $5,000 a ton, then later about $10,000 a ton. This was many times greater than the total prewar price of wolfram. Then buyers had to procure a license before they could export what they had bought. The Spanish government used the power to refuse or grant permission to export to bargain with both sides.

[3] The Spanish government required miners of wolfram ore to obtain a license. But there was widespread unlicensed and illegal mining of small deposits. The ore obtained was turned over to licensed producers, who sold it as their own.

As our campaign advanced, four connected obstacles defined themselves:

First, the Spanish production grew hugely under the rain of pesetas. New deposits were explored, new galleries were opened within old mines, old ones were equipped with new machinery, and thousands of Spaniards rushed out to work over alluvial sources. In early 1941 production had been at the rate of about 350 tons a year; by the end of 1941 it was at the rate of 800; by July 1942 it reached 1,300; at the end of November 1942 it was about 3,000; and during the next year at the rate of about 4,000 tons. The more we bought, the more there was to buy.

Second, the German government got ownership or control of some sources of supply. At first they amounted to little. But as the Allies began to corner the "free" market, they were greatly extended. By 1944 Germany could have obtained from sources of supply under its own control alone 500 tons or more a year.

Third—as already told—the Spanish government wished the competition to continue. Whenever one side seemed about to win, it helped the other to carry on.

Fourth, there was much smuggling, internal and external; smuggling from unregistered or illegal mines; smuggling across the Spanish-Portuguese frontier; smuggling across the Spanish-French frontier.

Growing awareness of these obstacles did not lead the USCC and the UKCC to renounce their aim. Undaunted, and with much larger sums, they went forward during 1942. They competed for the "free" ore. They bought up more Spanish mines. They contracted for the output of still others. They took measures to hinder operations in the German mines. They set a watch over enemy smuggling.

By these means the Allies managed to get much of the Spanish wolfram ore during 1942. Yet, because of the growth in production, Germany obtained more than during 1941. The combined supplies obtained from Portugal and Spain in 1942 were enough to defeat the hopes that animated the original British memorandum.

The Allies increased their effort. So did the Germans. Their purchases during the first quarter of 1943 were greater than ever: over 500 tons legally obtained, and a thriving flow of smuggled Portuguese ore as well. Germany was topping Allied bids and besting Allied staffs. It was determined to keep on doing so.

"Wolfram is to us almost what blood is to man," the German Ambassador told Carceller in March 1943 when demanding export licenses. Thus Germany spent by far the greater part of its Spanish funds for wolfram.

In February 1943 came the first of the deals with Germany, of which an account has been given. Germany did then what it had refused to do in 1940; it sent arms to Spain, arms of good quality, arms in advance, arms that might be needed to resist invasion in the west. The preliminary settlement provided means for paying for the large purchases made during the spring.

As the results of these German efforts began to show, Washington became fretful. The American government began to perceive that the joint program would turn out to have been futile unless new methods were used. Futile, at least, for the directly sustaining purposes, to impair German war production and make it easier to defeat the German armies. The IPOC began to consider blunter ways of bringing the struggle over wolfram to a swift end. But the decision was deferred because during this summer of 1943 it seemed as though the Allies might still win by default, by the power of the purse alone.

XXXV

NO MORE WOLFRAM

Would Spain Agree?

GERMANY ran short of current buying power. The Spanish government, as related, was refusing to pay the price asked for arms; and German accounts ran dry before a settlement was reached. The lapse permitted the Allies to slacken their buying. The price of wolfram fell to about a third of what it had been earlier in the year. At the same time the Allies were given the chance to extend the range of their "exclusive output" contracts with producers, thereby obtaining permanent control of an increased part of the supply.

Then in September came a turn-about. Germany, using the proceeds of deals traced out in other sections of this narrative, again became a determined buyer of wolfram.[1] The BEW decided that the time had come to call a halt to competition that was leading only into the Spanish Treasury. On October 7, 1943 Leo T. Crowley, who was now the Director of that organization, wrote Admiral Leahy for the Joint Chiefs of Staff that he thought it advisable to use the economic bargaining power of the United States to have Spain (and Portugal) limit or cease the export of strategic goods to Germany. He asked the approval of the JCS for whatever steps might best achieve this result. Perhaps, he wrote, Spain could be induced to end this trade if the Allies gave her new economic benefits; or perhaps Spain could be prevailed upon to do so if threatened by loss of those currently granted. If not, Crowley advised, the American and British governments should force her to do so by suspending shipments of certain goods such as oil, fertilizer, wheat, and cotton.

The Acting Secretary of State, Stettinius, was asked to comment

[1] See pages 186–7, 221.

on this call to action. Counseled by the political officers, he opposed it as a matter of common prudence. On October 11th he wrote Admiral Leahy that political considerations dictated a continuance of the economic policy thereto pursued. This, he explained, recognized the need to maintain at least a low level of economic activity in the Peninsula, in order to have political stability and avoid disturbances that might invite German intervention.

The letter reviewed the improvement in the Spanish treatment of Allied interests, with the implication that it was due to the policy of aiding Spain to maintain its economic life. This friendly trend would be destroyed by the measures advocated by Crowley even though they might be justified on the grounds of economic warfare. This opinion was shared by the British, and firmly sponsored by Ambassador Hayes and his staff. They wanted to approach the goal by another route—by bringing Spain more fully within the Allied economic orbit in all ways.

There were two solid reasons for thinking that the Spanish government would not comply with a mere request for an embargo: first, fear that Germany would strike back; second, the economic cost. As Spain made clear, this cost would be great and far-reaching. Wolfram was the lucky find, the buried treasure, the rich land in a country where there was so much poor land. If the wolfram trade went, thousands of Spanish workers would lose their livelihood, mine-owners and middlemen would lose great profits, the Spanish Treasury would lose much revenue, and the Bank of Spain would lose its greatest single source of dollars, sterling, and reichsmarks.[2] Countries cling to such kinds of trade as long and as hard as they can.

[2] The value of officially recorded exports of wolfram ore had risen from 2.1 million gold pesetas in 1940 to 102.4 million in 1943, and in the early months of 1944 was at the rate of almost 200 millions per year. Estadística del Comercio Exterior de España, 1940–4. This was increased by the proceeds of smuggled ore. The values are exclusive of the heavy tax. The official value of the gold peseta during this period was about 3 gold pesetas to a dollar but the values recorded for customs statistics were arbitrary—being arrived at, unless I am mistaken, by applying a "premium coefficient" of 2.57 to the value in paper pesetas.

According to the records of the USCC the American government spent for Spanish wolfram ore in the years 1942–4 about 58 million dollars, the British government about the same amount.

Should account be taken of these facts in formulating the demands upon Spain? Should the Allies offer other opportunities for growth and income that would make up for the one they were about to ask Spain to renounce? The political officers of the State Department thought such reward both fair and essential. But others differed. They cited various reasons in defense of the view that no recompense was called for. The expenditure that was enriching the Spanish economy was a forced wartime expedient. The United States could not increase shipments of most of the goods wanted by Spain without giving less to fighting allies and friends. If the invasion on the western front succeeded quickly, the trade would soon come to an abrupt end anyway. Spain would then have to make the same adjustment under more disturbed conditions. Such were their arguments for refusing to accord Spain any additional privileges or advantages as payment for ending wolfram shipments to the Axis.

To Bid or to Threaten?

In short, the debated question was whether to bid or to threaten. The views of the State Department, supported by the British Embassy, prevailed. It was decided first to find out whether Spain would agree to reduce exports to Germany in return for new economic favors. If Spain refused, it would be time enough to try other measures. The Embassy in Madrid, without waiting for the State Department's final word, tested the ground to see if it was soft and pliable. The first attempts, inquiring talks with the Under Secretaries of Foreign Affairs and of Industry and Commerce, met a hard crust. Neither of these Spanish officials thought it would be practicable to effect a quick or main change in the wolfram situation.

On October 21st Hayes submitted a trial proposal to Washington for approval. This glanced boldly toward a virtual trade alliance between Spain and the United States. Its main features were:

1. The Spanish government was to agree to an embargo not only upon wolfram but also fluorspar, strontium, and zinc.

2. The United States and Great Britain were in return to undertake (a) to end their price surcharges on oil and other products; (b) to increase substantially their purchases of other Spanish goods; and (c) to send free gold for any excess in the balance of trade in Spain's favor.

3. In the event that the Spanish government refused an offer of this sort, the Embassy should then turn to the other kind of persuasion. Notice could be given that the United States might have to cut off certain exports from this hemisphere to Spain, particularly oil. The Spanish government might thereby be stung out of its composure and make a satisfactory counterproposal.[3]

On the day (October 22nd) after the Ambassador had forwarded this program to Washington, he had a talk with Jordana, the Foreign Minister. Lacking reliable orders, he kept within the realm of general purpose. He reviewed the improvement in the Spanish economy that had flowed from the trade with the democracies. This had also, he pointed out, made it possible for Spain to supply our enemies. The American felt himself entitled to ask now two adjustments in Spanish trade policy, to even the balance: one, that Spain reduce its exports of foodstuffs and raw materials to the enemy; two, that Spain carry the Spanish goods we bought to the United States in its own vessels.[4]

Even though Hayes did not use the word "embargo," this was a bold advance. Washington had not yet made up its mind about what was to be asked and offered. On October 27th the State Department told Hayes that his ideas (of the 21st) had appeal, but should be kept in reserve. In Washington there was a fear—

[3] This general scheme of action was transmitted to the State Department by Hayes on October 21st. On the 26th, before the State Department sent any responsive comment, the Ambassador advanced a still more comprehensive program. In his book (page 184 et seq) Hayes refers by date to this alternative scheme as though it was the basis of his discussion with the State Department. But the message of the 26th went far beyond anything which the Department was ready to consider. The first program, that contained in the message of the 21st, is the pertinent one.

[4] Ambassador Hayes has published the text of what he terms a "personal" memorandum that he left with Jordana on the occasion of this talk of October 22nd. Hayes, op. cit., pages 185–6.

warranted or not—that Hayes might commit us to offer new inducements before we were ready, or even willing, to do so.

It is impossible to know how this situation would have developed had it trailed along as usual. A brisk scrap was in the making between the State Department and the other branches of the government represented on the BEW. These, particularly the Treasury and War Departments, had grown impatient and disposed to use crushing tactics to force all the neutrals to end exports of vital raw materials to Germany. They seemed to be sure that Franco's government, even though it might be resentful, would not dare to join Spain's fortunes to the Axis. They seemed to be ready—and apparently assumed that the whole government was—to deal with the unlikely chance that Spain would cast in its lot with Germany. In contrast, the State Department was afraid that the Spanish government would retaliate; that it would increase aid to Germany in the war even if it did not invite German intervention; that the Allies would not be able to prevent any such gesture of defiance except by the use of arms; and that they might in some way or other find themselves at war in or with Spain—to the derangement of strategic plans.

The British government was even more firmly of the view that the possible gain was not worth the risk. So the scale of arguments stood when, on October 25th, it was upset by a provocative incident.

XXXVI

NO MORE WOLFRAM (Continued)

To Threaten

THE Spanish government sent a congratulatory message to José P. Laurel, head of the puppet government set up by Japan in the Philippines. He was a servile mouthpiece. This news, coupled with the excuses printed in the Spanish press for the Japanese cruelties in the Philippines, aroused angry indignation.

The White House was much incensed. Nerves were tired of serving the cause of prudence, of coining soft words for the government at Madrid because of geography. The feeling dictated an order to Hayes on October 27th to suspend all talk and action *on any subject* until further instructed. This message agitated both the Spanish government and Hayes. The former seemed to be afraid that it forecast a demand for reparations. The latter feared that it would sever the threads of association which he was weaving. As the American government nursed its anger, Hayes tried to conciliate. The situation could be, he urged, turned to good use. But Washington took its time in deciding how to dispose of the wounding incident. Attempts made by Jordana in Madrid and Cárdenas in Washington to express the regret of the Spanish government were turned aside.

The surge of feeling turned the balance regarding the wolfram embargo. It knocked the blocks out of the way of a flat and uncompensated demand. The American government had been thoroughly advised, both by the British government and by Hayes, that such a demand might have critical consequences. But for the time being it was ready to ignore them. It seemed at least half disposed to sweep Franco out of the way, if need be.

Hayes in his book appears indirectly to suggest that this attitude was in disregard of the wishes of the Allied Military Command, that our gust of venturesome reproof was contrary to their ideas. He writes:

"The [Laurel] incident was discussed 'on the highest military level' where it was pointed out, however, that 'Allied war plans did not contemplate entry into Europe by way of Spain and that it was important to avoid any trouble which might require a diversion of Allied strength, and to see that no untoward incident should disturb the Spanish status quo in one direction or another.'" [1]

Whether this caution was withdrawn, or whether it was unheeded, or whether it was thought by the authors of Hayes's instructions to be beside the point is not clear. In any case Hayes was told on November 6th to ask the Spanish government to put into effect a complete and immediate embargo on exports of wolfram to all destinations without indicating that the United States would make any material payment. He was further told to suggest, if he found it necessary, that unless Spain did so, we might not find it possible to continue our supplies in view of the many other needs for them. In addition, he was requested to advance various other demands—including the removal of all German agents from Tangier.

During the preceding weeks the exchange of views between the American and British governments in regard to the embargo had grown skimpy, in both Washington and Madrid. The British government had shown itself in the past to be decidedly doubtful about any move that might have to be backed by compulsion. Now Hayes was told, in the message of November 6th, that while he should confer with Hoare, the State Department wished to avoid all delays in the presentation of American demands. Hayes warned by return cable that some delay in decision must be expected. Franco and the Cabinet would not, even if they could, hurry on so important a set of matters. This forecast was correct. Only an ultimatum—if that—could have won quick compliance.

---

[1] Hayes, op. cit., page 191. Neither the date of this discussion nor the military authorities are identified. No message from the Joint Chiefs or Combined Chiefs about this particular situation has been found in the records available to me. But the recommendation reported by Hayes is in accord with the attitude maintained by both groups toward the Spanish problem from the beginning to the end of the war.

On November 10th Hayes discussed our demands with Jordana. The Foreign Minister combined caution with indignation. He said that while he, himself, was well disposed toward our requests, the Spanish government could not be expected to heed them until the Laurel incident was smoothed out. Nothing could be done if Franco and the Cabinet felt that the American government was holding a pistol at their heads and taking an unfair advantage of what he called a trifling episode. The State Department decided to take heed of this reading of our conduct by the friendly Foreign Minister. Two days later it authorized Hayes to state that the American government regarded the Laurel incident as closed. Thus we returned to a state of grace; but this proved to be an unsettled realm. What next?

On November 11th the Embassy in Madrid sent a clarifying contribution to tactics. Hayes renewed his advice that our requests be coupled with an offer of compensation—such as the Embassy had previously submitted. Hayes recalled that Germany, master of the art of menace, had failed to frighten Spain. If, his advice again ran, Spain shouldn't accept a fair offer in a reasonable time, then we would be more justified in adopting other tactics. We might courteously but without prior warning interrupt our shipments of petroleum. Having done so, we could gradually make clear that, in view of Allied needs, they would only be resumed for a commensurate return. Such a plan, Hayes concluded, would have an excellent chance of success.

The State Department, checked in its demands, rewrote them in a reply to Hayes on November 15th. This message was like a bundle wrapped by a child. It used lots of paper and string, but the ends were flying loose. Whether or not it endorsed the program that the Ambassador had presented (on the 11th), he must have had trouble knowing. For the text seemed to suggest that the Spanish government be asked to grant an embargo as an expiatory offering, with trust that it would be rewarded later. Hayes may be excused for finding it curious if not "disappointing," as he did.[2] Attached to this message was another tag about time. The British government, Hayes was told, had been asked to make its opinions proceed anyhow to urge the Spanish government to impose a known quickly. But unless Hoare promptly concurred, he was to

[2] Hayes. op. cit., page 199.

wolfram embargo, leaving the question of a *quid pro quo*, should such be necessary, for later settlement.

Hayes found that his British colleague was without orders and without faith. Faced with this disconcerting fact, he construed his orders as well as he could in a talk with Jordana on November 18th. The memorandum that he gave to the Foreign Minister was well flavored by the salt of payment. This talk was vigorously followed up, both in Washington and in Madrid. Secretary Hull made plain to Cárdenas that he attached great importance to our requests. The staff of the Embassy worked hard during the following weeks to see that they obtained prompt attention. They sought to quell fears that Germany might, with justice, accuse Spain of a breach of neutrality. The American view on this point was correct. But this detail of legal propriety, we now know, was unreal. An explicit promise that the Spanish government had given the past August to the German government was in question, not merely an arguable international right.[3]

Thus the month of November went. The value of an embargo had become doubtful unless obtained at once. Or perhaps the time when it might count had already slipped past. The time, that is, to hinder German war production of weapons useful to resist the invasion of France, six months off. For if that attack succeeded, Spain would not be able to send wolfram to Germany. If it failed, Germany would be in a position to compel Spain to continue to send anything wanted.

But the Allies—still in November—were not willing to take either of the two decisive courses of action that might have led to a quick decision. One would have been to face Franco with ruin by completely severing all his overseas sources of supply. The other would have been to compensate Spain generously, and to promise Franco protection against both internal and external danger. Not finding it advisable to do either to end the wolfram trade, the Allies entered into the next mile of bargaining.

[3] See page 211.

XXXVII

DIVIDED WE FAIL

The Dots and Dashes of Evasion

WHAT a comfortable posture Spain had achieved by the end of 1943, on the edges of the great war! It was safe from invasion and drawing strength from the conflict. Poverty remained, but misery had passed; and the fortunate few were once more secure and prospering. How shrewdly Franco had used time to deal with dangers from both right and left! His canny patience, like that of a woodchuck, had served him well. The people had their wish—to stay out of war. Supplies of food and other essentials were becoming sufficient. Industrial activity was reviving. The value of Spanish trade was growing greatly and with it Spanish reserves of gold and foreign exchange.[1] A better paid and equipped army was firmly behind him. All the conservative elements in Spain, although divided, would support him against a radical or sectional revolt. Even a Communist victory, unless it spread to France, could not disturb his rule. As for the movement to restore the monarchy, he knew better than most the weakness of the aspirants and the opposed feeling of the masses.

Thus it was not surprising that he neither wished nor saw the need for any basic change in his policies. Tactical shifts now and again, but no alteration that would cost him any of his connections or sources of support. Germany was no longer in a position to compel him to change. He had little reason for genuine fear that the Allies would. The British government had shown its willingness, if not its wish, to have him survive. His talk gave clues to the belief that in any crisis the American government

[1] The value of exports from peninsula Spain alone increased from 395 million gold pesetas in 1940 to 877 million in 1943. Estadística del Comercio Exterior de España, 1940 and 1943.

would be of the same mind. For he was convinced that he would be wanted as an ally in that war against Communism that would follow the war that was being fought.

Thus sustained by fact and theory, he let the American demand for a wolfram embargo drift down the stream of time. The matter, Hayes was told, would require much further study. During this study period the Spanish government did not discontinue business with the other side. It went forward with discussions of its Civil War debt to Germany, knowing that any payments would be used to buy wolfram ore—ore that was later to be smuggled out of Spain with official connivance. Open defiance of Allied wishes was becoming harder. But by measures secret—of which an account will be given later—a break with Germany would be avoided.

The State Department and the Foreign Economic Administration (which had superseded the BEW) joined in a new instruction to Hayes on December 4th. This attempted to end the wavering in regard to what was wanted, and the terms on which it was wanted. The government reverted (though not quite) to the position stated in the original message of November 6th: that the embargo was to be sought without any definite promise of compensation. In that connection the point was made that the Allies had so far in 1943 spent over 50 million dollars to buy Spanish wolfram, exclusive of the huge tax.

The message also tried to correct the failure thus far to arrive at a concerted program with Great Britain. The intimacy between those officials of the two governments in Washington who dealt with the Spanish program had waned. It had centered in the State Department, and was not transferred with the gradual shift of activity to the FEA. Departures of individuals who were eager players for co-operation also made a difference. Impatience took the place of amiability. Less effort was made than before to attain unity before action, and more often failed.

A similar constraint prevailed in Madrid. Hayes and Hoare, though always in touch, worked apart. Hoare was adroit and sure of his judgment. He seemed—since his advice had proved itself so well during the dark period—to feel himself entitled to lead in the management of Allied relations with Spain. What hurt was that he seemed to enjoy getting ahead of his American associates. At times he seemed to seek to reap a special advantage for Britain.[2]

For knowledge of Hoare's feelings toward Hayes we are left to the arts of surmise. A person of Hoare's experience might have found his academic virtue trying, since it was not untouched by self-esteem. Then too (though this is only a guess), Hayes's hopeful thought that the Franco regime could evolve into a tolerable Spanish government may have been annoying to Hoare, whose vision was fixed on a monarchy. Here one verges on the subtle paradox that turns up repeatedly in Hoare's mission in Spain. On the one hand, he missed no opportunity, public or private, to declare how deeply he detested Franco and everything he stood for. On the other hand, he resisted every proposal that contained a threat of disturbing Franco's control. Currently, in the matter of the wolfram embargo, Hayes correctly found him to be indifferent and absorbed in other objects of British policy.

These personal tensions in Washington and Madrid made it a bit harder to stitch up the differences in policy. But—let this be clear—they did not create them. The American and British governments were really at a crossroad of judgment, if not of purpose. One was ready, or so thought itself, to force Franco to end all help to Germany, even though it might mean trouble within Spain. The other was not.

The State Department tried, during the first half of December, to achieve a combined program, along American lines. Again and again it urged the British Embassy in Washington to have Hoare ordered to cast full British weight behind the embargo demand. The British government was still going calmly forward with talks of their usual trade relations with Spain—wishing to be sure of supplies from that country. In short, the Allies were well on their way to market without agreement as to what they wanted most to buy or the price they could pay.

Little wonder, then, that their talks with the Spanish government continued to turn out the wrong way. On December 10th

[2] Hayes has given his impression of his British colleague at various points in his book (op. cit.), especially on pages 134-5. Hoare in contrast scarcely mentions his American colleague in his book. This was rather characteristic, and a mark of the loftiness of temper which proved so annoying.

Carceller showed himself master of the situation. He covered the canvas with objections. He said that an embargo would be the first step in a break with Germany. He made much of the fact that during the past few months Germany had provided Spain with substantial values of arms, machinery, and chemicals and was even about to send wheat. This wheat, it is now known, Carceller had induced the Germans to send in order the better to justify his refusal to the Allies.[3] The Minister asked directly what the Allies were ready to do to protect Spain against German anger, the cessation of imports from Germany, and the loss of income from wolfram. The Allies had not agreed upon the answers.

More Dots and Dashes

Hayes correctly concluded that the trail of Carceller's talk showed that Spain would dally long, while asking much. His earlier hopes drooped. Reproof seeped out of his cables (December 20 to January 1) as from one who felt himself *in loco parentis* for both the American and the Spanish governments. In his later account of the impasse reached at this time, Hayes seems to spray displeasure over everyone except the Spanish government—over Washington for not having long since stepped forward with a generous offer, over London for not being firm in the demand for an embargo, over the extremist American press for its attacks on Spain.[4] These, he wrote later, were "naturally" interpreted by the Spanish government as indicating a deliberate American purpose to utilize our wolfram demand for ulterior purposes.[5]

Despite these sentiments, Hayes bowed to the fact that the Spanish government must be dealt with firmly. However, he begged that Washington and London should first agree on how far they were prepared to go (a) in offering economic rewards for a wolfram embargo, (b) in using sanctions if promises failed.[6]

[3] See page 214.   [4] Hayes, op. cit., page 193.
[5] Ibid., page 207.   [6] Ibid., page 208.

How often over the years have American diplomats sent similar injunctions back home when dispatched upon dusty errands without assurance that the government knew its mind! Please measure before you move; please be definite in regard to what inducements we may offer or what force we may employ; please line up all potential allies before grappling with the opponent! What admirable prescriptions; how likely to remain unfilled!

Of all the points of trouble, the lack of unity between ourselves and the British was the most weakening. Hoare was expounding new reasons for not getting into a row merely to obtain a wolfram embargo. He argued that unless Portugal also ceased to supply Germany, it would be useless; and that neither the United States nor Great Britain was ready to force Portugal to impose an embargo. This point was pertinent but not conclusive, since Germany needed the Spanish supplies in addition to the Portuguese. Then, too, a similar demand on Portugal was in prospect.

But Hoare's main objection was that if we tried to force Spain to do what it did not want to do (or feared to do) by threatening to deprive it of the means of living, we would imperil aims more important than wolfram. This was, of course, a matter of judgment. Finally, he doubted the outcome of even combined British-American pressure. He recalled only too vividly, he said, the unfortunate consequence of the sanctions that had been imposed on Italy at the time of the Ethiopian affair.[7] This seems to be a twisted deduction regarding that episode, one which covered his own failure. Or was he implying that we, and possibly Britain as well, would, if defied, recoil from the risk of war with Spain in the same way as the members of the League of Nations had at the risk of war with Italy? In short, Hoare did not think that either the threat that we would cease to supply Spain or actual refusal to do so would cause it to give in to our demands.

In debate over such questions as these the year 1943 ended without any combined British-American program. With each passing month the subject of the difference lost importance. It mattered less and less whether Spain imposed a wolfram embargo or not.

The Spanish government let time pass and showed no inclina-

7 Ibid., page 209.

tion even to pursue the idea of compensation. So Hayes reported after talking with Jordana on January 3rd and 4th (1944). The Foreign Minister said in substance that an embargo was unfair and not to be had. The Ministers of Finance and of Commerce and Industry as well as the many private interests were against the sacrifice. Moreover Germany would not tolerate an embargo; it would mean a break. To be genuinely neutral, he said, Spain had to give to both sides, not merely to one. The many ways in which Spain had already served the Allies were being overlooked. Spain, he declared, had served as an impassable barrier between the Germans at the Pyrenees and Gibraltar and North Africa; our extended lines of communication could have been, and still could be, broken if Spain moved with Germany. The words were forcible, but the mood doleful. Hayes met assertion by assertion. All that he gained was a promise of a counterproposal.

The Spanish government was also refusing to dispose of any of the other matters that disturbed the Allies. It found new legal reasons for retaining Italian warships within Spanish ports. It formed a furtive tie with the scampering Mussolini regime. The Blue Division was being straggled out of the east rather than ordered out. German agents in Spanish Morocco and Tangier continued to inform about the movement of Allied convoys through the Straits. Both General Eisenhower and the Combined Chiefs of Staff were sure that the heavy air attacks against Allied ships in these waters were guided by these secret reports.

Spain was yielding to the German force of will and her own wish for continued profit. Doubt ended in Washington as to the need of strong countermeasures. The State Department took up Hayes's earlier suggestion as to the best way to begin—by a quiet notice that oil shipments would be suspended because of war needs. The British government swung to the same conclusion— as a result of what new talks or insight the available record does not show. Hoare was still advising that economic pressure should be delayed to coincide with Allied military action in the north. But early in January the Secretary of State for Foreign Affairs, Eden, stepped in. Hoare was told that the British government was also eager to suspend oil shipments at once, and to work with us. We were about to test how durable were the last Spanish ties to Germany in a time of crossed fortunes.

XXXVIII

THE BRUISES SPREAD

Sticks Beat, Tongues Clack

WHAT was to be started with a quiet word might end in a great clamor. Therefore, before speaking the word, the State Department consulted both the Combined (American-British) and the Joint (American) Chiefs of Staff. The letter to the Combined group seems to have been vague and the reply received seems to have been oracular. It was all right, the answer read, to use a stick against Spain, but not to the point of disturbing relations. The notice given to the Joint Chiefs was more definite; on January 12th they were informed by letter that the State Department intended to suspend oil shipments to Spain during February and possibly longer. It is more likely that the State Department knew the answer in advance. In any case, the proposed step was taken before a formal reply was received. On January 18th Smith was told to advise the Spanish Petroleum Director, without giving any reasons, that no oil would be provided on the February 11–12 loading date.

Reports just previously received from Hayes ended all doubt that the moment was more fit for slaps than for discourses. Carceller disdained Jordana's wish to please. It was true, he admitted, that Germany was coming into enough sums of pesetas to buy much wolfram; true also that, looking ahead, it was buying more mines. Well, the Allies might do the same; he would agree to give pesetas for as many dollars as they might care to spend. He was, in other words, willing to see that none of the bidders ran out of chips.

Not only that. He had a private winning word for each. Thus, he told Hayes that he was willing to work with us to force the price of wolfram up to the skies, so that Germany would get less for its pesetas. While he told the Germans they would not want, for he would help them when our backs were turned. This double ruse, it may be observed, worked. The Allies did not dare wait for Spain to come around. Thus they resolved, at the end of January 1944, to use all the funds they had to bid both ore and mines away from Germany. But not even Carceller could have thought that the United States would do so for long. It took oil to run the mines and transport the ore.

When Smith carried out his instruction (on January 22nd) the Petroleum Director showed no surprise.[1] As foreseen, the Foreign Office tried at once to find out what was afoot. Jordana consulted Hayes, who pretended no knowledge. Cárdenas approached the State Department.

The Department decided that it would be useless to deny the real reasons. Assistant Secretary Acheson prepared to explain them fully to Cárdenas. But he could not keep his first engagement because of a call to the Capitol. And on the day of his second (January 26th) he was ill. The scheduled interview was taken over by a group of junior colleagues: Charles P. Taft, who was concerned with economic-warfare operations; W. Perry George, of the European Division; and Henry Labouisse, of the IPOC. The reception by three officials when he expected to meet only one bothered the Ambassador.

Taft is not given to choosing words that soften his messages. They had been, in this instance, written with pains and cleared with care. Cárdenas was told that the American government was revising the whole Spanish economic program because Spain had failed to respond fairly. The causes of complaint were recited in detail. Cárdenas—for the first time—gave way to a fit of sullen depression. He said that the American statement made a failure of everything he and his chief (presumably Jordana) had tried to do, and left them with no course except to resign. This may be taken as the first natural response of a man who feared that he would be caught in the middle of the fight which might fol-

---

[1] Hoare, op. cit., page 256, seems to write that the news of the oil suspension came as a complete surprise to both himself and Hayes. But the latter had originally suggested the tactic, and the order to use it was sent to him. Hoare must have known we were on the verge of taking this action, even if not definitely told of the final decision. It is probable that Hoare meant to write that the later *public* announcement was a complete surprise.

low. But it also served to convey the thought that if the American government pressed, power would pass to those who would defy it. The message was hard, and probably disliked all the more because it was delivered by men beneath his own rank. They did not comment on the Ambassador's warning. Three days later Jordana denied that he had heard from Cárdenas about this talk. But the denial could not be believed.

The news of the angry crisis spread rapidly. Word of our action had seeped to the press and radio of both the United States and Britain. They poured forth long-hoarded dislike of the Franco regime and its aid to our enemies. The condemnation spread over the whole Spanish record of Fascist association. These public attacks were at first favored in some official spots, in both Washington and London. But they worried both Hayes and Hoare. The latter has expressed the judgment that the public criticisms—especially the broadcasts of the BBC—immensely increased the pains of reaching a settlement.[2] It does not seem possible either to confirm or to dismiss this opinion. The unpleasant things spoken spoiled the air in the room of compromise. They caused some Spanish officials to believe that we wanted to destroy the Franco government; this aroused an angry wish to resist. It is even possible that they were thought to be the opening curtain for an Allied attack on Spain—lifted in the German manner. The Spanish government long afterwards alleged that there was a plan for such an attack, and that the radio campaign died when the plan was abandoned.[3]

In such ways as these the public campaign may have caused the Spanish government, for the time being, to be more obstinate. But it is safe to conclude that these emotions did not govern Spanish policy. Broadcasts or no broadcasts, the Spanish government would have said no, as long as it had a choice. The reasons were in and on the earth, not the air. Franco wished to continue to draw resources from both sides; he did not wish to see Germany beaten. Binding these wishes was an obligation to provide

[2] Hoare, op. cit., page 262.

[3] Spanish White Book entitled *Reply to the Documents Relative to Spain Published by the State Department* (1946). This alleges that the plan was prepared by General Strong and sponsored by General Donovan, and proposed to the other Allied nations at the end of January 1944.

wolfram for Germany; the Spanish government did not dare to cancel this promise until it could plead that it had to do so to live; and even then only after sneaking supplies into Germany. The broadcasts pained so much, it may be surmised, because they brought home that trouble was ahead. Spain was going to have to hurt Germany or be hurt by the Allies. The bruise was being made by sticks and stones—not merely by words.

Jordana was then and later in the center of the trouble. He was upset but he did not resign. Instead, he searched for a way out. As a first step he promised (on January 27th) to do what he could to see that Germany received no export licenses until a settlement was reached. Franco said the same thing to Hoare the same day. Did they know of the help that Carceller was promising the Germans in getting along without licenses?

But the American will was stiffening. On the 27th the JCS sent a formal reply to the State Department's notice (of the 12th); this stated that there was no objection to the current suspension of oil shipments to Spain. Hayes was thereupon told to inform the Spanish government that no oil would be provided during the second February loading period. The ban was really on. However, the State Department laid aside a surprising suggestion by Eden that it be extended to other products, such as cotton and fertilizer.

Both Hayes and Hoare became more intense in their complaints about the harmful effects of the radio campaign. Hayes went further, warning that the public attacks in combination with our economic pressure might cause civil war. In that event, he pointed out, we might have to divert our armies to Spain.

Without retreating, Secretary Hull took heed of these tales from Madrid. He issued, on January 28th, a public statement, with which the British government was associated. This announced that we had suspended oil shipments to Spain "pending reconsideration of trade and general relations between Spain and the United States in the light of trends in Spanish policy." It then listed the causes of our grievances. The Secretary's purpose was to limit conjecture. The statement helped to do so. For it affirmed that his interest lay only in matters connected with the course of the war; he was not directing an assault on the Spanish regime itself.

The central question remained, could and would the regime meet our wishes? The signs were adverse. Hoare had come away from a talk with Franco on January 27th with a sense that Franco had decided to accept our demands and was only waiting for the instant when he could do so without danger from Germany.[4] But when Hayes saw Jordana on the 29th, he received quite a different impression. The Foreign Minister strewed the talk with reproaches. The Spanish government, he warned, would not be swayed by public threats; it would resist by reducing the use of overseas imports, such as oil, to the utmost, and make the reasons clear to the Spanish people. Hayes was touched because Jordana, who leaned toward us, was thinking such angry thoughts. He again sent word that we should not discount the chance that Spain would "be forced" into the war on the German side as a result of our disturbing public attacks. Secretary Hull again waved his staff of office over the air waves. He asked the OWI to pursue the subject no further and to use its influence to see that the American press and radio calmed down. They did so. The BBC carried on a short time longer. Then it, too, was restrained.

But still the marks of the dispute grew blue. On February 2nd the Spanish government announced severe reductions in the use of oil. The gasoline quota for trucks was cut in half, fishing boats were to have none, deliveries of fuel oil to industrial plants (except for olive-oil mills and electric power stations) were suspended. This was preface to a public statement which, after referring to the United States, said that Spain would not give way, in any manner, to pressure against its right to maintain a neutral position. The statement went on:

"The government furthermore has studied the measures necessary to cause its neutrality to be respected."

The American Government is Unmoved

Secretary Hull, having redirected the flow of the argument into safer channels of diplomacy, did not like this response. On Feb-

[4] Hoare, op. cit., page 256.

ruary 3rd he sent Hayes two starched messages. These, after disposing of the Spanish reading of our mind, centered on the point that every ton of wolfram that Spain sent to Germany might mean the death of American soldiers. They stated that Hayes's fear that Spain might break relations with us could be discarded. He was to continue to insist upon a complete and permanent embargo. Further, the Secretary said he was trying to persuade the British government to correct Hoare's pessimism.

But before these messages were decoded, talks marked by a wish to relax tension were under way. The Under Secretary, Stettinius, was amiable in a talk with Cárdenas, despite the Ambassador's remark that he was sure that Russian pressure was behind our policy. Hayes and Jordana met again (on February 3rd). Jordana's mood had changed; he was helpful and hopeful. He told Hayes that the Spanish government would meet Allied wishes on several matters, including the expulsion of German agents in Tangier and the suppression of German espionage in Spain. In regard to wolfram, he and Hayes found themselves coming together on an interim plan that Spain would maintain an embargo for a month or two, during which period both hoped the dispute would be settled. The United States was in return to renew oil shipments and to announce that the wolfram question was on the way to solution. During January 300 tons had been sent from Spain to Germany; and a brief embargo could have been easily excused.

Hayes, stating that Hoare was of the same mind, urged Secretary Hull to fall in with this interim plan. Then (on February 5th) he sent word that the Spanish Cabinet had issued orders to suspend all exports of wolfram for the time being. He asked to be permitted to discuss an accord limiting exports to Germany to the same quantity as had been sent in 1943. This was estimated by Jordana to have been about 720 tons.[5]

But Washington was cold. The tonnage allowed plus what could be smuggled would enable the German war machine to get along. For Portugal would stand up for the same privileges. By his

[5] Jordana's figures were wrong. During 1943, as Carceller stated later, export licenses for between 1,000 and 1,100 tons had been issued to Germany, including 125 tons that the Spanish government had itself requisitioned and delivered. In addition, about 200 tons had been smuggled.

message of the 8th, Secretary Hull turned down the idea. In doing so, he dismissed Jordana's notion that it was up to us to find a formula to save the face of his government. We wanted, Hayes was again told, a permanent embargo and intended to have it. Therefore the United States would permit no oil to move from the Caribbean to Spain during March. Our improved military situation, Hull pointed out, at last enabled us to insist that Spain should not strengthen our enemies.

Hayes took a deep breath before facing the Spanish government with so unbent a claim. He asked, on February 11th, whether he might not, in doing so, at least promise that we would increase both our purchases of Spanish goods and our shipments of certain products that Spain obtained from Germany, particularly machine tools, machinery, and dyestuffs. The State Department granted permission to give a "lick" without a "promise."

Our British connection was again awry. Despite the earlier messages from Eden which the British Embassy in Washington had conveyed to the State Department, Hoare still hung back. He insisted that his instructions were very clear; Britain was ready to support the American demand and he had been doing so, but it was not ready to risk a break with Spain.

All other attempts to end the difference in judgment having failed, President Roosevelt himself tried. He cabled Churchill on February 12th that he believed that if the British and the American governments stood firmly together, Spain would grant a complete and total embargo, which would be a lifesaving achievement; that he perceived no danger to the Allied position in so doing; that he understood Hoare wished to give in and that he hoped the Prime Minister would instruct him not to waver.

> Oh, the little more, and how much it is!
> And the little less, and what worlds away!

Churchill leaned toward the President's eager wish. Then almost at once another and better offer came out of Madrid.

XXXIX

ALL OR NOTHING

How Near to Our Wishes

ON THE 15th of February Hayes made clear that the United States wished all or nothing. He reviewed his troops of fact and logic with gloomy dignity and Jordana, in his turn, did the same. But without result. A copy of Jordana's memorandum of this talk has come to hand. Its final sentence leaves a pleasing light upon what must have been a painful talk:

"With this [the avowal that each appeal to God to interpose His omnipotent power in the present situation] and with the conventional salutations, this interview which, notwithstanding the unpleasantness of the matter discussed, was carried on in cordial terms, was ended, having lasted five hours."

Faithful as Hayes's statement of our position was, it did not dispel the Spanish idea that we would accept less than we asked. Probably some sense of Hayes's inner wish to avoid a break came to the surface, despite his words.

Hoare, having heard from Churchill, talked with Jordana on the 17th. Again—as in his earlier talk with Franco—he thought the task achieved. He told Hayes that the Foreign Minister, besides granting all else that Britain asked, offered to limit future wolfram exports to Germany to so small an amount as hardly to count. Hayes, when sending on this report, stated that he would refrain from again trying to advise the State Department. But his analysis of the bargaining situation clearly added up to advice that we should amend our demand. He said that he thought that the Spanish government could be persuaded to continue the embargo for six months and thereafter send a little. This would serve our purpose. While if we insisted now on an absolute all, we might lose all. Spain could, if it chose, make do with its oil supplies for between four to six months, during which time Germany could heap up ore for the rest of the war. This was so. Memories revived of the dispute with Hayes earlier in the year over how close to keep Spain to the margin of her need for oil.

The British government did not wait for proof that Jordana could give effect to his offer or for reliable detail. The British Embassy in Washington sprang forward with the statement that it would net us ninety-five per cent of our desires. On February 21st Churchill cabled the President that reports from Madrid indicated the chance of a settlement that seemed to him most satisfactory on all points if we acted quickly. On the same day the British Ambassador gave the Under Secretary of State a note of the same purport. It suggested that if Spain pledged itself to maintain an embargo for the next half year, ways and means could later be found to extend it.

Almost at once the State Department received a report from Hayes that seemed to confirm the nature of the offer. The embargo was to be extended for some time forward, and Germany was to receive a trivial amount (disguised by a formula) during the rest of 1944. We were to buy the rest of Spanish production at a fair price in order to avoid the abrupt ruin of the industry. The President, on February 23rd, said he would accept these terms. Our ends seemed gained. Presently faults would appear in German armor. All Allied activities in and about the Iberian Peninsula would be smoother and safer henceforth. That evening the officials who had worried over Spain since the dark days of 1940 went home early and cheerful.

But this mood lasted only overnight. Obscurities emerged in regard to the meaning of Jordana's offer. Somewhere in transit from Jordana to Hayes to Washington it had been misconstrued. Scattered through many cables, the details of this confusion are no longer of interest.

For the real trouble was deeper. Jordana was unable to go through with the general type of settlement he had proposed—one that would almost end all wolfram exports to Germany. An important section of the Cabinet—led by Carceller—would not accept the loss and take the chance. Germany was using accusation and blank threats to keep its Iberian wolfram supply. For it was not to be had elsewhere. The Nikopol supply was gone; the Finnish supply was about to be overrun; and most recent attempts to run the blockade from the Far East had failed.

Jordana, on March 7th, pleaded with the American government to resume oil shipments while he unraveled the hindering obligation to Germany. But it refused. The Madrid movie houses featured their newest American importation, a film called *Boom Town*, a drama fought out over gushing oil wells. The crowds laughed.

The Council of Ministers rejected Jordana's formula. Carceller now taunted us for thinking that Jordana could have his way. The Spanish government could go so far to please us, he said, but no farther. Some wolfram must be sent to Germany; 209 tons, he suggested, between then and the end of August. What was to be done later could be talked over later. This would have meant legitimized export to Germany of over 500 tons between January and the end of August; over 300 tons, it has since become known, were smuggled during this period. This total of 800 tons compared with total legitimate exports to Germany during the whole of 1943 of 1,000–1,100 tons.

Again Hayes reviewed in his reports to the State Department the possible penalties of saying no, of continuing to refuse oil. The Spanish government might defy us and lift the temporary embargo. The internal strain and dispute might cause a civil war, which might derange our military plans. But Secretary Hull was now angrily set. He told Hayes on March 16th that Carceller's offer was neither good nor clear. We sat still and refused to permit oil to cross the ocean.

The Spanish government made no overt act of defiance. With the patience that had served so well in other bargains, it crocheted new formulas. Under their changeable hues the British found an acceptable pattern. First Hoare and then the rest of the British government became impatient with Washington. Other benefits, they said, useful in the fighting, were being lost while the American government tried to force Spain to its will. Wolfram was not the end-all, the be-all of Allied effort. They wanted to settle on a Spanish promise to extend the embargo for a further short period and thereafter reduce the exports to Germany. This wish was supported by all the familiar arguments and an urgent new one—that Britain had a vital need for such Spanish products as iron ore and potash. The British Embassy tried to persuade the State Department to accept less than all, and failed. Hoare tried to convince Hayes, who upheld the American position with spirit.

Churchill next carried these views to the President in a long personal message of March 30th. He sent a carefully reasoned plea for taking what was offered. But there was a snap in its tail; he could not, he said, any longer support in public the policy that was being forced upon the British government.

A day later Hayes reported that the issue had reached a crisis in Spain. Jordana had sent him a signed personal letter, saying that if his latest offer was refused, Spain would be forced to lift the embargo and enter into a trade agreement with Germany. Hayes had warned Jordana at once that such action might compel the American government to sever all of Spain's overseas supplies. He had also pointed out that before long Spain might have to face the future alone. It was, he had informed the Foreign Minister, up to Spain to decide. But beneath these resolute words Hayes was discouraged. The Spanish government would not give in and the British Embassy had quit the fight.

The situation could not be protracted. If the American government stood fast, it might have to (it was being told that it *would* have to) manage without Britain and face the consequences of a smash-up within the Spanish government. It was not ready to test these opinions. The President told Churchill that for the sake of unity he would recede from the demand for a total permanent embargo, and that he was asking the State Department to work out with the British Embassy in Washington a mutually agreeable line. Anxiety speeded this effort. On April 4th Hayes and Hoare were given identical instructions to make a new offer. Its two chief features were that the embargo should be kept in force until July 1st and the total exports to Germany in 1944 should not exceed 600 tons (including the 300 already shipped).

But this step toward concession did not end the high-strung clash. The Spanish government clung to the wish to soften Germany's anger by making small shipments before July—20 tons a month during April, May, and June. The British government was eager to agree and wipe the slate of grievances clean. But the American government would not do so.

For Spanish wolfram had now become the touchstone for the whole range of neutral trade with our enemies. On April 9th Secretary Hull had condemned this traffic sternly. He had declared:

"It is now clear that our strength and that of our Allies now makes only one outcome of this war possible. That strength now makes it clear that we are not asking these neutral nations to expose themselves to certain destruction when we ask them not to prolong the war, with its consequences of suffering and death, by sending aid to our enemy. . . . We ask them, but with insistence, to cease aiding the enemy."

All over the country this firm statement had been praised. Could he go back on it? The War Department and the FEA were also determined not to recede. Churchill in a talk with Under Secretary Stettinius, who was in London, warmly praised Hull's speech, especially its bearing on Eire. But the Foreign Office remained of the same mind; we were risking too much for very little.

On April 11th Assistant Secretary Acheson tried to convince Lord Halifax to the contrary. If we gave in to Spain, he stressed, we would have to yield elsewhere, let Portugal also send tungsten, Turkey ship chrome, Sweden and Switzerland provide ball bearings and machine tools. But Whitehall was not convinced that this was so; facts and force, not logic, would govern the settlements with these other neutrals.

The Allies were near separation in their dealings with Spain.

XL

THE LAST TRANCE AND END OF THE AFFAIR

Churchill Forces the Issue

OVER the remaining tongue of difference excited ghosts of argument chased. The Spanish government, about the middle of April retouched its figures. It offered to limit shipments to Germany before July to 60 tons and to send only 240 more during the rest of 1944. The British government again urged acceptance. On April 15th Churchill sent word that he hoped Secretary Hull would realize that a settlement along these lines would be regarded throughout the world as a triumph of the Allies over German diplomacy—which would be widely ascribed to his speech. Two days later he again informed Roosevelt that he did not think that for so trifling a difference we ought to risk the loss of so many benefits. The invasion of France was two months away. To end before that event all German war services in and by Spain, he said, was far more useful than having our way about a few tons of wolfram.

The appeasing message failed. Hull was angry at the British desertion. For he was almost sure that Spain would have given in long since were it not for the British protection.[1] Then too,

---

[1] He might have found confirmation in the message that Dieckhoff had sent on to the Foreign Office on April 4, 1944, reporting that Carceller had told the Counselor of Embassy that in view of this discrepancy between the English and the American attitudes, the Chief of State, Franco, had directed the Foreign Minister to give the two enemy powers the alternatives of accepting within a short period the informal oral agreement or of refusing it and at the same time considering the negotiations a failure.

Also from the later (April 16, 1944) report that Dieckhoff sent to the Foreign Office, explaining and condoning Franco's fears of a break with the Allies. Franco, he related, had to take into account the strain under which the Spanish people had so long been living; he was afraid of a possible attack on the Spanish islands in the Atlantic; and in the event of a break it may be surmised, he saw a stimulating chance to show he had no soft feelings for Franco.

Irritation tinged the Secretary's remarks to Lord Halifax on the 17th. Britain, he said, wanted to compromise. The United States did not. American public opinion would no longer stand for a continuation of those branches of neutral trade with our enemies which had fatal results for our soldiers. Therefore, he continued, further effort to agree seemed vain. The only way out seemed to be one that allowed each to follow its own bent. Why, since Britain affirmed a special interest in the situation because of its need for Spanish strategic materials, should it not sponsor the oil shipments that would be the counterpart for the goods that Britain received from Spain? It is hard to tell, and Lord Halifax seemed to find it so, whether this idea was advanced out of resentment or was really meant as a way out of an impasse that had become intolerable. Its defect was plain: the advertised split on this issue might spoil the feeling of unity needed for the vital joint military venture that lay ahead.

The President answered Churchill's beckoning message with another appeal to stand firmly for a complete embargo through June. But the Prime Minister became impatient. On the 22nd he expressed a fear, derived from Hoare's reports, that unless the Spanish offer was accepted within a few days, Jordana and the even more friendly Under Secretary for Foreign Affairs, Pan de Soraluce, would resign. The control of the Spanish Foreign Office would then pass to our opponents and the large stocks of ore that had been gathered by Germany would pass over the frontier. The Prime Minister then broke loose. Referring to the talk between Hull and Halifax on the 17th, he said he was ready to take the whole responsibility for the proffered settlement. Would the President please confirm his assent to this course at once? For he had already told Hoare to advise the Spanish government of his intentions, as soon as he heard from the President. If diplomatic tremors were marked by a sensitive machine, the sheet for that day would have borne deep lines.

But the tremors were cut short. Secretary Hull was persuaded

---

feared the possible consequences of intensified Allied propaganda or recognition of Negrín. Even Carceller and Asensio, the report added, were afraid of Allied economic, political, and military pressures.

to yield. Late on the 25th he told Hayes to join the British in reaching a settlement within the realm of the latest Spanish offer. His reason for doing so, he explained, was that Churchill was set to carry it through himself. In that event he would have to make a public statement that would clearly reveal the break. The terms of the Spanish offer—as it was understood in Washington—was that Spain would limit its shipments to Germany to 20 tons in May, 20 in June, and 40 each month thereafter, a total for the rest of the year of not over 280 tons. Spain would, as well, meet Allied wishes in regard to all other requests, which had been on the table for months. On these terms Hayes could start the Spanish tankers toward the Caribbean.

The confused crisis dragged out three days longer (April 26–8). It was made worse by delays in the receipt of cables and mist in their language. But the basic cause was our reluctance to cry quits. Now Hayes, too, preferred to carry on further by putting the issue squarely before Franco. The American tactic still seemed to include one more attempt to have our way; the British tactic was to force an end. Hoare was annoyingly self-assured. It is no longer useful to trace out the crisscross messages of these few final days. Hull dropped the idea of appealing to Franco. In view of his knowledge of the British position, a refusal was certain. If then the American government granted to Franco what had been so stubbornly refused to Jordana, the standing of the Foreign Minister would be impaired.

Hayes and Jordana, each stretching the limit of his authority to the utmost, reached agreement on the morning of the 29th. The wolfram crisis was over. Arrangements were made at once to resume oil shipments and to renew other trade relations with Spain.

All through the spring of 1944 the sky had been clouded in the direction of Spain. Now it quickly lightened. But the White House and the State Department did not smile as they looked up. They felt cheated of a popular victory. Thus their first impulse was to avoid all praise of the accord. Premature newspaper comment, thought by the British to have started with American newspaper men in London, was critical. Word came that Churchill was preparing a full and proud defense in the House of Commons.

In response to Hayes's report on the accord, Secretary Hull

had salted his commendations. He said that he thought the American government must make clear that it took these terms only because the British government felt it had to obtain wartime supplies from Spain. It would not be popular; the public felt itself entitled to a complete cessation of neutral aid to the Axis war effort.

Hayes thought this was a mistake. He reviewed the many benefits to the Allied cause that made the accord a signal triumph. He urged the Secretary of State so to present it publicly, taking a full share of the credit for our side.

The text that issued out of the press room attributed our acceptance of the terms to British needs and ideas, but otherwise was calm and free of reproach. Eden, in the House of Commons, greeted the settlement as good in its military and economic benefits, and a notable step toward strict neutrality. On May 24th Churchill, after doing the same, expanded into a tribute to Spain for not having joined its enemies in the grim period of the war.

". . . Well, I say we speak the same words to the Spaniards in the hour of our strength as we did in the hour of our weakness. I look forward to increasingly good relations with Spain and an extremely fertile trade between Spain and this country. . . ."

Franco was forgiven. But not in Washington. There was no outflow of warm satisfaction either from public officers or in the press. Rather, a sense of a job half done. But the moving reason was probably deeper and beyond this dispute over wartime trade.

Was it not the knowledge that the crisis had come and gone, and left the *"Spanish problem,"* not the wolfram problem, unsolved? Germany and Italy would fall, but Franco would stand, his past behind him. He would remain part of our universe, an affront to our sense of justice. We were committed, and in some ways more firmly than ever before, to continue to supply Spain with the means to maintain its economic life. But no document of the time records such thoughts. They are only dim notions that have rubbed off this page of the past like dust on the hands of the scholar. Or perhaps the other way about—dust rubbed over the documents by the hands of the scholar. In either case they are only dust.

XLI

HOW THE AGREEMENT WAS DENATURED

Spain and Germany during the Crisis

THE wolfram agreement had been glued with bad grace. For the German thumb was always in the glue-pot. Left alone, the Spanish government would have been unhappy about the ending of the wolfram trade. It was scared as well. Only when and as Spain could show that it could not get along without oil did it dare offend even the falling German power.

The German government glowered and cajoled. Yet the Spanish did not fall into confusion. Even as the Allies (from November to April) were led along from one waiting station to another, so was Germany. By adroit steps and soothing words the German protests were sheathed. The teasing German offers were inspected with warm interest, used, and said to be wanting. One by one the Allied demands were met. But before giving in, the Spanish government insured itself against German wrath. It saw to it that Germany secretly got its portion, and more, of Spanish ore.

The German government does not seem to have directly threatened to use force to compel Spain to obey. Its warnings sometimes took the guise of prophecy that the Franco regime would suffer in the event of German defeat. Thus, for example, Dieckhoff remarked to Franco on December 15, 1943:

". . . it would be a very dangerous policy for Spain to make concession after concession to the English and Americans; Spain would thereby find itself on the downgrade and she would become more and more dependent upon the Anglo-Saxon powers." [1]

To which Franco replied that he knew that:

[1] Memorandum, conversation Dieckhoff and Franco, December 15, 1943, State Department Document No. 15.

". . . a victory of the Anglo-Saxons, in spite of all the pacifying declarations which would be made to him from time to time in this respect by the English and American side, would mean his own annihilation."

At other times blunt bluffs were tried—such as the one that, on February 22, 1944, Ribbentrop told Dieckhoff to make; he was to tell Franco that Germany would not tolerate any talk of reduced wolfram shipments regardless of what Germany did or did not deliver to Spain. Or again, on May 22nd, after the signing of the agreement with the Allies, when Dieckhoff was instructed to tell Jordana that Spanish statements did not change Germany's view at all about either wolfram or the closing of the Tangier Consulate. Without German and Italian help, he was to remind Jordana, there would have been no Nationalist Spain.

But the "don'ts" came from a distance. Ribbentrop did not go to Madrid, nor could he summon the Spanish Foreign Minister to Berlin. In what ways, if defied, Germany would punish Spain was not set forth.

The German government knew itself to be unable to prevent Spain from giving in to the Allies. When, in the midst of the January crisis, the situation was reported to Hitler by Doenitz (in connection with the question of whether or not to send surface blockade runners to the Far East) the conclusion as reported in the minutes of their talk seems to verge on acceptance:

"The Fuehrer considers that there is also imminent danger that tungsten shipments from Spain and Portugal might cease. He has therefore given orders to bring in as much tungsten as possible now." [2]

But the Spanish government could not be sure of what lay beneath the stormy surface. A fringe of terror hung along the edges of messages from Berlin. Ships could be torpedoed without a trace. Even crazed and wanton attacks from the air leave cities in flame and people in agony. Who knew what Hitler might not do on his way to ruin? He was showing no pity for the Germans.

Thus Jordana and Carceller strove to keep Germany calm, while trying to reduce Allied demands to a minimum. Carceller failed at no stage to give assurance that German needs would be kept in mind. He, along with Franco, was ingenious in finding

[2] Conference, Hitler-Doenitz, January 18–19, 1944. "Fuehrer Conferences," 1944, page 4.

reasons for each concession made to the Allies. Now it was the fact that the Allies might stop imports of wheat and cotton as well as of oil; and if this happened, Communist and Separatist influences would increase. Next it was that Germany need not worry, for Spain would certainly hold out for the right to send the minimum amounts that Germany needed.

Such quieting promises suited Spain's purpose. But they were, it is probable, honestly meant. For Franco long was sure that the Allies could be brought to compromise. As late as March 17th he passed on to Dieckhoff for immediate relay to Ribbentrop "the very secret facts" on which this certitude fed. These were a long and twisted account of recent secret diplomacy among the Allies—with a simple conclusion. The USSR had managed to compel Britain and the United States to start the attack on the "Atlantic Wall" in the very near future, and they, therefore, would not want to get into a fight with Spain on the eve.

German offers progressed from the possible provision of more arms, to hints that Germany would be able to send most, if not all, of the basic products for which Spain depended on the Allies, such as grain, oil, cotton, and rubber. The Spanish government, at each turn of the Allied screw, asked how much of these Germany could deliver.[3] Dieckhoff urged his government to do its utmost to meet the Spanish bill. Committees in Berlin worked out long lists of everything that a lean industry or a fat housewife could wish. But these tended to be spectral. For they shrank in size whenever the Spaniards came close; and when pinched hard, they vanished completely. Germany did exert itself, however, to send in the course of the spring small amounts of wheat, potatoes, machinery, and even aviation gasoline. The German armed forces gave up this gasoline grudgingly on the score that it would serve to win the favor of Vigón, the influential Air Minister, in the matter of wolfram exports.[4] Spain took in all that was to be had and went on to the next point.

[3] As later related by Dieckhoff to American interrogators, Spain naturally asked what Germany could offer in return for continued shipments of wolfram; for example, Franco wanted 600,000 tons of wheat. He was authorized to offer 60,000.

[4] The small deliveries appear to have been on a monthly basis. It also seems as though some deliveries were made after the agreement with the Allies in connection with a wish to secure Vigón's help in smuggling.

During the final April crisis, while Franco was threatening to deal with Germany if his last offer to the Allies was refused, there was much searching about, both in Madrid and in Berlin, to locate the wanted goods. But it became clear that Germany could or would not provide what was wanted. Thus Franco was forced ultimately to conclude that he had to sign with the Allies.

It was by a ruse that Spain, while doing so, also managed to succor Germany. Wolfram in large amounts was illicitly moved over the frontier during the first half of 1944. These shipments were illicit because they were contrary both to Spanish public decrees and to promises made to the Allies. But in another sense they were not. For they were arranged with the cognizance of various branches of the Spanish government. This compliance began as soon as Allied pressure became earnest. On January 18th the Spanish government was notified by us that oil shipments would be suspended unless wolfram was embargoed. On January 27th the German Embassy informed Berlin that Carceller had confidentially pledged his full support for such illegal transactions as might be necessary.[5]

On February 3rd Jordana agreed to a temporary embargo, and on February 5th the Spanish Cabinet ordered one to be placed in effect. This was thought to be our safeguard as the talks dragged on. But Germany was told, at each necessary interval during the following weeks, not to fear its effects. Thus, on April 4th, Dieckhoff reported to Ribbentrop that while Carceller was elusive in discussing with the Counselor of the German Embassy the terms of the prospective agreement with the Allies, he stated that this did not need to trouble Germany; for, in agreement with the Caudillo and the Spanish Military, he would see to it that Germany—without detriment to the settlement attained with the Allies —would receive the tungsten it needed from Spain by another

---

[5] Carceller's experience in such operations was, as the narrative will have illustrated, extensive. Another instance may be recalled. In 1942 the Allies wished to buy mercury. Spanish production and export was subject to regulation under a cartel arrangement with Italian producers. Carceller gave secret consent to the sale. In order to keep knowledge of it away from Italy, the books of the Spanish producers were falsified. The mercury was smuggled into Portugal in box cars on which rode an official of the Ministry of Trade and Commerce along with a representative of the USCC; his presence took the place of an export license.

route. This must, Carceller argued, be the sole deciding factor for Germany.

It is not necessary to judge whether the bold activities of the Minister of Industry and Commerce were shaped solely by regard for the public interest or not. Fritz Kolbe, a Personal Assistant (*Referent*) to Ritter, Ambassador for Special Assignments within the German Foreign Office, later informed American questioners that the Spanish authorities, especially the Minister of Industry, Carceller, were aware of this traffc, but their acquiescence was purchased by payment of funds transmitted through the German Embassy from the Economic Division of the Foreign Office. The meaning of this is obscure.

In any case, the German official Trade Organization (Sofindus) was given much help in its smuggling operations. Its able head, Johann Bernhardt, was later to state that everything his group had done in Spain had been done with all due correctness, and if occasionally there were curious actions, these were always with consent.[6] Sofindus made the most of its chances during this agitated spring. All available pesetas were poured into the free market. Technicians and mining machinery were rushed to the German-controlled mines in order to increase production. Large stocks of ore were stored in warehouses near the frontier. Sham delivery contracts were signed with Spanish producers and brokers; this was to swell the German claims which the Spanish government could portray to the Allies.

The ore was smuggled out in trucks. Two devices were used. False declarations were made. Legitimate export permits were used twice, once for the proper shipment and once again for the improper. The shrinkage in the stock piles was made up by substituting "black earth" for the wolfram ore.

The first big illicit shipment was on April 6, 1944, when 184 tons were put across the frontier. This was only managed, Berlin was informed, through the close collaboration between Sofindus and Carceller, who participated actively and thereby jeopardized himself considerably. Then on May 2nd, shortly after the conclusion of the accord with the Allies, another 103 tons were sent, and 18 more a few days later. A shipment of 24 more tons was

[6] See Supplementary Note IV on Bernhardt.

reported on May 19th and 111 in June. This made, in all, illicit shipments of about 443 tons since April 1st. The Allies sooner or later learned of these operations. But the ore was gone before the complaint came in; and the warnings, which grew sterner, did not bring back the ore.[7]

Export licenses had been granted for 342 tons since the beginning of the year. Thus Germany had obtained from Spain during the first half of 1944 about 785 tons of wolfram ore, a substantially greater amount than in any similar previous period. Further, during the spring about 100 tons a month of Portuguese ore were shipped first into Spain and then passed on toward Germany. Thus the agreement was denatured.

And, although this narrative has slighted this vital factor in the wolfram problem, there was Portugal besides. A larger source of supply than Spain, and still open. Even a real and complete denial of Spanish supplies would count for little unless imports from Portugal were also stopped. The Allies had forborne pressure on that country because of a wish to secure peaceful consent to the use of the Azores as an air and naval base. This Salazar had granted. He felt Portugal to be entitled to special treatment in return. Britain did not like to coerce its oldest ally. But after the Spanish agreement was signed, our will became less forgiving. The wish for quick victory dominated.

The Allies pointed out that the trade was unhealthy and would end when the war ended. But the Portuguese government would not give it up. Thus on May 24th, after patient attempts to arrange a compromise, the British government agreed to join the American in demanding a complete embargo. Evasion was followed by a

[7] When first asked by the State Department about reports of these activities, the Embassy in Madrid replied on May 9th that a check of all border points failed to provide any substantiation. But a week later the OSS secured a full account of them through an informant of the German Ambassador.

Hayes, op. cit., page 229, writes: "As for the wolfram part of the agreement, the Spaniards gave us every facility for seeing that it was scrupulously observed and that smuggling was prevented or, if detected, was heavily penalized." And on page 230: "In May, 1944, Spain exported the agreed-to 20 tons of wolfram to Germany. It was the first that had gone since January. But when our agents at the border got track of the Germans smuggling out a few additional tons in May, Spain volunteered to deny Germany the 20 tons promised for June. Hence from the end of January to the beginning of July 1944, the Germans obtained from Spain only 28 or 30 tons of the indispensable mineral. . . ."

threat to suspend oil shipments. News of the invasion of France was in the air. In June Portugal gave in. The end of the legitimatized trade between Germany and the Iberian Peninsula came into sight.

Smuggling was still being planned. Germany in June was preparing to sell its accumulated stocks in Spain (some 800 tons) to a Spanish "dummy" group, which might find ways of moving it across the border. It is impossible to know what might have happened next, had not the American armies come southward to the Pyrenees. Had the transport route not been cut, the fight with Spain might well have flared up again.

Did the Allied attempt to corner the wolfram hurt the German war effort at all? The information so far in hand does not permit a complete or conclusive answer—certainly not a precise one. The decline in the receipts of tungsten ore during the second half of 1943 caused a small decrease in the production of tungsten metals.[8] According to several reliable intelligence sources, Germany was forced to dispense with tungsten in important uses, including ammunition cores and to use it most sparingly in others.[9]

But by economy Germany seems to have been able to keep itself supplied for the most vital purposes up to the end. The essen-

[8] Some tables regarding tungsten needs, production, and supplies are contained in a report prepared by the Planning Branch of the Speer Ministry, June 29, 1944. But I am unable to interpret them with confidence. It is observed in this report that "total Spanish supplies for 1944 will probably amount to 900 tons of tungsten concentrate as compared with a planned 1,200 tons before export restriction went into effect." This estimate is not greatly different from one that may be arrived at from the figures given in the text; 785 tons before July 1st and the 240 allowed under the accord with the Allies give a total of 1,025 tons. However, the tonnage figure given in this report was probably in terms of 65 per cent concentrate, while much of the ore sent to Germany was a poorer grade.

[9] As stated in *The Hidden Weapon*, by two former officials of FEA, David L. Gordon and Royden Dangerfield, page 115. They write that from 1943 on, Germany "had to abandon the use of tungsten in important (though not vital) items such as ammunition cores. . . . Even in essential uses the proportion of tungsten had to be drastically cut: for example the tungsten content of carbide tool tips was reduced from the normal 10–18% to 2–3% at times, with a consequent forced reduction of machinery speeds by 60–75%; the use of tungsten carbide for cutting tools other than in armament production was also forbidden, excluding it from many essential applications not only in the machining of metals but also in coal cutters, rock drills, etc." A similar statement is found in an article by Lindley and Weinthal, *Harper's Magazine*, December 1944.

tial minimum need had by 1944 been reduced to about 3,800 tons per year, and Germany always managed to obtain at least that amount. As of January 1944 the situation (as summarized for Hitler by the Naval Staff) was deemed tight but not critical.

"The tungsten situation is also such that there is no need for using surface blockade runners [to Japan]. This remains true only so long as imports from Spain and Portugal remain at their present level and so long as combat submarines use freely the possibilities of transporting tungsten." [10]

The imports from Portugal and Spain were, as recounted up to the required schedule of need for the first half of 1944 and beyond. Even before the receipt of the last illegal shipments, Ribbentrop was advised by his staff that Germany had enough wolfram to last twelve months even though no more was imported from the Iberian Peninsula.

In several important, though indirect, ways, the Allied wolfram-buying program hurt the German war effort and helped ours. It was compelled to use all but a small part of its resources in Spain to buy wolfram and wolfram deposits. Thus it had to cease buying other products—such as woolen goods. It was less able to compete for, and thus make more costly and scarce, the Spanish products that the Allies needed for their own war production.

In summary, it would seem as though the effect upon German power to resist was real but not conclusive. Only had the battle in the west been longer fought might it have been so. The Allied tanks arrived first. They outpaced our diplomacy. But was it not because they could get behind the Germans in the Pyrenees in a way diplomacy could not? When the routes through France were cut, the Germans still had many hundreds of tons of wolfram ore stored near the frontier. The world lost interest in them. No longer could they make a difference in the price of victory.

[10] Report submitted by Naval Staff for Conference Hitler-Doenitz, January 18–19, 1944. This report estimated German needs to be about 3,840 tons; quantities obtained recently, 3,500 tons, including 860 tons within Germany, presumably scrap; stocks on hand January 1, 1944, 380 tons. "Fuehrer Conferences," 1944, pages 3, 4, and 13.

XLII

DOWN A BRANCH ROAD OF HISTORY

An End without Grace

THUS the wartime struggle with and over Spain passed down a branch road of history. The Allies, for better or for worse, had chosen to let events evolve in Spain rather than dictate them. The decision was made when, in the spring of 1944, Spain's concessions were accepted and oil shipments were resumed. For Spain could not have gone without oil much longer. By summer a crisis would have come—which would have forced Franco either to make way for a government more pleasing to the democracies, or to have defiantly thrown in his lot with Germany. Either would have caused a division within his government, in the Army, and among the Spanish people. What the scene in Spain would have been at the time of our landing is—for me at least—an unanswerable question. Franco still in power—ruling with strong measures? A parliamentary government and a satisfied people? A weak government and a sullen people, which would have later come under Communist control? Or no government—anarchy and cruel civil war again?

These questions loomed sharply and then were passed on, unanswered, to the future.

The results of the brief oil suspension were severe despite, or in a way because of, the drastic rationing. Private automobiles disappeared. Only buses and taxis equipped with charcoal burners were allowed to circulate. The reduced movement of trucks caused food shortages. Railway transport services, freight and passenger, were jammed. The government did its utmost to meet farm needs for harvesting and threshing, but only partly succeeded. Some industries were shut down completely, including glass factories, which created a bottle shortage in the wine and brandy business. The fishing catch was reduced. Had supplies ebbed much further, Spanish economy would have been near collapse—if only for lack of lubricants alone.

Had Spanish stocks at the beginning of the suspension been smaller, the crisis would have been briefer and sharper. The stocks gave the Spanish government time to curvet its way through opposed demands and secret liens. The original American oil program, as we have noted, had been based on the idea that maximum Spanish stocks should never exceed amounts needed for two months' use, three months' for lubricants. The Spanish government showed that under duress they could make what they had last for much longer. This hedge of time was, perhaps, a decisive historical fact.

The April 1944 agreement brought the Allies various military benefits of certain and prompt value. These—rather than the end of the wolfram trade—had been the primary objects of British effort in Spain. The German Consulate in Tangier—the directing center of German activities throughout Morocco—was closed, though not without wrangling. The expulsion of many—but by no means all—German agents from both Morocco and the Spanish mainland was hurried, though only after nagging. The last remnants of the battered Spanish army unit in the east was withdrawn, though not without an attempt to absorb its men into the German forces. Most of the interned Italian merchant ships were released, but not all. Though all these actions had been promised, they had to be hauled out of the lax net of Spanish decision.

With the resumption of the oil shipments, the stale three-cornered differences over how much oil to send and how large Spanish stocks should be re-emerged. The American government wished more than ever to keep the supplies low. But the British government remained of the contrary mind. In fact, it now pushed hard to get a share of the trade for British oil companies and to secure an equal place in the administration of the system of oil control. During this last period of the war, small squabbles took the place of big ones. They have no special interest or importance. They might even be regarded as an advance signal of the ending of the war. The nations were beginning to feel themselves free to relapse into their customary commercial rivalries.

As our troops moved across France, our trade with Spain ceased to have vital wartime significance. Government offices in Washington began to figure out how they could prevent Spain from becoming a safe haven for the property and persons of the defeated Germans. They had cut off all the spreading branches of German influence. Now they wished to pull out the roots. For the memory was still green of those anxious times when only the misery of the Spanish people, their proud independence, and the divisions among them prevented the crooked cross from flying over the vital Straits.

Spain ceased to be a main focus of Allied diplomacy. The beams swept across the vaster sky of the continent, writing as they moved: "unconditional surrender." The last remaining guards poured oil over the dead bodies of Eva Braun and Hitler. Of all the leaders who had once been near his side and wished him victory, Franco alone survived in power. Survived to see, during the few years that have gone by since, the beams of Allied diplomacy scatter and crisscross in lost confusion. Survived to see them separate into two great hostile bolts, as he had been so sure they would.

This end without grace cannot be an end. But who knows what the end will be?

SUPPLEMENTARY NOTES

ONE
(see Chapter VI)

ON CERTAIN ACTIVITIES OF CAPTAIN THORKILD RIEBER

The large exports of oil from the United States to Spain were mainly arranged by the Texas Company. This company contracted in July 1935 to supply the Spanish government oil monopoly, Campsa.

When, a year later, the rebellion against the military government began, it had five tankers on the high seas bound for Spain. Rieber ordered them to deliver their oil to General Franco on credit. Other shipments followed, some on manifests that falsely declared the shipments were destined to France—for which offense the company was fined $22,000 by the American Treasury. Under Rieber's direction, the Texas Company continued to keep Franco supplied, thus risking some six million dollars on the outcome of the Civil War.[1] After Franco won, the debt was paid off and the contract was renewed. Under its terms Campsa undertook to purchase specified minimum amounts of oil and secured options for much greater amounts. The Texas Company undertook to do its best to supply all Campsa requirements.

It did very well. Texaco shipments to Spain were as follows:

Dates	Metric Tons			
1936	344,000			
1937	420,000	(part	to	Canaries)
1938	478,000	"	"	"
1939	624,000			
1940 (first half only)	432,000			

The Texas Company before the war had built up a good market in Germany. Captain Rieber had intimate friends there. He had

[1] See article by Joseph L. Thorndike Jr., in *Life*, July 1, 1940.

traveled around Germany with Goering and other influential Nazi officials. Captain Rieber put his German intimacies to good use. Thus, as related in the article already cited:

"A spectacular proof of the power of the Rieber personality was the tanker Skandinavia which the Germans allowed Texaco to take out of Hamburg and through their Baltic blockade in March [1940]. The Texas Company had the Skandinavia built in Hamburg as part of the ships-for-oil deal made with Germany before the war. By the time she was finished, however, Germany was in no mood to release any ship which might be used to supply the Allies and when Rieber landed in Italy on one of his transatlantic trips he was told that the Skandinavia had been interned in Hamburg.

"Rieber flew to Berlin and was ushered into the presence of high Admiralty officers. The officers said they were sorry but Germany could not possibly release the tanker. . . . Rieber heartily agreed that in their place he would take the same position. But, the Captain went on, it would seem a shame to break up the long and honorable relations between Germany and the Texas Company. As naval men, they would understand, too, how an old captain felt about his boats, how he loved them like children, what pride he took in them. And finally, said the Captain, if the Germans ever caught the Skandinavia carrying oil for the Allies they would have his hearty permission to fire a torpedo into her."

The Captain was persuasive.

"The Skandinavia sailed triumphantly through both German and British blockades. . . ."

In June 1940 both the French and the British governments accused him of pro-Axis activity. They passed on reports that Rieber was personally doing his utmost, through the manager of the Texaco interests in Italy, to assist Spain to charter tonnage and accumulate stocks of oil, part of which was destined for Italy. For example, the S.S. *Dungannon*, a tanker owned by the Texas Company, sailed from Port Arthur destined for the Cepsa refinery. It arrived in Santa Cruz on June 24th, at which point it proceeded to discharge the oil into the holds of three Italian steamers.

Rieber's activities were brought to an end by chance public disclosure of his intimate associations with Dr. Gerhardt Alois Westrick, Special Economic Representative of Germany and

Adviser to the German Embassy. The American press featured the fact that Rieber had provided him with an automobile, the better to carry out his secret tasks. The publicity frightened the Texas Company. The directors became afraid of the role in which it had been cast by its bold head. In August 1940 they forced his resignation, but granted him a very large pension. For a time he acted as general purchasing agent in the United States for Campsa. Then he went into the shipbuilding business; one of his associates was the German pilot who had flown him about in the company of Goering.

TWO
(*see Chapter VI*)

ON THE SPANISH OIL SITUATION IN 1940

The first American decisions, those made in June and July of 1940, in regard to the Spanish oil supplies were taken in the haze of uncertainty regarding the facts of the situation. The available information was unsystematic and turned out to be in part wrong. The State Department did not have a reliable record of either (a) total recent shipments to Spain, (b) actual recent Spanish consumption, or (c), and of greatest interest, the size of accumulated stocks.

The rushed efforts to collect this information from British, American, and Spanish sources brought in most divergent estimates, especially in regard to the size of the stocks. For example, in the memorandum presented by the British Embassy on June 17th, stocks in the Spanish peninsula alone were estimated to be about 400,000 tons; in another statement transmitted by the Embassy on July 23rd, they were said to be equal to ten months' supply (21 months' for lubricants). In contrast, the American Naval Attaché at Madrid reported, on the basis of information supplied by the Spanish oil monopoly, that Spanish stocks of gasoline and fuel oil were lower than normal, and if the current flow was reduced, they would become critically low. It has not been possible to trace back the statistical record with precision. But it is certain that these early British estimates were too high. In later negotiations regarding navicerts, the British government, after investigation, was guided by lower estimates. On the other hand, the figures sent by the American Naval Attaché were too low.

The evidence that was immediately available to the State Department in June–July 1940 regarding the recent rate of exports to Spain seemed clearly to warrant some action. American records of shipments during the first nine months of the war (September 1939 to May 1940) from the United States alone showed them to have been far greater than during the corresponding months a year previous—25 per cent greater for gasoline, 400 per cent for lubricants, 200 per cent for fuel oil. The number of tankers known to be under charter to transport oil to Spain was much greater than ever before. The schedule of shipments seemed to indicate that if unchecked, the imports during the summer months would exceed 100,000 tons a month. The increase in the flow to the Canary Islands had been even greater. The rate of operations in the Spanish refinery at Teneriffe, which used American and South American crude, reached capacity in June for the first time since the Civil War. The destination of the exports of its refined products was a closely guarded secret. Storage space on the islands, estimated to be 115,000 tons capacity, was reported to be full.

Nevertheless, the Spanish government throughout the summer made both private and public denials that accumulated stocks were of unusual size.

Presently the State Department was able to put together from information provided by the American oil companies a rough comparative estimate of the course of their shipments from the Western Hemisphere to peninsular Spain and the Canary Islands. They were as follows:

Years	Shipments to Peninsular Spain	Shipments to Canary Islands
	THOUSANDS OF METRIC TONS	
1935	275+	44
1936	543	64
1937	588	116
1938	716+	102
1939	868+	221
1940 (first half)	433+	234

As of interest, the figures for later years were as follows:

1940 (full year)	777
1941	509
1942	230

It is clear that beginning in 1939, despite a shortage of dollars, the Spanish government greatly increased its oil purchases. It is also clear that during the spring of 1940 the Spanish government tried to secure even greater amounts. There is a strong probability that its main purpose in doing so was to increase its reserve supplies.

The effort to accumulate stocks might under the circumstances have been governed by any one of several of various purposes. It was only prudent for any neutral government to try to assure itself of a continued supply of vital fuel. No country could be sure that the hazards of war might not interrupt the trade. Reserves were insurance against economic disturbance. They also could be a means of preserving independence of action. A country that lacked oil might have to pay a high premium to one or the other of the belligerents, or both, in order to secure it. For these reasons the attempt of the Spanish government to accumulate reserves was not, *in itself*, subject to proper objection. If it had not been for Spain's geographic position and the obvious tendencies in its policy, the attempt would not have been hindered.

But after the downfall of France, there was much reason to fear that, no matter what the original reasons for accumulating reserves, they might be used in the war against England. There were solid reasons for suspicion that the intensified effort made in June 1940 to increase shipments was for that very purpose. The unwillingness to permit Spain to accumulate larger stocks was due to a fear that it would join the Axis in an assault on Gibraltar and Morocco; even if it did not, that it would transfer supplies to Germany and Italy.

The steps taken by the American government from June on caused the inflow into Spain to be much smaller than would otherwise have occurred. The Spanish government during the summer of 1940 tried to preserve supplies by extending its restrictions on consumption. Nevertheless, during the last half of 1940 Spanish stocks were substantially reduced. On August 27th the British government, after a special investigation, estimated Spanish stocks, as of August 1st, to have been around 217,000 tons; and it reckoned that if Spain had to rely on its own tanker fleet, this would be reduced by October 1st to 146,000 tons.

The American government did not, during 1940, enter into direct discussions with the Spanish government with regard to the rate of supply—though the United States was the chief source of supply and the trade was handled by American companies. It was willing to permit the British government to manage the matter through its blockade and navicert system. But the British government consulted us often. It had persuaded us to restrict the outflow in the summer of 1940. But after this early period of alarm, British policy was to permit, even to encourage, a generous rate of supply for Spain, provided it was currently consumed. The British government was ready to permit Spain as much oil as it wished to use. The goodwill of the Spanish people, it was thought, could best be gained by showing its own. During the tense autumn months of 1940 when Spain was debating whether or not to enter the war, Britain wished to be sure that advocates of such action could not persuade the Spanish people that Britain was responsible for their troubles.

After consultation with the State Department, the British government in early September signed an agreement with the Spanish government for the regulation of supplies during the rest of 1940. This was on what later came to be regarded as lavish terms. Navicerts were promised for about 36,000 tons during the rest of September and 65,000 tons in each of the succeeding months. The British were willing to provide more if Spain removed the restrictions on consumption. It was reckoned that under this supply program Spanish stocks at the end of 1940 would be about 160,000 tons, about two and a half months' supply at the current rate of use.

The American government co-operated in the effort to make this agreement work satisfactorily. It consented to the use of tankers that were American-owned but operated under foreign flags. It also tried to adjust the issuance of cargo licenses to fit the program. But still, because of the difficulties in obtaining tankers and delays in clearance, actual imports into Spain during the remainder of 1940 were smaller than the scheduled amounts. A similar arrangement was worked out between Great Britain and Spain for the supply of the Canary Islands and other Spanish colonies.

Subsequent management by the American government of the shipments of oil to Spain have been recounted in the main text.

THREE
(see Chapter XXVII)

FUEL FOR THE SPANISH AIRLINES?

Would the United States provide fuel and lubricants during wartime for the airlines that connected Spain with its colonies and the outside world? Washington rejected, it will be recalled, the proposals made by the Embassy in Madrid in regard to the shipment of aviation gasoline and lubricants in 1942.

The decision centered on the system controlled by the Spanish government—the Iberia Line. This flew not only between Spanish towns but from points in Spain to Portugal, Tangier, Spanish Morocco, the Balearic Islands, and the Canary Islands. The flight to Tangier provided quick touch with Gibraltar. The flight to Lisbon provided connection with the Atlantic air services.

Germany owned a substantial part of the stock and was represented on its Board of Directors.[1] It had also penetrated the operating branches, although these were mainly Spanish, as were the flying and ground crews. The services of the Iberia Line were of utility to the officials and agents of the Allied governments. But they were of even more use to servants of the Axis—especially the line to Spanish Morocco. Members of the German armed forces and secret services filled its places.

Hayes transmitted the Spanish requests for aviation fuel and lubricants in January 1943 with supporting comments. He said that if we refused, Spain would be forced to seek other sources, and he passed on a report that Germany might provide the fuel in return for a greater share of control. On February 18th the State Department answered that it would not decide the question

[1] The American government thought this interest was only 24.5 per cent, but it was in reality twice that size, half being in the name of Spanish dummies.

until it knew more about Spanish stocks, civil and military. It discounted the chance that Spain would transfer control to Germany.

In March 1943 the Iberia Line came to the end of its supplies. Hayes sent a series of vigorous messages advocating that we send 320 tons a month for its services, as well as 100 tons a month for the use of the Spanish Air Ministry. A variety of reasons were summoned in support of this policy. Most were familiar, but a few were special to the case. Suspension of operations would greatly handicap the travel of officers of the American and British Embassies, couriers, and petroleum observers. By refusal we would lose the chance to gain the support of General Vigón, Minister for Air, to draw him farther out of the German camp. He had recently helped to provide good treatment for and the ultimate release of American aviators forced down in Spain or escaping from France.[2]

Hoare concurred with these views. But those officials of the State Department and the BEW who were engaged in the economic-warfare program did not find them convincing. They thought that Germany was getting more benefit from the Iberia Line than the Allies. They did not want to sustain a line in which the German government had a large interest. But the European Division of the State Department was unhappy about the rejection of the pleas and the serious inconvenience to our mission in Spain. These views were merged in a proposal to provide minimum amounts of fuel for selected routes provided the Allies could secure certain positive advantages in return. The first of these was the elimination of the German interest in the ownership and management of the line.

On April 3rd the Combined Chiefs of Staff approved such a policy. But Assistant Secretary Acheson and others continued to question it. The Secretary of State, on their advice, postponed the decision. Hayes tried to hurry it. He cabled that Hoare knew of the opinion of the Combined Chiefs of Staff and was asking authority to advise the Spanish government. On April 15th the

---

[2] He was simultaneously doing his best to secure planes from Germany and to arrange for German help in training Spanish pilots. Germany in 1944 drew upon its scant supplies of aviation gasoline to hold his favor and help in wolfram smuggling.

State Department replied that such action would be premature. Hayes next suggested that when we informed the Spanish government of our willingness to provide limited amounts of fuel, we might ask permission for an American commercial airline to operate from the United States to Spain. Again he was told to defer action. Spain and Germany were tying themselves closely together in new economic accords. Washington wanted a chance to judge their meaning before helping Spain further to carry on its revival.

But the British government did not wait. On May 7th it agreed to grant navicerts for 320 tons of aviation gasoline a month for civilian airlines. Spain was to take measures to prevent the air services from being a menace to Allied convoys or a source of intelligence to the enemy. Further, it was stipulated that the German interests in the Iberia Line should not be increased. The British government informed the State Department of this agreement, but the Department still hung back. On June 7th Hayes reported that the Spanish government agreed in principle to permit an American commercial airline to operate to Spain. On the 17th the Joint Chiefs of Staff stated that this privilege was much to be desired.

A joint program finally emerged from discussions with the British held in Washington. On June 23rd the State Department cabled Hayes that we were ready to agree to permit the import of 320 tons per month for the use of the Iberia Line: provided, first, that no flights would be made to the Canary Islands or the Spanish colony of Río de Oro without American or British permission; and, second, that Spanish planes would not enter or pass over enemy-occupied or enemy-controlled territory. We would like, it was added, to secure a promise that the Iberia Line would not carry any enemy nationals to Tangier or Spanish Morocco. We would not insist upon this, but Hayes was asked to do his best. Further, he was informed that the Joint Chiefs of Staff thought it would be most useful to secure landing and other rights for an American airline to Spain. The Department, finally, suggested that this program be presented jointly by the British and American Embassies in Madrid, to end the troublesome rivalry.

Hayes took up the offer with alacrity and vigor. Despite hard German opposition, he managed to obtain all we asked—either then or later. In July the Spanish government bought back the

Axis share of the Iberia stock; Vigón secured German consent to this resale by posing as an opponent of a fictitious American demand that the German share be transferred to the United States. The Spanish government argued that the service to the Canary Islands was needed, but by September 20th agreed not to resume it until or unless the British and American governments approved. It also promised that no Axis nationals would be permitted to travel on the lines to Morocco or Tangier. The way thus seemed open to the quick resumption of gasoline shipments and of flight operations.

But this was delayed again by letters of protest that Harold Ickes, the Petroleum Administrator for War, on September 21st sent to Secretary Hull and Leo T. Crowley, head of the BEW. This protest was based on principle, not on the ground that the small quantities in question could not be spared. The dispute was referred to the Munitions Assignment Board, which approved the contemplated arrangement. The first shipments were sent. The Iberia Line began to resume limited operations. In November it asked consent to fly from Barcelona to Mallorca in the Balearic Islands. This consent was given on the condition that no Axis nationals would be carried and that no increase would be asked in the total supply of gasoline.

Again the need for our oil had served us well. Injurious German activities in and about the western Mediterranean were thereafter reduced to ground speed. Axis agents found it long and wearing to move about the area; their spy, sabotage, and naval operations were hurt.

It may be added that in 1944 the Spanish government renewed its request for gasoline for the use of its military Air Force. It was wanted to keep the training program going. Not only Hayes, but the Military and Naval Attachés in Madrid urged that we supply small amounts in return for various favors—such as greater help in moving our stranded fliers out of Spain. But the American government again refused, for it continued to doubt the ultimate wisdom of contributing to the perfection of Spanish air forces.

FOUR
(see Chapter XLI)

ON JOHANN BERNHARDT, HEAD OF SOFINDUS

Sofindus was the name of the company through which the German government conducted its trading relations with Spain—except in arms. It also ran many enterprises in the fields of mining cork, and wool; it owned wolfram, tin, fluorspar, lead, and iron-ore mines.[1] It operated a fleet of merchant ships to take goods through the British blockade, and a large trucking system of over-land shipment to and from Germany. It carried on the illicit and illegal smuggling of wolfram—of Portuguese wolfram into Spain, and of Portuguese and Spanish wolfram from Spain over the French frontier to Germany.

Johann Bernhardt ran Sofindus with vigor and skilled cunning. He was one of its founders and the most influential of its directors. He could rely upon inner connections in Germany and Spain, gained by his services at the opening of the Spanish Civil War. He had been a sugar broker in Hamburg during the years of the inflation and had ended up in a fraudulent bankruptcy. There-after, he found work in a German trading firm in Tetuán, Spanish Morocco, with a wage of $65 per month. This firm sold stoves and other supplies to Spanish Moroccan troops. Bernhardt traveled between the army camps seeking orders. He became intimate with the local German Nazi leader in Tetuán, and the local leader sprang forward at the first sounds of rebellion against the Re-public.

In July 1936 General Franco had no way of bringing his troop battalions into the fight in Spain. The two Germans flew home. They persuaded Bohle, Chief of the Foreign Organization of the

[1] On these alone American experts later estimated that Germany spent some 40 to 50 million dollars.

Nazi Party, and Rudolf Hess that the German government should seize the chance. Hitler was at Bayreuth, listening to the music of Wagner, in council not only with the gods but also with his party friends. Before Bernhardt and his friend had finished talking, Hitler had given the necessary orders. German planes left for Morocco the next day. By August 2nd a large German troop-transport system from Tetuán to Jerez de la Frontera and Seville was in operation. Each plane made four daily flights with thirty fully equipped soldiers; within a week Franco had 15,000 troops on their way across Spain.

Bernhardt did not pause. Within the next two months he had convinced the German government that it should supply aviation parts and equipment, gasoline, and technical troops. He gathered a staff to manage the troop and supply transport operations, to service the German planes, to provide fuel, to build and control airdromes at Salamanca and Talavera de la Reina. He also set up a special establishment at El Ferrol to handle ships and the shipment of goods. For the conduct of these activities he maintained direct telephone lines to the headquarters of two leading rebel generals, Franco and Queipo de Llano.

Goering approved these supply activities. But he wanted payment, or as much as could be had. Bernhardt was given the task of getting Spanish materials in return. His organization—which became known as Hisma—thus grew into the manager of Spain's trade with Germany. Wherever the rebels went and won, the trade grew. When, after the end of the Civil War, the trading company was reconstructed, and renamed Sofindus, Bernhardt was left in effective charge.

His working position was strong both in Germany and in Spain. He had independent authority and much discretion in the use of large secret funds. By many branches of the Spanish government he was treated with special favor, and not only because of past services rendered. He contributed to the well being of various Spanish officials and personages and procured benefits therefor. He was shrewd, without scruple, an able organizer, and a persuasive man. His own wealth grew rapidly along with that of his friends. He is supposed to have lost Franco's friendship in 1943. But he retained other important protectors, among them General Asensio, Minister of War.

At the start of the war Sofindus managed to secure a far greater sum of Spanish goods than it delivered. Gradually, as related, Spain grew firmer and would only send as much as it got. Sofindus began to lose its control over the meager Spanish surpluses. But in the most vital field—wolfram—it fought ably to the end. In the face of the tumbling German military fortunes in the winter of 1943-4, Bernhardt retained enough influence within the Spanish government to arrange the important wolfram-smuggling operations that have been recounted.

Bernhardt has often been questioned by American investigators in search of knowledge and control of German assets in Spain. Adroit and almost as sure-minded as ever, he told what he had to, no more. He has been of help despite himself. While he has long been on the repatriation list to be sent back to Germany, he was, at last report, still getting along most comfortably in Spain.

INDEX

i

IN THE NORTON LIBRARY